Cognitive Capitalism and its Reflections
in South-Eastern Europe

Sozio-ökonomische Perspektiven in Südosteuropa

Socio-Economic Perspectives in South Eastern Europe

Herausgegeben von
Siniša Kušić / Slavko Kulić / Vladimir Cvijanović

Band 2

PETER LANG
Frankfurt am Main · Berlin · Bern · Bruxelles · New York · Oxford · Wien

Vladimir Cvijanović / Andrea Fumagalli /
Carlo Vercellone (eds.)

Cognitive Capitalism and its Reflections in South-Eastern Europe

PETER LANG
Internationaler Verlag der Wissenschaften

Bibliographic Information published by the Deutsche Nationalbibliothek
The Deutsche Nationalbibliothek lists this publication in the Deutsche Nationalbibliografie; detailed bibliographic data is available in the internet at http://dnb.d-nb.de.

Cover Design:
Olaf Gloeckler, Atelier Platen, Friedberg

ISSN 1864-483X
ISBN 978-3-631-60461-8

www.peterlang.de

Contents

List of Contributors

Vladimir Cvijanović, Associate at University of Zagreb, Faculty of Economics and Business.
Andrea Fumagalli, Professor of Economics, Department of Economics, University of Pavia, Italy, Vice-President of Bin-Italia (Basic Income Network, Italy).
Nadica Jovanovska, MSc in Economics, Assistant Lecturer, Faculty of Business Administration, Southeastern European University – Tetovo.
Aleksandar Kešeljević, Assistant Professor, Faculty of Economics, University of Ljubljana.
Siniša Kušić, Assistant Professor, J.W. Goethe-University Frankfurt.
Stefano Lucarelli, Assistant Professor of Political Economy, Department of Economics "Hyman P. Minsky", Faculty of Economics, University of Bergamo.
Cristina Matos, Assistant Professor at Escola de Economia e Gestão, Universidade do Minho and Researcher at Dinâmia-CET, ISCTE, Lisbon, Portugal.
Matko Meštrović, Senior Research Fellow (Emeritus), The Institute of Economics, Zagreb.
Jean-Marie Monnier, Professor in economics at the University of Paris-I, Panthéon-Sorbonne, CES CNRS.
Natalija Nikolovska, PhD. in Economics, Full Professor, Faculty of Economics, University "Ss. Cyril and Methodius" – Skopje.
Cosma Orsi, Researcher at Florence University (History of economic doctrine), Visiting Professor at University of Lugano.
Carlos Prieto del Campo, Ph.D. in Philosopy (Universidad Complutense de Madrid), independent researcher, member of Universidad Nómada, Spain.
Pasquale Tridico, Assistant Professor, Department of Economics, University of Rome III.
Carlo Vercellone, Assistant Professor in Economics at the University of Paris-I, Panthéon-Sorbonne, CES CNRS.

List of Tables

List of Figures

List of Abbreviations

BIS – Bank for International Settlements
BRIC – Brazil, Russia, India, and China
CAP – Common Agriculture Policy
CC – Cognitive Capitalism
CEE – Central and Eastern Europe
CEECs – Central and Eastern European Countries
CIS – Confederation of Independent States
DB – Defined Benefit
DC – Defined Contribution
DC – Developed Country
ECB – European Central Bank
EE – Emerging Economy
EES – European Employment Strategy
EFDGA – European Found for Development and Guarantee of the Agriculture
EMU – European Monetary Union
ERDF – The European Regional Development Fund
ESF – European Social Found
ESM – European Social Model
ETEs – Emerging and Transition Economies
EU – European Union
EU-27 – 27 member states of the European Union
FDI – Foreign Direct Investment
FED – The Federal Reserve System
GDP – Gross Domestic Product
GNP – Gross National Product
GSI – Guaranteed Social Income
HDI – Human Development Index
HPI – Human Poverty Index
HQG – High-Quality Growth
ICT – Information and Communication Technologies
ILO – International Labour Organization
IMF – International Monetary Fund
IP – Intellectual Property
IPR – Intellectual Property Rights
ITR – Information Technology Revolution
LDC – Less Developed Country
M&A – Mergers & Acquisitions
MBO – Management-Buyout
NDC – Notionally Defined Contribution System
NGO – Nongovernmental Organisation

OECD – Organisation for Economic Co-operation and Development
OMC – Open-method of Coordination
PAYG – Pay-As-You-Go System
PPP – Public-Private Partnership
PPP – Purchasing Power Parity
R&D – Research and Development
SAA – Stabilisation and Association Agreement
SLA – Sustainable Livelihoods Approach
TE – Transition Economy
TNC – Transnational Corporations
UBI – Universal Basic Income
UK – United Kingdom
US – United States (of America)
USA – United States of America
USD – United States Dollar
USSR – The Union of Soviet Socialist Republics
WBO – Worker-Buyout
WTO – World Trade Organization
WWII – World War II

Introduction*

Vladimir Cvijanović, Andrea Fumagalli, and Carlo Vercellone

The contributions in this book are the proceedings of the International Conference held in Dubrovnik, May 23-25, 2008, and entitled *Innovation and Social Development: Cognitive Capitalism. What Are the Conditions for Social Development?* The conference was one of the few occasions on which scholars from the Eastern and Western European countries can meet for discussion, and especially on a topic that is unusual in the economic field. The book, in fact, deals with a subject that only in recent years has attracted the attention of sociologists and economists, at least those more interested in analysing the transformation of capitalist society since the crisis of the Fordist paradigm. Moreover, much of this literature is in Italian and French, while the literature in English is scant. The articles in the book highlight different aspects of *cognitive capitalism* (henceforth CC), which is considered to be a new stage in the historical evolution of capitalism. The point of view of the French "Annales school" and "theorié de la regulation" allows discussion to focus on current structural changes from a historical and long-term perspective.

A distinctive feature of capitalism, unlike other previous social and economic systems in the history of mankind, is its capacity to reproduce itself through continuous transformations of social relationships and the valorisation of capital. This peculiarity was much emphasised by Fernand Braudel, especially when he recognized that economists tend to assimilate "real capitalism" only with the industrial stage of capitalist dynamics. In fact, according to Braudel, "Capitalism is an old adventure, which anticipates and spans the industrial revolution and the economic growth. It continuously adjusts the means of its domination" (cf. Braudel, 1979: 311).

Structural crises – that is, the transformations of capitalism – are moments when capitalism's capacity for adjustment as recalled by Braudel is able to produce a dynamic metamorphosis which changes the evolution of history; but it does so within the capitalist structure. Even more than the previous crises of industrial capitalism, the creative destruction driven by the social crisis of Fordism was indubitably one of these moments of bifurcation when the long-period, almost imperceptible, time of structural change encounters the contingent time of events often represented by major social conflicts, which make the system fall over. History then accelerates, and the question of transition between one order

* The authors would like to thank Luka Grgić and Denis Redžepagić for their help with technical editing of the book.

and another gradually arises. To quote Christian Marazzi, the time of transition is a time of uncertainty, "a tragic time: of the new, we glimpse outlines, of the ancient, we undergo the limits" (Marazzi, 1997: 8). In this framework, previous categories and tools of analysis enter into crisis and the researcher is confronted with a difficult methodological choice between two options:

a) The first option relates to the temptation to privilege elements which militate for continuity in change. This stance makes it possible to develop the reassuring vision of a world which on the whole moves only marginally, and which, *mutatis mutandis*, does not require revision of the old analytical categories. This approach characterizes a number of works which, by concentrating on the former driving industries of Fordism, have interpreted the current transformation in terms of a transition from the mass production model to that of flexible accumulation or Toyotism. The latter is largely conceived as being a part of the previous Fordist industrial paradigm. The vagueness of categories such as "after-Fordism" or "post-Fordism" reveals this tendency to conceive the new capitalism as a simple development of the laws and trends of the capitalism that sprang from the first industrial revolution.

b) The second alternative consists in privileging, not what seems stable and as confirming previous regularities, but rather what in the previous order comes undone, what is being born, the phenomena now developing and which can thus prefigure the movement towards the upcoming order. This therefore requires identifying the trends and the structural and institutional forms of capitalism's new configuration, also by audaciously questioning industrial capitalism's logic of development and the tools devised by political economy to understand its functioning.

The second option has been the basis for the elaboration of the program of research around the thesis of the CC that this book is going to present. According to this thesis, the origin, meaning and the stakes in the crisis of Fordism did not correspond to a simple major crisis of one of the modes of accumulation which succeeded one another since the development of industrial capitalism. The crisis of Fordism corresponded to a higher level of crisis, and with regard to the concept of crisis of the accumulation regime described by the French "de la Régulation" school (Boyer and Saillard, 2002). It was at the same time a deeper and more radical crisis in some of the most fundamental invariants of industrial capitalism itself.

We are thus confronted with the comparable metamorphosis which, between the eighteenth and twentieth centuries, led to the transition from mercantilist capitalism to industrial capitalism, and which both the classical economists and Marx had succeeded in describing as an emerging power. Although still unfinished, this metamorphosis expresses a process of structural change which marks the transition, after industrial capitalism, towards a new system of accumulation termed *CC* or *bioeconomics*. As defined by Monnier-Vercellone and Fumagalli in this book, these expressions denote a new logic of capital accumulation in which the cognitive and intellectual dimension of work plays an increasingly important role by replacing the fixed assets and material work at the core of the accumulation process.

In the context of this transformation, the first pillar in the valorisation of capital directly concerns control over the production of knowledge and its processing into fictitious goods. Most of the laws and tendencies which characterized the growth process of industrial capitalism, and which were at the basis of political economy, are deeply affected. Hence, this new transformation of capitalism raises a series of issues requiring deeper analysis and which this book intends to resolve on the levels of both theory and empirical research as regards the Eastern European countries.

In what sense can we speak of a new and driving role of knowledge, and what is its impact on the social organization of production, the dynamics of innovation, and the orientation of scientific research? To what extent does the increased importance of cognitive work and the new composition of the labour market modify the determinants of the value of goods, the structure of welfare, and the forms of income distribution? What is the nature of the conflicts and contradictions engendered by the endogenous dynamics of CC and which may lead to its destabilization?

* * * * *

The book is divided into two parts. The first is theoretical, the second empirical; the latter especially deals with the transition of the former socialist countries to free-market capitalism, with particular regard to the diffusion of CC.

In the first paper, Andrea Fumagalli and Stefano Lucarelli discuss some of the structural characteristics of CC by providing a theoretical framework in which it is understood as a financial economy of production. Financialization, on the one hand, and the internationalisation of production due to the exploitation of dynamic learning and network economies, on the other, have structurally changed the accumulation regime. The instability at the basis of the present global economic crisis can be analysed by updating theoretical tools employed by the monetary circuit approach of the 1970s and 1980s. The paper argues that, during the 1990s and 2000s, the financial market has increasingly replaced the credit market and the Keynesian welfare state in influencing and determining investment choices and the distribution of income.

This has been made possible not only by the change in social relations since the crisis of the Fordist paradigm and the new international division of labour, but also by qualitative changes in the regime of accumulation and exploitation. In the second paper, on the concept of bio-economy, Andrea Fumagalli argues that the basis of capitalist accumulation is being expanded not only intensively but extensively as well, with the consequence that life activities such as consumption, social relations and reproduction are being affected. All of these are activities that Fordism considered to be unproductive; but today, by contrast, value is set on life and accumulation becomes more "bio-economic".

In line with the first two essays, the one by Matko Meštrović emphasizes that the process of globalization intrinsic to CC on the one hand promotes a new form of the cognitive division of labour based on differential access to knowledge, and on the other, promotes the total subsumption of human life to the capitalist organization of society. The consequence is a distortion of human capabilities and the need to redefine value theory, which must increasingly deal with the obstacle of immaterial immeasurability.

The following two essays analyse the problem of the role of welfare in CC. Jean-Marie Monnier and Carlo Vercellone start from the consideration that most recent analysis of the rise of knowledge-based capitalism has obscured the crucial role played by the welfare state and the system of gender relations associated with Fordism. Similarly, research into the various forms and functions of the welfare state has suffered from an essentially static and taxonomic approach which ignores the changing dynamics of capitalism as well as the importance of gender. In their essay, Monnier and Vercellone show how the development of the welfare state and the system of gender relations affected the transition from Fordist industrial capitalism to "cognitive" capitalism. The transition to CC has been, however, a complex and contradictory process that may go in opposing directions in the future. Cosma Orsi first discusses the insufficiencies and invalidity of the mainstream approach in economics (what he calls the "political economy of freedom") and contrasts it to a novel approach – the political economy of reciprocity. Drawing on the latter, he proposes measures that should be implemented in order to adapt Fordist welfare to welfare in which knowledge is a common good. Some proposals are put forward in this regard: a basic income as a means to develop individual potentialities better, and the conception of the state as a partner on the basis of a contract of mutual solidarity.

The challenges of the new millennium and the specific properties of knowledge are analysed by Aleksandar Kešeljević's essay, which argues that a new understanding of knowledge is required. Knowledge can be studied from three interrelated perspectives, namely the perspectives of substance, subject (i.e. individual and an organisation), and a holistic aspect. Because some forms of knowledge are more strongly embedded in social relations, Kešeljević emphasises the need for a holistic perspective on knowledge. This would require a new epistemological approach that enlarges the boundaries of economic theory.

In the last essay in the theoretical part of the book, Carlos Prieto del Campo introduces some innovative aspects relative to the socio-economic policy that should be implemented in the era of CC. The essay's main concept is represented by the idea of "common", and it argues that accumulation and valorisation are increasingly based on the exploitation of social cooperation among human beings (the idea of the *general intellect* put forward by Marx in *Grundrisse*). However, this outcome cannot be achieved as the result of a social and political compromise within a progressive and reformist framework. On the contrary, it requires a dialectical process resulting from a dynamic conflict whose context is still to be defined.

The essays presented so far seek to describe the elements of rupture induced by the transition to cognitive capitalism. They apply especially to the Western countries. However, with appropriate additions, they concern the economic growth and development of the Eastern European countries as well. This issue is particularly addressed by the second part of this book, which comprises four papers.

Because model(s) of capitalism(s) in the Eastern European countries may be heavily influenced by the European Union, an important question is the direction in which the EU is heading. Natalija Nikolovska and Nadica Jovanovska stress that the European Union's model of capitalism has recently come to resemble the US (neoliberal) model of capitalism, which relies on financial markets. Since European monetary union has opted for the stability of prices and of the exchange rate, the authors suggest that the trade-off between unemployment and the inflation rate has been forgotten. The immense importance of financial markets for the competitiveness of the US economy is contrasted with the potential of those markets to provoke economic crises. The authors analyse the institutional steps in Europe's shift to the US model of capitalism. They underline that the EU still faces the dilemma of whether convergence to or divergence from the US model of capitalism is better. This dilemma is even more important for the "New Europe" because it may be crucial in determining its economic growth and development.

One of the capitalism's subsystems is social security (pension systems), which is the topic of the paper by Cristina Matos. She discusses pension reforms in the EU-27 countries. According to Matos, pension innovations have been similar in the EU-27 countries, so that cultural and institutional determinants have contributed to some of their specificities. Trends in pension reforms, like the development of complementary pensions and the promotion of later retirement, are addressed by questioning their cognitive validity and socio-economic sustainability. Pension reforms in the post-socialist countries are recognised by the author as part of "a more general ideology of privatisation and state disengagement".

Pasquale Tridico conducts econometric analysis on a sample of 50 emerging and transition economies in the period from 1995 to 2006 in order to determine whether economic growth has been connected with the socio-economic development of these countries. The transition countries in South-Eastern Europe included in the sample are Albania, Bulgaria, Croatia and The Former Yugoslav Republic of Macedonia. Tridico's paper presents strong arguments against claims that the economic benefits accruing from economic growth in those countries have trickled down in terms of greater equality. After discussing concepts of socio-economic development in the literature, as well as pertinent variables, Tridico's main finding is that economic growth has occurred despite negative trends in development indicators.

Siniša Kušić seeks to answer the questions of why capitalism in South-Eastern Europe exists in such a rough form and why it has developed as such. The transition process in the countries of South-Eastern Europe has been gradual and slow. These post-socialist countries started the transition process from a very low level, and/or rather late, because of war and political instabilities. They have experienced a slower process of elite change, with the old elites rent-seeking within the open confines of the new institutional arrangements. Hence the planning horizons needed to create a new socio-economic system have been severely limited. While capitalism in South-Eastern Europe is still in the making, it is unclear whether the countries in the region can advance towards a social market economy. Kušić argues that (radical) changes in the socio-economic systems of these countries are influenced by the EU because of the enlargement process.

References

Boyer, R. and Y. Saillard (eds) (2002), *Regulation Theory: the State of Art*, London: Routledge.

Braudel, F. (1979), *Civilisation matérielle, économie et capitalisme, XVe-XVIIIe siècle*, Tome III, Paris: éd. Armand Colin.

Marazzi, C. (1997), *La place des chaussettes*, Paris: éd. De L'Eclat.

Part I: Theoretical Papers

1. Cognitive capitalism as a financial economy of production

Andrea Fumagalli and Stefano Lucarelli

It is interesting that the stability of the system and its sensitiveness to changes in the quantity of money should be so dependent on the existence of a variety of opinion about what is uncertain. Best of all that we should know the future. But if not, then, if we are to control the activity of the economic system by changing the quantity of money, it is important that opinions should differ. Thus this method of control is more precarious in the United States, where everyone tends to hold the same opinion at the same time, than in England where differences of opinion are more usual (Keynes, 1936).

1. Introduction

The structural changes that occurred in the last 30 years have substantially modified the capitalistic organization of society, both at national and international level. In order to understand the evolution of social and economic systems it is necessary to focus on the relations of production, that is, on those social relationships that explain the valorisation process. Since the economic crisis of the 1970's until the late 1990's the structure of production in the developed countries has been characterised by the development of highly flexible forms of production. The organizational revolution that occurred within production activity has been achieved through introducing new information technologies and restructuring of production within increasingly wider territories.

A new regime of accumulation devoid of a stable mode of regulation and centred on financial valorisation of new socio-economic growth perspectives has been consolidating. Conditions imposed by financial markets in order to create the shareholder's value consisted of promoting downsizing, reengineering, outsourcing and *Merger & Acquisitions* processes (*M&A*). The flexibilization of labour force and precarization of existence has thus been the result of the established valorisation norm. But why should the corporate restructuring sustain the enterprise value by creating income stock?

In order to answer this question it is necessary to analyse the importance of knowledge in the production process. For this purpose, we shall use some categories of the so called French Regulation School. The definition of a new regime of accumulation involves a research on the criteria of valorisation and the prevailing technological paradigm. The main changes of new capitalism concern mainly two spheres: the role played by knowledge in the new technological paradigm and valorisation process and the importance of finance. The dominant technological paradigm and the role played by knowledge within it are not enough to explain the evolution of the accumulation regime. It is needed to introduce further elements necessary to explain the expectations that sustain the investment choices made by capitalists; these are the conventions or collective beliefs (Orléan, 2008).

Then, after describing the main features of the accumulation paradigm that many scholars have not hesitated to name as *cognitive capitalism* (henceforth CC – see Corsani et all, 2001; Azais, Corsani, and Dieuaide, 2001; Vercellone, 2003, 2005, 2006; Fumagalli, 2007; Moulier-Boutang, 2007; Fumagalli and Vercellone, 2007; Colletis and Paulré, 2008), we shall attempt to provide a theoretical framework of it intended as a financial economy of production. We shall therefore proceed to the reformulation of the schemes of monetary circuit (Graziani, 2003) by taking into account the structural changes induced by CC.

2. The main features of cognitive capitalism

2.1. A critique of the liberal theories of knowledge-based economy

CC is a *regime* of accumulation without a viable mode of regulation between entrepreneurs and workers as regards knowledge exploitation and capital gains allocation. On the demand side, the increasing polarization of income distribution – in absence of suitable welfare policies – risks to penalize not only aggregate demand, but even knowledge-learning process and network economies. A too high share of precarious works can negatively affect social productivity, with the risk to worsen financial gains. On the contrary, a constant realization of capital gains and their fair allocation provided by financial markets should guarantee a stable growth of CC (Fumagalli and Lucarelli, 2007).

The hypothesis of CC develops from a critique of the political economy of the new liberal theories of knowledge-based economy.

> Understanding of the meaning at stake in the current mutation of capitalism cannot be reduced to the mere constitution of an economy founded on knowledge, but in the formation of a knowledge-based economy framed and subsumed by the laws of capital accumulation (Vercellone, 2007: 2).

The notion of CC has also been developed as a response to the insufficiency of the interpretations of the current mutation of capitalism in terms of the transition from a Fordist to a post-Fordist model of flexible accumulation. David Harvey has defined flexible accumulation paradigm by a direct confrontation with the rigidities of Fordism:

> It rests on flexibility with respect to labour processes, labour markets, products, and patterns of consumption. It is characterized by the emergence of entirely new sectors of production,

new ways of providing financial services, new markets, and, above all, greatly intensified rates of commercial, technological, and organizational innovation. It has entrained rapid shifts in the patterning of uneven development, both between sectors and between geographical regions, giving rise, for example, to a vast surge in so-called "service-sector" employment as well as to entirely new industrial ensembles in hitherto underdeveloped regions [...] it has also entailed a new round of what I shall call "time-space compression" [...] in the capitalist world – the time horizons of both private and public decision-making have shrunk, while satellite communication and declining transport costs have made it increasingly possible to spread those decisions immediately over an ever wider and variegated space (Harvey, 1990: 147).

This vision is not completely exhaustive and may lead to distorted political implications: the knowledge economy has been a central element of the Third way, pinpointing the role of public intervention for education and new information technologies: knowledge economy seems, to the optimists, to be a nicer kind of capitalism, an "opportunity economics", a new economic egalitarianism that was truly dependent on "exploiting the potential of all".

An opportunity economics would be one that frees opportunity for individuals to grasp, and gives them the means with which to realise their inherent potential:

The Third way's notion of emancipation is this notion of everybody's freedom to fully realise their potential – of "bridging the gap between what we are and what we have it in us to become". However, emancipation does not seem to be the dominant feature of what the knowledge economy brings. There is sufficient critical analysis of the post-fordist production order to point to the possibility that while it might hold the potential for emancipation for some, it also brings about new forms of exploitation for others, a relationship that is obvious and yet still poorly understood. [...] Clearly, contemporary social democracy does not speak of capitalism as a system of the exploitation of labour in the interest of capital, or at least, New Labour doesn't, while there are varieties of this in social democratic discourse. The Third way denies, in fact [...] that a distinction between labour and capital can be made in knowledge capitalism, since labour *is* capital (Andersson, 2006).

The category of post-Fordism model of flexible accumulation appears to be inadequate for comprehending the real transformation of the antagonistic relation of capital to labour related to the development of an economy founded on the driving role of knowledge. The notion of CC aims to overcome these difficulties by explaining the formation of a knowledge-based economy framed and subsumed by the laws of capital accumulation.

To deeply comprehend the role of knowledge in the evolution of capitalism we need to re-read the history of workers. Let us consider the case of Italian economic boom: the starting point for the formation of CC is the process of diffusion of knowledge generated by the development of mass schooling and the rise of the average level of education. The experiences of the *new employees* were radically different from those of the previous generations of individually unskilled workers. The intellectual quality of the labour force led to the assertion of a new primacy of living knowledge, mobilized by workers, in contrast to the knowledge incorporated in fixed capital and the managerial organization of firms (Vercellone, 2006).

When between 1978 and 1979 the so-called "new employees" walked into Mirafiori (a FIAT factory), their experiences were radically different from those of the previous generation of workers, who were "individually deskilled, neo-immigrants and new to city living, yet socialised en masse in this highly mechanised 'factory'" (Alquati, 1975). They would rise up against both the wage "structure", its "form" and the necessity to work for the whole duration of one's life itself, to receive an income rather than a salary [see Citizenship income]. The subjectivity expressed by this new labour force certainly failed to undermine the factory regime overall. If anything, it made it more viable and eased the restructuring moves towards flexibility. This is due to the rigidity of the offer of labour caused by the rising levels and spread of education. Whilst it had been previously possible to interpret the productive behaviour of the labour force as an articulation of the technical composition of class, now this was made impossible by the growing penetration of the "social" into the productive sphere, which limited its normative power over the behaviour of the workers (Zanini and Fadini, 2001).

The subjectivity expressed by this new labour force failed to undermine the factory regime overall and yet it eased the restructuring move towards flexibility: it means that the process of wealth creation is no longer based upon homogeneous and standardized scheme of labour organization.

Whereas within the Fordist factory productive activity is mute, and work is performed by a silent human chain, in the post-Fordist metropolis, the material labour process can be empirically described as a complex group of linguistic acts, a sequence of assertions, and a symbolic interaction. This is because labour activity is now performed alongside the system of machines, with regulating, surveillance and coordinating functions; but also because the process of production uses knowledge, information, culture and social relations as its "raw materials" (Virno, 2001: 181).

2.1.1. The life cycle of knowledge

The generation of knowledge and its spatial diffusion through learning and network processes are the basic features of CC. The life cycle of knowledge comprises three phases: from tacit to codified, to exploited codified knowledge (Fumagalli, 2007). The socialization of tacit knowledge occurs via a slow and expensive process entailing the sharing of personal experiences and social context. Whilst tacit knowledge holds out the specialised learning economies, the development of industrial production needs that part of tacit knowledge is formalised in abstract codes (Becattini and Rullani, 2000: 105). The process of codification depends on organisational decisions and behaviours. The codes can be used as means of appropriation: a high degree of routine can represent a precondition for perpetrating expropriation and codification of workers tacit knowledge[1]. Knowledge of organisations resides in routines that are also "a locus of conflict, governance and way of codifying microeconomic incentives and constraints" (Coriat and Dosi, 1998, quoted in Cassi, 2007: 78).

If important tacit knowledge cannot be effectively spread through an organization, it means that training in an organization becomes more time consuming. In order to collectivize and spread tacit knowledge, organizations should invest greatly in the human capital of their members by offering high wages. But there is another important variable: education. Education inside the society may represent a form of social control.

> Orthodox treatment of education has been dominated, however, by references to codifiable knowledge. This can be seen below, for example, in the central role given to targets (for literacy, numeracy and so on) in New Labour policy towards primary and secondary schools. Targets are premised on knowledge that can be codified.[...] Tacit knowledge points away, therefore, from a classroom environment (Prabhakar, 2002: 44).

If knowledge is the basis of accumulation, it becomes unavoidable to analyze how its exchange and diffusion affect the dynamics of productivity. It is reasonable to assume that the greater is the share of codified knowledge dedicated to the accumulation activity, the higher is the achievable level of social productivity. The ability to enlarge both knowledge-learning process and network economies, respectively, depend on the degree of *cumulativeness*, *opportunity* and *appropriability* (Nelson and Winter, 1982) and on the level of income and positive externalities. When knowledge-learning process is constrained by intellectual property rights (IPR), we shall see that the consequence is that the greater is the degree of *appropriability* of knowledge, the smaller becomes its capacity of diffusion – affecting, *de facto,* its ability to positively influencing the associated productivity.

To a higher level of knowledge corresponds, in terms of its generation and diffusion, more *potential* innovative technologies. It may be useful to define innovation in economic sense: from a systemic perspective, an innovation is a change in the economic process occurred as a result of the investment activity. Whether

---

1 Cassi (2007: 76) defines a *code* as a *set of signs and symbols with a pre-determined, accepted meaning and some rules to combine them*; he also points out that "sharing a code is necessary but not sufficient condition for an effective communication among agents ... The institutional and social context shapes the feature of knowledge in terms of non-excludability and non-rivalry" (Cassi, 2007: 79).

the investment is devoted to the already existing technology or to new technologies will establish the amount of innovation.

2.2. Investment activity and the internet convention

The crisis of Fordism led to a new investment activity based on new sources of growth: electronic marketing, informational goods, encoding software, control over the quality of information, branding, control over the lifestyles, etc. Then social system is geared around innovation and immaterial production and investment policies depend not only upon R&D, but also "learning by doing" strategies and process. But in CC the impact of new ICT based on computer science, micro-electronics and the new organizational productive changes (just-in-time, zero stock) have sped up the "learning by doing" processes, spreading them well beyond the firm (Venturini, 2006). At the same time, part of the R&D process unfolds itself within territories each having one or more specific competencies. Where to locate economic activities is mainly determined by the search on the part of the firm of advantages in the development of its competencies (Mouhoud, 2006: 300). Consequently the productivity entailed by the exchange of knowledge cannot be assimilated to material productivity. High tech production systems define organisational decisions and behaviours and indirectly both the process of codification of knowledge and the exploitation of codified knowledge.

Investment is a primary source of productivity increases and it may be split in two parts: 1) *routine* investment; 2) investment in innovation, knowledge (learning and human capital) and *branding*[2]. These are investments that are used to produce and subsume the value produced outside the directly productive processes. Routine investment traditionally depends on demand expectations and on realized production level in the previous period.

---

2 Adam Arvidsson (2007) delineates the ideal-typical model of what he calls the "logic of the brand". He argues the logic governing how brands create value, represents a paradigmatic example of the dominating value-logic of informational capitalism. Value is less based on the control of salaried labour and more on the ability to appropriate and commodify a socially produced immaterial externality. This externality consists in forms of knowledge; sociality and affect that arise in (relatively) autonomous processes of media enhanced sociality. It is the new empowered capacity to create what Arvidsson calls an "ethical surplus" that result from new information and communication technologies, that constitutes the real foundation for the wealth that brands valorise. Arvidsson suggests that the logic of the brand is applicable to a range of other socialized production processes, from the ethically conscious company to the contemporary participatory online economy, or Web 2.0.

Investment in innovation and knowledge is characterized by very high potential returns and, at the same time, by possible catastrophic losses. In CC they represent the most relevant part of the firm's strategies. Whilst the investments in production and transmission of knowledge (education, training, R&D, management, that is immaterial goods) increase, there is a significant reduction of the costs of codification, transmission and acquisition of knowledge, due to the generation and diffusion of linguistic and communicative technologies (ICT, Internet, and the like).

Not only knowledge has become an increasingly mobile resource, but also, and above all, better codify-able (Rodriguez, 2000; Rullani, 2004), and therefore directly exploitable via IPR. In a context where the exploitation of knowledge is the final goal, the labour market becomes even more fragmented as a result of the shift from mechanical-repetitive to linguistic-communicative technologies (the so called high tech) where both quality and modality of the performed work are irreversibly modified. It allows the exploitation of individual knowledge and relational skills and generates technological unemployment and work precariousness.

Vis à vis the levels of remuneration, this process has led to the individualization of wages accompanied by a wage dynamics even more disjointed both from productive gains and working hours. At the same time, increased quotas of postponed salary are expropriated, as a result of the tendency to privatize the welfare system (Figure 1).

Figure 1: high tech production systems (internet convention)

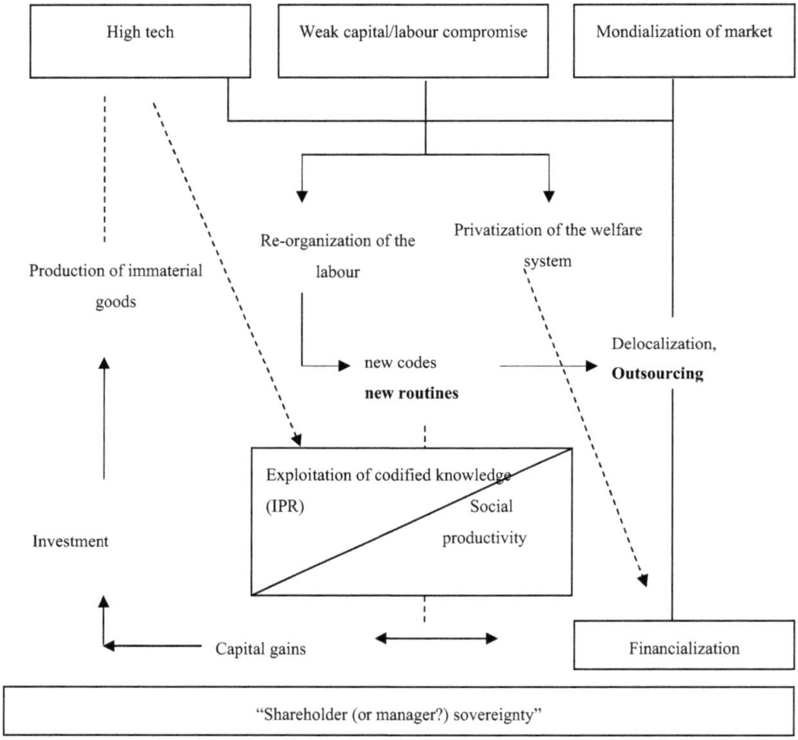

In the 1990s, financialization, in as much investment of the collective savings in the stock market, generated additional incomes. The incomes were created in the markets through business debt to the banking system[3]. In the period between 1993 and 2000, the New York Stock Exchange upwardly exploded (the Dow Jones from 4000 to 11700, Standard & Poor's from 450 to 1530): the apprecia-tion obtained in the market favored real growth thanks to the exploitation of the

3 The disinvestment in fixed capital that freed up liquidity from productive processes should be taken into account. This liquidity was used to increase the market value of capital. If in addition to the increase in liquidity, consequent to the reduction of investments in fixed capital, the increase of business debt to the banking system is added, we can understand why the financialization of the economy (payment of dividends, interest, Merger & Acquisitions, the buyback of already exposed stocks) was an extraordinary transfer of wealth to the class of stock investors and the managers that were responsible for financialization processes. On this point see Marazzi (2008).

knowledge and productivity of labour involved in the high-tech sector above all. The valuation of financial markets began to depend on the organizational change geared toward favoring innovative cooperative forms between relatively autonomous workers. The dynamism of the organizational change became – thanks to the attention that the financial markets gave it – a new modality of valorization of productive capital. Thus a finance-led growth regime asserted itself (Boyer, 2000). In the second half of the 1990s, the idea of a digitalized society, with liberating effects on the world of work and life, became a convention (Marazzi, 2008). Whether true or false, there is no doubt that this convention pulled the real transformation processes of the world ahead. Joseph Stiglitz's lucid critique of the roaring '90s confirms this:

> Modern American-style capitalism was pivoted around what would later be called the New Economy, symbolized by the so-called dot-coms that were revolutionizing the way that America – and the rest of the world – did business, modifying the rhythms of the very technological shifts and increasing the growth rate of productivity to extraordinary levels, that had not been seen for over 25 years. [...] Halfway though the '90s, the manufacturing sector had slipped to a scarce 14% of total production, with a percent of employees even lower in respect to the active population (Stiglitz, 2004: 4).

A convention determines more than just the definition of a "scenario of reference":

> We must go further, and also consider the battery of specific criteria it constructs to serve as a basis for the concrete valuation of companies. Thus, in the case of the "New Economy convention", faced with the difficulty of accounting for stock market prices solely on the criterion of profits, as most "dot.com" businesses were loss-making, a new basis for making estimates appeared, in the form of "value per user". So the potential number of subscribers, visitors or customers was adopted as the strategic variable, supposed to enable the level of value creation to be assessed (Orlean, 2008)[4].

In this accumulation system, various forms of remuneration tied to the whole of business yield developed: not only stock options for managers, but also the very retirement or investment funds that mostly involve wage labourers. These forms of remuneration made financial market liquidity grow but, in the absence of an adequate redistribution rule, inside a capitalism in which the rule is to command

4 Following Keynes, André Orlean (2004) proposed a definition of "collective belief" that is essential for studying financial markets: an individual *i* believes that the group *G* believes the proposition *Q* if he believes that, in the majority, the members of the group believe that the group *G* believes *Q*. The definition is "self-referential", it does not involve any reference to the "primary beliefs" of individuals, but only refers to beliefs that bear directly on what the group *G* believes. The self-referential hypothesis therefore reconciles the *ex ante* existence of a heterogeneous set of individual fundamentalist estimates and the *ex post* emergence of a unique representation that gives the price its significance.

living labour in any case, this also compressed wages, leading to systemic instability. This is what happened in the March 2000 crisis: beyond having distributed new stock incomes unequally, the command bridge of the New Economy made them by destroying wages and employment stability, in line with a new common sense: the conditions over financial markets to create stock value encourage extreme organizational innovation, promoting the processes of downsizing, reengineering, outsourcing and *M&A*. Hence, finance translates and betrays the real innovative processes in act by devaluating living labour. To attract investors to the stock markets, businesses offered increasingly higher yields precisely through merger and acquisition operations of other businesses, acquiring their own shares, and even rigging their accounts. The necessary capital for this restructuring aimed at controlling the technological trajectory was done by taking remuneration from the work force.

The March 2000 crisis marked the passage toward another diffusion and generalization of financialization: a new phase characterized by a marked decline, with losses of 40% in the Dow Jones, 50% in Standard & Poor's and 80% in the NASDAQ. In the meantime, wage deflation advanced, under the effects of the Asian (Indian and Chinese) industrial army reserve but also put into action by outsourcing.

2.3. The Chinese and real estate convention

The market recovery came in 2003. Christian Marazzi has talked about this as the "China convention" (Marazzi, 2004); a convention – which, in our opinion, should be understood as a change on the margins of the internet convention – that rests on the idea that valorization depends on the outsourcing towards developing countries with a high exploitation of labour and the environment, but still within the same technological paradigm. This triggered a mechanism that could be defined as an industrial reserve army of financial origin. The financial crisis of March 2000 is the first one after 1987 which involved the western stock exchanges, a new convention raised up. It deals with the increasing role played by China, India and other newly developed countries (like Brazil and Russia, but also South Africa and the so called Asian tigers[5]) in the internationalization of production and cognitive division of labour (Figure 2). From an institutional point of view, the "China convention" started to work after the entrance of the

5 Jim O'Neill, global economist at Goldman Sachs, argues that the economic potential of Brazil, Russia, India, and China (BRIC) is such that they may become among the four most dominant economies by the year 2050. These countries encompass over 25% of the world's land coverage and 40% of the world's population and hold a combined GDP (PPP) of 15.435 trillion dollars. On almost every scale, they would be the largest entity on the global stage (Goldman Sachs Global Economics Group, 2007).

Republic of China in the WTO in December 2001. The role played by China in dragging the world economy is quite known in this decade. The increasing Chinese export, especially towards the western economy, characterized by low prices, favored the stabilization of inflation rates and the diminishing of real interest rates. Stock exchanges market were able to recover after the internet convention crisis and to provide liquidity to the speculative activity, even thanks to the increase of indebtedness of American and western families, in order to keep up with the living standard of the previous decade. Chinese surplus started to finance the USA internal and external deficit[6].

6 In November 2008, China became the first country which finances USA public and foreign deficit, surpassing Japan after 2005.

Figure 2: Chinese and real estate conventions

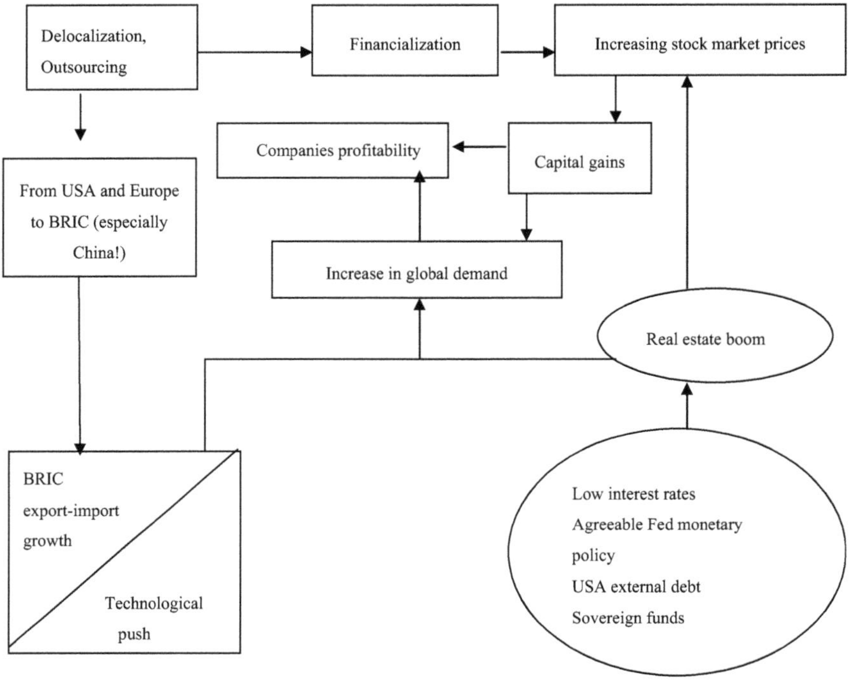

In the two-year period following the March 2000 crisis (2001-2002), the FED drastically lowered the interest rate from 6% to 1%. That pushed the economic agents to go into unreasonable debt to benefit from the discrepancy between their own capital yield and the interest rate. This incentive to accumulate debt means that the wealth-effect was articulated in different ways in respect to the roaring years of the New Economy: the prices on real-estate markets rose and the FED's monetary policy supported the buying power of American consumers. American families could thus obtain practically unlimited credit from the banking system, putting up a real-estate patrimony with increasing value as a guarantee. The expected earnings came back high, sustained by a negative real interest rate. Stock prices came back up in March 2003 (at the eve of the American intervention in Iraq). It is possible to find a precise description of financialization as practice of social control in the words of Stiglitz (2007, our emphasis):

The story goes back to the recession of 2001. With the support of Federal Reserve Chairman Alan Greenspan, President George W. Bush pushed through a tax cut designed to benefit the richest Americans but not to lift the economy out of the recession that followed the collapse of the Internet bubble. Given that mistake, the Fed had little choice if it was to fulfill its mandate to maintain growth and employment: it had to lower interest rates, which it did in an unprecedented way – all the way down to 1%.

It worked, but in a way fundamentally different from how monetary policy normally works. Usually, low interest rates lead firms to borrow more to invest more, and greater indebtedness is matched by more productive assets.

But, given that overinvestment in the 1990's was part of the problem underpinning the recession, lower interest rates did not stimulate much investment. *The economy grew, but mainly because American families were persuaded to take more debt, refinancing their mortgages and spending some of the proceeds.* And, as long as housing prices rose as a result of lower interest rates, Americans could ignore their growing indebtedness.

In other words, the population was involved in the production of (financial) wealth, first through the construction of the New Economy, then – after the diffusion of a new swarm of innovations and innovative instincts that fed financial euphoria, but over time transformed into positional rents for only the most aggressive businesses – repositioning the financial level to the real-estate sector after having disciplined a euphoric society through outsourcing toward developing countries that highly exploit labour and the environment. Monetary policy facilitates this process without governing it: from Spring 2003 to January 2007 the FED extraordinarily increased the liquidity available to the markets. 97% of the American population hit by wage deflation – through which the devaluation of living labour is understood – continued to preserve its quality of life through rising real-estate prices, the generosity with which the American credit markets operated, and the low price of imported goods. Nevertheless, this financial lever sustained financial earnings without any relation with the capacity to generate profits in the "real" economy: insolvency risk was high. Credit of the same nature was grouped and converted into bonds and derived products that were put into financial markets. Thus risk was transferred to the operators of these financial activities, which increased bank solidity, but was susceptible to leading to a bigger crisis.

A positive effect on financial market begun to be developed by credit-debt relationship on housing market (the "real estate convention"), favored by low interest rates, financial innovations (new types of derivatives) and increase in the house prices. The convention has lasted until September 2007, after the first disease in the mortgage market.

2.4. A finance-led capitalism?

The previous analysis says that CC is not simply a stage of capitalism where knowledge assumes a new role after the transformations in the capital/labour relation. CC is a finance-led economy based on a particular theory of the firm – the so called *shareholder sovereignty theory* – that legitimates the shareholder control of the company (Aglietta and Rebérioux, 2005: 1)[7]. To complete the analysis of the knowledge/power relation in the development of the division of labour we need to consider together new form of production and financialization. CC is mainly based upon the globalization of financial markets, utilized by the investors both for financing the economic activity and for stimulating investments via the increased financialization of the productive activities.

The dismantling of the Welfare system, favouring the growth of the quotas of income to be allocated to the financial market, shows the irrelevance of the intervention of the State in economy and the diminishing its regulatory and distributive role. The so-called "Washington consensus", named after the Washington-based institution of the IMF and the World Bank has conquered the policy agenda in most countries, by providing the key policy justification for financing and supporting financial markets throughout the world.

The realization of production is compensated by financial markets acting as a *multiplier* of aggregate demand, and by the processes of globalization (delocalization, outsourcing, lower labour costs).

The efficiency of the system is assured by both the growth of financial markets – primary source of surplus distribution – and by massive processes of outsourcing and delocalization characterizing advanced countries (which are by definition the places where the accumulation of knowledge occurs more intensely).

The power of finance capital depends on its ability to impose the criteria of financial returns. Markets move in waves of conventions – internet, China, real estate market have produced movements of public opinion that are historically determined to divert towards the objects of desire-investment. Conventions are

---

7 The doctrine of shareholder sovereignty does not consider that, being dispersed, shareholders do not have the real means to exercise their sovereign control. But external and internal controls compensate for the shareholders' inability: externally auditors, financial analysts and rating agencies are responsible for accounting information for investors; internally, the board of directors assumes the task of re-establishing shareholders' real rights. Aglietta and Rebérioux (2005) demonstrates the logical contradictions of outside controls and the real collusion between management and market finance.

never real; they have real effects on the economic growth, though. Conventions are market trends originated within the investors community according to a logic of self-referential rationality. Self-rationality has to be interpreted as a prodigious mechanism for amplifying rumours. Conventions are historically determined, that is they epitomize a high number of heterogeneous factors that contribute to determine the qualitative trends of market. Internet convention is based on diffusion of communication and information technologies at domestic level, on a feeling of unlimited development of digital market and the infinite power of interconnection.

Companies, in order to obtain liquidity for *M&A* run into debts. Through the *M&A* strategy the company controls technologies, skills and know-how of other potential competitors.

The crisis of financialization of cognitive and innovative labour occurred in March 2000 involves the impossibility to reproduce the virtuous circle of s*tart up* and *M&A* on the base of the ongoing influx of capitals in the USA. The loss of capital gains (of risk premium and goodwill) is compensated by reducing drastically workers' wage and through processes of delocalization and outsourcing – China and India represent extraordinary areas of low cost labour force that is ready to enter the global circuits of high-tech production. Those new strategies concerning the re-launch of financial markets take place by weakening the generation of workers, whose skills made the New Economy grow in the developed economies.

New convention needs to sustain consumptions even in the presence of an income redistribution to the disadvantage of workers. Monetary policy of the Fed had to adapt itself to make this apparent contradiction possible. Between the end of 2000 and 2003 the maintenance of high levels of consumption had been assured by interest rates at 1%, therefore negative in real terms, set by the Fed (Asensio, 2007). This occurred thanks to the elimination of savings and the re-mortgaging for home-owners who chose it rather than facing the inflation of real estate value.

Thus, business expectations should increase, managers should sustain the positive dynamics of shareholder values on the one hand, and pay the debts to the banks, on the other hand. More importantly, indebtedness is not directed to capital expenditures, but it is a powerful means of satisfying the financial criteria of shareholder value (Figure 3).

Figure 3: finance-led growth

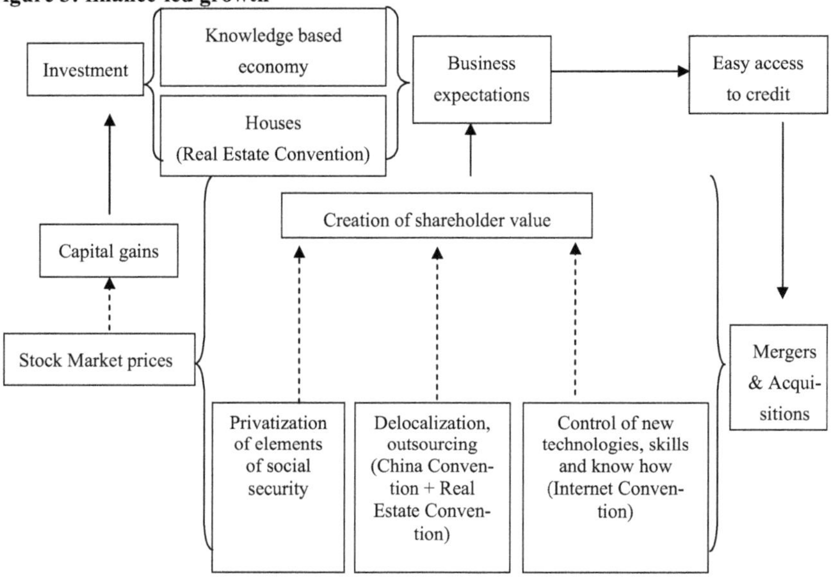

Such a process requires specific monetary policies by a massive injection of liquidity and lowering of interest rates to prevent the emergence of financial bubbles[8]. Macro-economic changes depend entirely on monetary policy: the USA Fed has played a decisive role, averting deflation by bringing the interest-rate curve to very low levels over 2001-2008 period. The result is a massive transfer of corporate risk onto households, which thus saved company profitability (Aglietta and Rebérioux, 2005: 4).

But, as the US situation in the '90s shows (Aglietta, 2006: 11-14), the financial boom has a double result: from one side, the positive dynamics of shareholder values favours the increase in aggregate consumption, from the other, because of its unequal allocation, leads to a distorted income distribution.

8 The term "bubble" describes a situation in which current stock market prices are no longer justified by future dividends.

3. Monetary economy of production and financial economy of production: a comparison with the circuitist approach

3.1. The monetary circuit scheme in its original form (Graziani 1984)

Within the economic theories that have a descriptive function of economic reality in order to formulate analytical rules concerning its functioning, an important role is played by the so called theory of the monetary circuit. It is an analytical scheme embedded in Quesnay's *Tableau économique* and in Marx's reproduction schemes that fixes the conditions of reproduction of a given system. It is not necessary then to define functions that synthesize the behaviour of the agents. The monetary circuit schemes consist of a macroeconomic analysis based on social structure rather than on individual behaviour. As it occurs in the classics researches, the characteristic behaviour of each social group is not given by free individual choices but by the specific social location that therefore expresses itself in a functional distinction of the economic agents who play a well specific role in the economic process according to the class they belong to. According to the indications of Keynes (but also of Schumpeter and Wicksell), banks, enterprises and workers are the social groups to take into consideration while individual's behaviour is determined by the functioning conditions of the whole system.

In the traditional individualistic analysis (the neoclassical one) the economic process seems like a whole of simultaneous and multilateral exchanges that involve all agents in an equal way: money and credit have any other function but to allow agents to make their exchanges. Exchanges that took place in an hypothetical perfect competition market determine the prices producing both the subjective equilibrium of each agent (that is the maximization of utility or individual profit) and the objective equilibrium of market (i.e. equilibrium between demand and supply). Money, that makes exchanges easier while avoiding the drawbacks of barter, does not change market equilibrium, that is the quantity produced or relative prices. In case monetary circulation alters market equilibrium it means that there is something incorrect in the management controlled by monetary authorities. The whole relative prices can therefore be analysed even assuming that economy works without money whereas determining monetary prices is due only to the quantity of existing money.

The monetary circuit as social macroeconomic analysis rather considers modern economy as a monetary production economy and thereby it involves a completely different mechanism from that of a barter economy. Monetary economy means that all exchanges are settled in money and this raises immediately the problem of how money is created and introduced into the system. In modern economies, money is created by the interaction between banking and enterprises sectors and it is then made available for the latter through granting credit. Because just those who have money can enter the market, the decisions made by banks as regards to whom grant credit and also how much credit they wish to grant become crucial elements to the determination of the final equilibrium of the system. Creating money contributes thus to determine the quantity produced as well as the distribution of national income. The result is that money is never neutral.

First of all it is necessary to explain how money enters the economic circuit, who owns it and on which conditions: In a capitalist economy, liquidity created by banks is loaned to enterprises. Enterprises make use of liquidity to buy labour force and put into action the technical process of production. When the production process is completed, enterprises sell their products and repay the loan.

Obviously an important point about such a description of capitalist mode of reproduction process is that categories and problems that have been removed by neoclassical equilibrium analysis re-emerge as being analytically crucial:
a) the classical concept of capital as monetary advance which allows for production process to take place is taken up: capital is not thus a result of abstention from current consumption but it rather represents the possibility to get a loan to start-up the production process;
b) there is not equality among economic agents. The distinction between those who have chances to get a loan and those who do not is simply an expression of the class structure of capitalist society;
c) workers are excluded from the decision-making process concerning the management of the production process: loan beneficiaries are the firms thereby it is them that manage the production process and therefore choose the technology involved in the process as well as the quantity they wish to produce and the nature of the product itself;
d) the acknowledgement that enterprises – by managing the production process – have the power to determine the nature and quantity of production brings about the abandonment of another theorem of the neoclassical theory, i.e., that in market labour workers can bargain the level of their wages in real terms. As a matter of fact, if bargainings are not simultaneous and labour and goods market are regarded as different markets any chance to concretely contract real wage fails since workers lack knowledge of the actual prices of goods until when they go to buy them;
e) in the neoclassical view, the issue of the realization of products and profits is not taken into account whereas in the view of the capitalist process as a monetary cycle the issue of such realization emerges again with all its implications concerning the distribution of income and the accumulation of capital (and the

theory of value). This occurs not just because one or more agents can decide to accumulate liquidity and thereby interrupt the monetary circuit but especially because the enterprises, at the end of the production process, have to find adequate liquidity to pay off their loans including the agreed interest rates. Although this can happen, it is necessary that some conditions occur in order to solve the problem of the realization faced by the enterprises. Those conditions can be considered neither normal nor automatic: the monetary circuit in itself does not have endogenous elements that assure its equilibrium.

In the traditional version of the monetary circuit scheme (Graziani 1984) there are three classes (bankers, capitalists, and workers) and two sectors (producing consumption and investment goods). The capitalist production is described as a process characterized by sequential phases, the first one being the creation of money by banks. Firms set the amount of both the consumption and investment goods to be produced. The initial amount of credit that firms obtain from banks is less than the amount that they should pay back at the end of the period. Augusto Graziani, the founder father of the Italian circuitist approach, posed the problem since the early 1980s (Realfonzo, 2006; Fumagalli and Lucarelli, 2008). In France the circuit theory has been analytically developed by three main groups of authors: 1. the so-called Dijon school headed by Bernard Schmitt (Rossi, 2006); 2. the group headed by Alain Parguez, strictly connected to French-Canadian authors; 3. the group of Bordeaux, active mostly in the 1980s, formed around François Poulon.

i. The opening of the monetary circuit (initial finance)

The first step in the economic process is to found funding so that either the industrial or business entrepreneur comes into possession of the means of production and labour force necessary to start up his business activity. The trust relationship established between agents of goods and services markets is guaranteed by money in its function of credit money. Credit money enters the economic process under entrepreneurial demand. When industrial enterprises increase the flow of investments, money demand addressed to the banking sector is met through the ex novo money creation. The amount of money used to fund the production activity is not just endogenous in the demand side – since it varies according to the changes in the investment plans of the enterprises – but also in the supply side because it depends on the availability of monetary policy and the selecting and rationing criteria in force in the banking sector.

In the monetary circuit approach, the separation between banking and enterprise sector represents a fundamental characteristic of capitalism. Money is not neutral at all and it has direct consequences on the level of investments made by the enterprise sector and therefore on the final level of production. Money does not just affect the level of effective demand (as in Keynes' General Theory) but being the only means of funding it also heavily influences the productive activity of the enterprise sector, which is the effective supply.

ii. The production process

The production process lies at the heart of the capitalist economic system. Most of the existing social conflict due to the conflict of interest between entrepreneurs and workers lies in the transformation process of the factors of production into finished products. Such a distinction is mainly established by the opportunity for entrepreneurs to directly manage the production activity and to take initiative autonomously thanks to their free access to credit market, against the subordinate role played by workers who passively have to express their willingness to work according to changing productive needs.

Particularly, the management of production techniques becomes a fundamental variable to explain the evolution of production dynamics aimed at the valorisation of goods produced and introduced into the market. Production plans chosen by entrepreneurs can be affected by two main economic factors:
1. the availability of liquid assets in order to fund new investments;
2. the expectations concerning the placement of products on the market aimed at the valorisation of production.

Thus it would seem that the only actual constraint for production activity is given by monetary conditions established by the banking sector. The risk of not selling all goods that have been produced represents a constraint that can be easily removed: enterprises have the opportunity to issue stocks and bonds and thus regain liquidity to pay off their bank debt.

iii. The closure of the monetary circuit

Here it is about analysing the problem of regaining the amount of liquidity that enterprises have spent. They have to be able to pay off not just the loan granted to them at the beginning of the production process by the banks but also the interests accrued over the same period of time. Issuing securities does not represent an authentic expenditure for enterprises. Because part of liquidity paid in the form of interests or dividends constitutes the income of the working class, it can be used to buy new consumption goods or other securities issued by the enterprises.

3.2. Description of the role played by financial markets in the traditional circuit schemes

In the circuit schemes introduced by Augusto Graziani, financialization emerges as a scenario linked to the budget results of enterprises. The so-called phenomenon of an increasing weight of the financial sector is explained not so much by a decline in entrepreneurship, but rather by a high government deficit coupled to a credit squeeze.

> The analysis of the circulation approach shows that, for finance to increase its weight as compared to production, a fall in entrepreneurial spirit is not enough and that additional technical factors are needed. More precisely:
> a) A first condition is the presence of firms having earned profits not only in kind (which would only be a case of self-financed investment) but in the form of money. [...] a considerable increase in financial activity to the detriment of real production can only take place in the presence of disequilibria in the balance sheets of single agents: for instance when whole groups of firms suffer conspicuous losses while other groups earns corresponding profits; or in the presence of a considerable government deficit. [...];
> b) A second condition is also necessary, namely that agents in debt towards the banks be prepared to obtain loans from agents endowed with liquid holdings, thus replacing bank debt by debt towards other agents. This can easily happen when the government tries to finance its own deficit by issuing new securities. The same can happen whenever a credit squeeze occurs and firms having financial problems, and unable to get the required amount of credit from a bank, try to take advantage of liquidity holdings existing in the non-banking sector. It is after all a well known consequence of a credit squeeze that a reduction in the money stock, or in its rate of growth, give rise to an increase in the velocity of circulation (Graziani, 2003: 157-158).

In other words, financial markets are relevant in the traditional circuit framework only in the closure of the monetary circuit: it plays the role to recuperate the liquidity not collected through the sale of goods. Hence, the financial market could not even operate if money has not been previously created by the credit market, the only one which is able to provide "money ex-nihilo".

Figure 4: monetary production circuit in Fordist capitalism

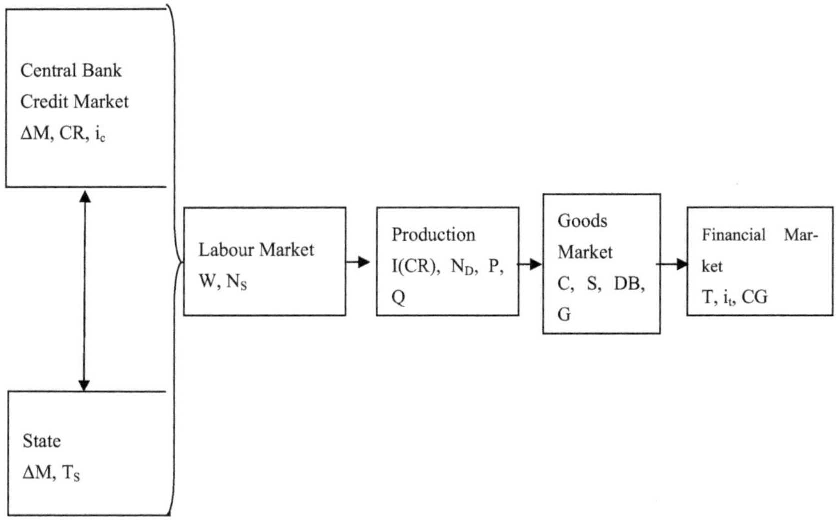

Legend

ΔM = Money creation flow (initial finance)
CR = Bank credit
i_c = rate of interest on credit
W = wages
T_S = Public bonds
N_S = Labour supply
I(CR) = Investment activity financed by credit
N_D = Labour demand unilaterally fixed by firms
P = production prices
Q = Output level
C = Consumption
S = saving
DB = bank deposit
G = Public expenditure
T = bonds
i_t = interest rate (or dividend) on bonds and shares
CG = capital gains

3.3. The monetary circuit scheme in cognitive capitalism: towards a financial economy of production scheme

Following the crisis of Fordism and the fall of the Bretton Woods system, money increases its power of control. It is the triumph of virtual money that is no longer tied to the real economy – and therefore to goods – and it mainly assumes a double function.

The former, prevailing in the 1980's, has an informative nature. Throughout the 1980's the strong increase of economic uncertainty, that started with the adoption of a flexible rate regime, the downward rigidity of interest rates and the reduction of the referential time horizon (becoming increasingly short term), has facilitated the arising of financial tools (the so called derivative products such as options and futures) aiming at insuring themselves against risk and pre-dating the deadlines for trading and thus at predetermining the value of the exchange itself. Such operations allow to advance exchanges liquidity within financial debt and credit operations mainly concerning public securities or operations on the foreign exchange market. Thereby, it is possible to meet an increasingly inescapable need of modern post-Fordist economies, that is to advance the monetary realization of exchanges which may partly concern also merchant activity and thus insure themselves against insolvency or unsold risk. Besides, there is a need to regulate the international financial flows in order to support disciplinary and international hierarchilization mechanisms through processes of discriminant reallocation performed by the financial capital – former credit money already created and now reallocated by saving activities on global scale and aimed at the mere reproduction of money by means of money in the short term (D-D'). This is accompanied by the international concentration of control of monetary and currency policies in supranational bodies that are out of any national political control. Monetary policy authorities exercise a disciplinary power. It can be seen through the European Union "stability plan" or the so called "structural adjustment plans" that IMF imposes on indebted countries of the third and fourth world. But such a disciplinary power, especially in the richest areas, is subjected to the dynamics of international capital and foreign exchange markets and therefore it cannot manifest itself in absolute terms as it could do in Fordism since it does not control the issue of monetary liquidity in toto.

As a matter of fact, it is since the 1990's, with the development of the "Internet Convention", which financial markets start to play a key role in creating virtual money, by now completely dematerialized and therefore subjected to the evolution of conventional and trust mechanisms that are created within the financial markets themselves. To explain the evolutionary process informing today capitalism, the monetary circuit framework must change aspect (Fumagalli and Lucarelli, 2007). In the following pages we propose a financial economy of production. Monetary policy is more and more depending on the dynamics of financial markets and the first goal is to support the creation of positive capital gains as engine to favour economic growth[9]. The institutional channel for money creation becomes less and less important. Public creation of money through deficit social spending policies is strongly reduced. They play a subordinate role according to the dynamics of stock exchange prices in an anti-conjunctural perspective[10]. We face a fourth channel of money creation, after credit channel, State channel and balance of payment: financial market channel. With the shift towards cognitive capitalism, the first two channels become almost irrelevant, whilst the amount of liquidity which is necessary to finance internationalised production depends on the latter two.

9 If we look at the Fed balance sheet, we can observe that the direct creation of money reached the minimum level in the 2007 just before the crisis: total assets were about 880 billion $ (6,2% of total USA GNP), whose the creation of money due to Treasury Securities was about 90% and only 10% was justified by creation of private credit money. This means that the role played by Fed in creating money ex-nihilo has become more and more irrelevant. At 31 December, 2008, the Fed total assets reached the level of 2.109 billion $ (14,8% of total USA GNP), whose 48% is constituted by credit money creation (1.001 billion $). It is easy to note a sort of substitution effect in the creation liquidity between the credit and the financial market.

10 Public expenditures in the USA increased after the Internet convention collapse, dragged by military reason, too. European restrictive fiscal policy starts to decline after the Chinese-real estate convention collapse.

Figure 5: financial production circuit in cognitive capitalism

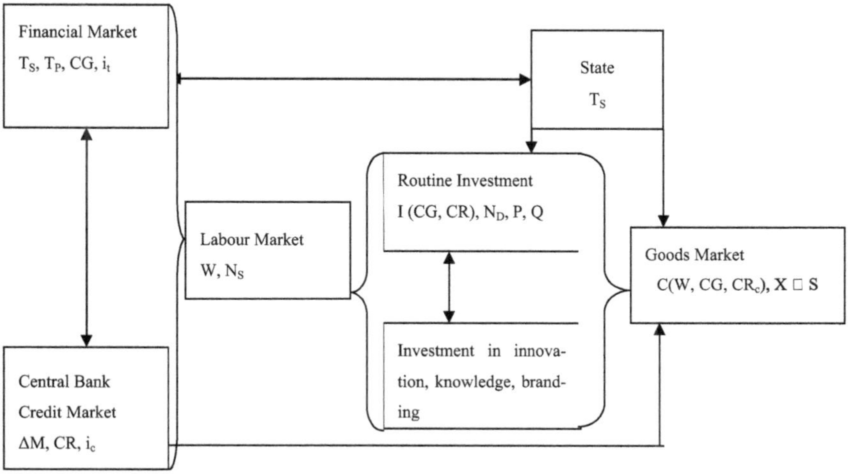

Legend

ΔM = Money creation flow (initial finance)
CR = bank credit
i_c = rate of interest on credit
T_S = Public bonds
T_P = Private bonds
CG = capital gains (financial money creation)
W = wages
N_S = Labour supply
I(CR) = Investment activity financed by credit
N_D = Labour demand unilaterally fixed by firms
P = production prices
Q = Output level
C(W, CG, CR_c) = Consumption depending on wages and capital gains dynamics
CR_c = credit to consumption
X = esport
S = saving
i_t = interest rate (or dividend) on bonds and shares

i. The opening of the financial circuit

Enterprises enter into debt towards the bank system in order to have the liquidity necessary to the buyout and merger of other firms by pursuing a strategy of growth and control of markets and also to avoid bothersome competitors. In a context of effervescence of financial markets, such strategy leads to an increase in common stock, allowing to earn capital gains able to pay off (more in a virtual than in a real way) the debts previously contracted from the banking system and possibly to accrue profits to be returned or to be used as self-funding to consolidate the productive activity. The realization of accrued capital gains is the condition for creating such a virtuous circle. The growth of financial markets becomes therefore conditio sine qua non for keeping the balance sheet in balance.

This represents a deep change in the funding process of the enterprise activity that it is worth dwelling on. Firstly, it is necessary to point out that the loan agreement provided by the banking system to enterprises is not aimed at the investment activity but rather at financing the buyout of one or more businesses. The purpose of such operation is to take possession of the technologies and know-how that can then entail an increase in the stock value of the enterprise itself. In the last analysis, bank funding becomes necessary to obtain capital gains on the stock market and not to obtain – as in the traditional productive investment activity – monetary profits due to the realization of production on the consumption goods market. In the United States since long time productive and technological investments of the enterprises listed on the stock exchange (capital expenditure) are financed for 98% by the enterprises themselves (self-funding) whereas the expenditures to pay dividends, interests and prospective merger and buyout (mergers & acquisitions, M&A) and buyback are financed by bank loans.

Under a qualitative analysis profile, the relative movement of the monetary creation space from the sphere of the central bank to the sphere of financial markets[11] involves a change in the very nature of sovereignty. Whereas bank liquidity creation is pre-eminent, the sovereignty of the nation state is affirmed. Whereas, instead, financial liquidity creation is the priority, it is the sovereignty of the socio-financial convention that historically belongs to it, to be affirmed.

ii. The production process

In cognitive capitalism, as we already pointed out (see part 2.1), the production process is based on two new elements:

1. The horizontal extension of the basis of accumulation, based on the necessity by firms to use external source of knowledge. The exploitation of intellectual property (IP), notably patents, is increasing "not only by incorporating protected

---

11 *It has to be noted that this does not mean that the financial markets create their own specific currency, different from the one created by the central bank; it means that the central bank in order to create money and to assure the circulation of values, is obliged to follow the movements of financial markets.*

inventions into new products processes or services, but also licensing them to other firms or public research organizations" (cf. Kamiyama, Sheehan, and Martinez, 2006: 1). But we can add more. External sources of knowledge arise not only by intra-firm relationships but more and more by the human capital, social context, educational processes, diffused general intellect and consumption activity which characterize territory. In this context, accumulation and valorisation do not depend only on the direct production activity, but on the whole material and immaterial production cycle. The role played by advanced services is quite relevant in the direct valorisation process.

2. When social life is one of the sources of the production process, new scale economies becomes more and more strategic in the competitive market economy. They are both dynamic scale economies, related to learning and network processes. Both learning and network economies derive from the inner society. It follows that, as much as production is diffused within a territory, externalities play a different role respect to the Fordist paradigm. Therefore, positive externalities are in CC quite important in order to improve generation (learning) and diffusion (network) of knowledge. They need a special analysis. In this context, investment activity, at the basis of accumulation dynamics, is composed by two elements. A first one has to do with the traditional investment activity in material production (such as manufacturing goods), the second one with immaterial production (investments in devices of production and subsumption of the value produced outside the directly productive processes). In the current regime of accumulation, profits derive from this latter form of investments.

iii. The closure of the financial circuit

Consumption and the demand regime are directly affected by financialization. In order to avoid a demand crisis, the wage de-regulation ought to be compensated upon the wealth effect stimulated by capital gains. The capital gains of financial markets function as multiplier of real economy just like the deficit spending did during fordism and Keynesian times[12]. If control of the financial activities is distributed in a distorted way, unlike the redistributive effects of the welfare state, the result is an increase in revenue polarization. The stability condition of the economic system depends on the propensity to invest and the wealth effect, both produced by capital gains allocation. But when financial gains misrepresent the

12 Over the 1992-2001 period, the USA experienced the most extensive and longest growth ever seen in the history of capitalism (110 moths) – three months longer than the one registered in Kennedy's time. The average annual growth rate has been between 3,5% and 4%, virtually twofold higher than the European one. On the threshold of the year 2000, 60% of American families had invested their savings in the stock exchange through shares directly owned or purchased through pension funds and common investment funds. In 1989 the percentage was not higher than 30%.

real effects of investment, dynamic scale economies and static scale economies on productivity, then financial bubbles may emerge.
If the wealth effects generated by the capital gains fail, the facilitated access to credit is used to sustain consumption (CR) and guarantee, even if provisionally, the closure of the circuit. Necessarily, the final result is an ever-growing debt affecting more and more families that leads to an increase in the risk of debt insolvency. Without a mode of regulation that guarantees that the overall produced wealth will be re-invested into the dynamic learning and network economies and without a policy which controls financial bubbles, a finance-led growth is always at risk of instability[13].

4. Preliminary conclusions: the present global crisis

We argued that financial markets are today the pulsing heart of cognitive capitalism. They finance the activity of accumulation: the liquidity attracted to the financial markets rewards the restructuring of production aimed at exploiting knowledge and the control of spaces externalities to traditional business.

Furthermore, in the presence of capital gains, financial markets play the same role in the economic system that the Keynesian multiplier (activated by public deficit spending) did in the context of Fordism. However – unlike the classic Keynesian multiplier – this leads to a distorted redistribution of revenue. So that such multiplier is operative (> 1) it is necessary that the financial base (i.e. the extension of financial markets) constantly grows and that the matured capital gains are on average higher than the average wage depreciation (that, since 1975, has been about 20%) (see Fumagalli and Lucarelli, 2009). On the other hand, revenue polarization increases the risk of debt insolvency which is at the base of the growth of that same financial foundation and lowers the median wage. Here is a first contradiction whose effects are visible today.

---

13 But, in the current situation there are not any economic or political premises sufficient for a new social pact (or New Deal). It is therefore a mere illusion. The Fordist New Deal was the result of an institutional assemblage (Big Government) that was based on the existence of three assumptions: a nation state able to develop national economic policies independent, even if coordinated, from other states; the possibility of measuring productivity earnings and therefore see to their redistribution between profits and wages; industrial relations between social components that were reciprocally recognized and were legitimized on an institutional level, able to sufficiently and unequivocally represent (not excluding margins of arbitrariness) entrepreneurial interests and those of the working class. None of these three assumptions are present in today's cognitive capitalism. No innovative New Deal is possible, if not one that is pushed by social movements and by the practices of autonomous institutionality through the re-appropriation of a welfare system ravaged by private interests and frozen in public policy.

Thirdly, financial markets forcefully, redirecting growing parts of labour revenues (like severance pay and social security, other than revenues that, through the social state, are translated into state health programs and institutions of public education), substitute the state as the principle provider of social securities and welfare. From this point of view, they represent the privatization of the reproductive sphere of life. They therefore exercise biopower (on this point see Lucarelli, 2009).

Lastly, the financial markets are the place where capitalist valorization is fixed today, which is to say the exploitation of social cooperation and the rent from general intellect.

Hence, in a financial economy of production, there is no more separation between the real sphere and the financial one. Financial markets to be able to support phases of expansion and real growth need a constant increase of the financial base. In other words, it is necessary that the share of global wealth redirected toward financial markets continually grows. This implies a continuous increase in the relations between debt and credit, either through the increase of the number of people in debt (the degree of financial market extension) or through the construction of new financial instruments that feed on pre-existing financial exchanges (the degree of intensity of the financial markets). Derivative products are a classic example of this second modality of expansion of the same financial markets. Whatever the factors taken into consideration, the expansion of financial markets are necessarily accompanied both by the increase of debt and by the speculative activities of the risk associated with them. It is an intrinsic dynamic in the role of financial markets as a founding element of cognitive capitalism. Speaking of an excess of speculation due to manager or bank greed has absolutely no sense and can only serve to deviate the attention from the true structural causes of this crisis. Necessarily, the final result is the unsustainability of an ever-growing debt, especially when high-risk sectors of the population begin to be too far in debt: the social strata that, following the process of labour precariousness, find themselves in the condition of not benefiting from the wealth effect that participation in the stock earnings permitted to the more well-to-do social classes. The insolvency crisis in real-estate mortgages thus finds its origin in one of the contradictions of contemporary cognitive capitalism: the irreconcilability of an unequal revenue distribution with the necessity of widening the financial base to continue to push the process of accumulation.

A distorted income distribution does not only penalise the capacity of financial market to keep high aggregate demand dynamics but negatively affects learning and network economies. Consequently, the loss of productivity gains reduces the efficiency of the system. An enduring uncertainty deeply affects the learning process of the individual and his relational ability, with the result to reduce the impact of dynamic economies upon productive returns.

Aggregate demand is influenced both by the dynamic of the financial markets and by the capital gains deriving from the internationalization of production. With the weakening of the wage-productivity nexus, these dynamics had a greater impact on consumption and the investment activity. In a finance-led economy in order to avoid a demand crisis, the wage regulation ought to be based upon the distribution of capital gains. However, the shortcomings intrinsic to this approach are, firstly, that given the widespread uncertainty generated by working precariousness, knowledge loses its generative capacity, and, secondly, as there is no guarantee that the overall produced wealth will be re-invested into the financial market or elsewhere, a finance-led growth is always at risk of instability.

As far as supply side is concerned, changes in the ability to generate new knowledge, as a basic condition for the spread of new technologies, depend on the characteristics of the environment in which R&D activities are organized. This environment is positively affected by the income level and by a set of variables, such as education, an overall macroeconomic and political stability, fair wealth redistribution, a balance between material and immaterial activities, and the existence of a good system of infrastructures, which we define as positive externalities. That is the challenge that also Eastern European countries need to face.

References

Aglietta, M. (2006), "The future of capitalism", in B. Coriat, P. Petit, and G. Schméder (eds), *The Hardship of Nations*, Cheltenham-Northampton: Edward Elgar, pp. 9-35.

Aglietta, M. and A. Rebérioux (2005), "Regulating finance-driven capitalism", *Issues in Regulation Theory*, (51): 1-5.

Andersson, J. (2006), "Socialising capital, capitalising the social: contemporary social democracy and the knowledge economy", paper presented at the conference *Debating the Knowledge Economy* at the Institute for Advanced Studies at Lancaster University.

Arvidsson, A. (2007), "The logic of brand", *European Journal of Economic and Social Systems*, 20(1): 99-116.

Asensio, A. (2007), "Inflation targeting drawbacks in the absence of a 'natural' anchor. A Keynesian appraisal of the FED and BCE policies over the period 1999-2006", paper presented at the conference *Third International Post-Keynesian conference of Dijon*.

Azais C., A. Corsani, and P. Dieuaide (dir) (2001), *Vers un capitalisme cognitif?*, Paris: L'Harmattan.

Becattini, G. and E. Rullani (2000), "Sistema locale e sviluppo globale", in G. Becattini (2000), *Il distretto industriale*, Torino: Rosenberg & Sellier, pp. 93-116.

Boyer, R. (2000), "Is a finance-led growth regime a viable alternative to Fordism? A preliminary analysis", *Economy and Society*, 29(1): 111-145.
Cassi, L. (2007), "The economic interpretation of knowledge", *European Journal of Economic and Social Systems*, 20(1): 65-80.
Colletis, G. and B. Paulré (2008), *Les nouveaux horizons du capitalisme*, Paris: Economica.
Corsani, A., P. Dieuaide, M. Lazzarato, Y. Moulier-Boutang, B. Paulré, and C. Vercellone (2001), *Le capitalisme cognitif comme sortie de la crise du capitalisme industriel: un programme de recherche*, Paris: Actes du Forum de la Régulation.
Fumagalli, A. (2007), *Bioeconomia e capitalismo cognitivo. Verso un nuovo paradigma di accumulazione?*, Roma: Carocci.
Fumagalli, A. and C. Vercellone (eds) (2007), "Le capitalisme cognitive. Apports et perspectives", *European Journal of Economic and Social Systems* (Special Issue), 20(1).
Fumagalli, A. and S. Lucarelli (2007), "A model of cognitive capitalism. A preliminary analysis", *European Journal of Economic and Social Systems*, 20(1): 117-133.
Fumagalli, A. and S. Lucarelli (2010), "Instability and uncertainty in cognitive capitalism", in C. Gnos and L.-P. Rochon (eds), *Money, Finance and Crisis*, Cheltenham: Edward Elgar.
Fumagalli, A. and S. Lucarelli (eds) (2008), "Money and Technological Change. The Role of Financing in the Process of Evolution", *European Journal of Economic and Social Systems* (Special Issue), 21(2).
Fumagalli, A. and S. Mezzadra (eds) (2010), *Crisis in the Global Economy. Financial Markets, Social Struggles, and New Political Scenarios*, Cambridge, MA: The MIT Press.
Goldman Sachs Global Economics Group (2007), *BRICs and Beyond*, Goldman Sachs, available at http://www2.goldmansachs.com/ ideas/brics/book/BRIC-Full.pdf.
Graziani, A. (1984), "Moneta senza crisi", *Studi Economici*, (24): 3-37.
Graziani, A. (2003), *The Monetary Theory of Production*, Cambridge: Cambridge University Press.
Harvey, D. (1990), *The Condition of Postmodernity: an Enquiry into the Origins of Cultural Change*, Cambridge: Blackwell.
Kamiyama, S., J. Sheehan, and C. Martinez (2006), "Valuation and exploitation of intellectual property", *OECD Science, Technology and Industry Working Papers*.
Keynes, J. M. (1936), *The General Theory of Employment, Interest and Money*, available at http://homepage.newschool.edu/het//texts/keynes/gtcont.htm.
Lucarelli, S. (2010), "Financialization as Biopower", in Fumagalli, A. and S. Mezzadra (eds) (2010), *Crisis in the Global Economy. Financial Markets, Social Struggles, and New Political Scenarios*, MIT Press, Ma, USA, pp. 101-120.
Marazzi, C. (2004), "Dietro la sindrome cinese", *Il manifesto*, 1 July.
Marazzi, C. (2008), *Capital and Language: From the New Economy to the War Economy*, Cambridge, MA: The MIT Press.
Mouhoud, E. M. (2006), "Global geography of post-Fordism: knowledge and polarisation", in B. Coriat, P. Petit, and G. Schméder (eds), *The Hardship of Nations*, Cheltenham-Northampton: Edward Elgar, pp. 293-307.
Moulier-Boutang, Y. (2007), *Le capitalism cognitif. Comprendre la nouvelle grande trasformation et ses enjeux*, Paris: Ed. Amsterdam.
Nelson, R. R. and S. G. Winter (1982), *An Evolutionary Theory of Economic Change*, Cambridge, MA: Belknap Press of Harvard University Press.
Orlean A. (2010), *Dall'euforia al panico*, Ombre Corte, Verona.

Orlean, A. (2004), "What is a collective belief?", in P. Bourgine and J.-P. Nadal (eds), *Cognitive Economics*, Berlin, Heidelberg, and New York: Springer-Verlag, pp. 199-212.
Orlean, A. (2008), "Knowledge in finance: objective value versus convention", in R. Arena and A. Festré (eds), *Handbook of Knowledge and Economics*, Cheltenham: Edward Elgar.
Prabhakar, R. (2002), "Markets, tacit knowledge and education", *Economic Affairs*, (22): 41-46.
Realfonzo R., (2006), "The Italian circuitist approach", in P. Arestis and M. Sawyer (eds), *A Handbook of Alternative Monetary Economics*, Cheltenham-Northampton: Edward Elgar, pp. 105-120.
Rossi, S. (2006), "The theory of money emissions", in P. Arestis and M. Sawyer (eds), *A Handbook of Alternative Monetary Economics*, Cheltenham- Northampton: Edward Elgar, pp. 121-138.
Stiglitz, J. (2007), "America's day of reckoning", available at http://www.project-syndicate.org/commentary/stiglitz90.
Stiglitz, J. E. (2004), *The Roaring Nineties: A New History of the World's Most Prosperous Decade*, New York: W. W. Norton & Co.
Venturini, F. (2006), "How much does IT consumption matter for growth? Evidence from national accounts", in A. Malgarini and G. Piga (eds), *Capital Accumulation, Productivity and Growth*, London: Palgrave-Mcmillan, pp. 81–133.
Vercellone, C. (2006), "Cognitive capitalism and models for the regulation of the wage relation: Some lessons from the anti-CPE movement in France", paper presented at the conference *"Immaterial Labour, Multitudes and New Social Subjects: Class Composition in Cognitive Capitalism"*.
Vercellone, C. (2007), "From formal subsumption to general intellect: elements for a Marxist reading of the thesis of cognitive capitalism", *Historical Materialism*, 15: 13-36.
Vercellone, C. (ed) (2003), *Sommes-nous Sortis du Capitalisme Industrielle?*, Paris: La Dispute.
Virno, P. (2001), "Lavoro e Linguaggio", in A. Zanini and U. Fadini (eds), *Lessico Postfordista*, Milano: Feltrinelli, pp. 181-185.
Zanini A. and U. Fadini (eds) (2001), *Lessico Postfordista*, Milano: Feltrinelli, "Introduction", translated in English by Arianna Bove, *http://www.generation-online.org/it/postFordismo.htm.*

2. Bioeconomics and the valorisation process

Andrea Fumagalli

1. Introduction

The capitalist economy is driven by an accumulation activity that has gradually freed itself from natural constraints. As a result of human and social action, it assumed artificial and discretional forms that, starting from the industrial revolution, would have taken on the structure of manufacturing. Being unable to keep a constant form in time such an activity varies according to the dialectic process that accumulation itself triggers. During the XIX century, the accumulation process depended upon the combination of two factors: the factory workers' knowledge and the early processes of mechanization attached to the development of heavy and textile industries. In the subsequent phase, namely during the development of the Taylorist-Fordist model, the accumulation process, via the complete expropriation of workers' knowledge and the consequent implementation of the production of goods, brought to its apex the process of the *Smithian* division of labour. At present, with the advent of cognitive capitalism, the accumulation process rests *upon* and takes shape *from* the exploitation of an individual's vital faculties via a net-shaped structure of social cooperation. Hence, in this context, it is fair to say that it is the very same knowledge that is to be[come] the expression of the *bios*. In other words, the accumulation process presupposes the existence of a power mechanism (*dispositif*) able to transform existential activities into productive relations. From this point of view, *bio-economics* is the complementary and symmetric aspect of *bio-politics*: if by *bio-politics* is meant here the ability to put in place a mechanism of social and juridical control, by *bio-economics* we mean its analogous *vis a vis* productive, accumulative and redistributive mechanisms.

2. Bioeconomics as critique of political economy

As bioconomics deals with the forms assumed by capitalistic processes of accumulation and valorisation, it should be understood as a tool of the critique of political economy. Both classical and neoclassical economic analyses have always been concerned with the critique of political economy. Marx's reflections represented the apex of the critique of Smith and Ricardo's classical political economy. According to Smith (1991: 3) only labour, intended as fatigue and pain, is the active element that creates "all the necessaries and conveniences of life" (Smith, 1904: Vol. I, para. II.1). As a result of an increase in labour demand that, according to Malthus principle, is superior to the demographic trend, the accumulation deriving from the exploitation of labour favours an increase in real wages. Upon this assumption, Smith establishes a positive correlation between capitalism and the betterment of working conditions. Against Smith, Ricardo maintained that, since labour is a cost of production, value and not labour is the engine of capitalist growth. The accumulation process rests upon the existence of a surplus value that guarantees its growth. This triggers a redistributive conflict between labour and capital that heavily questions Smith's positive correlation noted above[14]. Ricardo's political economy sheds Smith's ethical-moral features, and defines the object of its study: the analysis of capitalism, economic growth, redistributive conflict based upon the idea of labour as the production of value.

The traditional reading of Marx's critique rests upon the idea that exploitation is the material basis for capitalist accumulation via the distinction between labour (in both its abstract and concrete forms) and the labour-force. Furthermore, failing to guarantee a stable and balanced accumulation process, exploitation tends to produce deep crises.

Following the XIX century prevalence of the vulgar economy – that would lead to the development of Walras theory of economic equilibrium and the marginalist theory of production – in the 1920s Sraffa and Keynes opened up a new phase of the critique of political economy. Sraffa showed, beyond any reasonable doubt, the baselessness of the marginalist approach to redistribution. In a "real" production economy, the distribution of surplus is not regulated by a divine harmony: neither a "natural" level of wages, nor a redistributive configuration of social product, can exist. The range within which the distributive quotas may vary is rather significant. Within such a range the situation is determined, above all, by the historical influences gradually exerted by social and political pressure. However, according to Sraffa, the coefficients of the system of simultaneous equations from which we obtain both wages and the rate of profit, given the wage (or the wage, given the rate of profit) may be expressed as a quantity of labour, but a theory of value labour becomes superfluous. Put differently, although not a necessary condition, it is possible to trace back the prices of production to the quantity of labour. In this way, Marx's critique of Ricardo becomes insufficient.

Moving from the idea of a monetary production economy, Keynes established the impossibility for the capitalist system to reach full-employment equilibrium merely by recurring to market arrangements. Focusing upon money as the decisive element both in delineating the economic hierarchy and in determining in-

14 As Bellofiore reminds us, for Ricardo the conflict between profit and rent was even more important (Bellofiore, 2005).

vestment activities, Keynes challenged the very foundations of free-market theory. In his Premesse ad una critica della teoria economica (cf. Sraffa, 1979), Sraffa not only shows the irrationality of the bourgeoisie's economic theory, but also invites us to search beyond Marx's critique. Both Sraffa and Keynes left unfinished their critique of the valorisation process. Today, we are faced with a new phase of critical analysis of political economy. It originates from a heterodox reading of Marx's Grundrisse, based on Marx's idea that capital is value able to valorise itself (Bellofiore, 2005: 919).

"The two fundamental theoretical passages are represented, in the first part of *Grundrisse*, by the definition of the *law of value in its form of surplus-value*, namely in the first fully flagged formulation of the law of surplus-value and, in the second part, by the *extension of the theory of exploitation* (the law of surplus-value) within *the mechanisms of reproduction and circulation of capital*, namely in the transposition of the law of exploitation in law of crisis. [...]" (Negri, 1998: 18-19).

This new approach to Marxism, which sees it not only as a methodology of inquiry but also as a perennial idea of the becoming of exploitative social relationships (the two are irreducibly linked), finds its synthesis in the evolution of the notion of machinery from physical means of production to *general intellect.* In these respects, it is necessary to underline an analytical symmetry between the break-down operated by Panzeri's and the Italian *Operaism* with the analysis of the "capitalistic usage of machinery" occurred in the 1970s, and that occurred in the 1990s concerning the re-reading of the well-known passage in the *Grundrisse* about the *general intellect* – intended as the ultimate transformation of "machinery" – that undergoes a transformation from physical to human element: in other words, the passage from physical to *human capital*, which better than anything else describes the transformation from economic to bio-economic accumulation.

"In the *Grundrisse*, in fact, Marx not only elaborates a certain number of categories of the critique of political economy that he would use lately in *The Capital*; not only he defines the methods of the critique of the capitalistic history and economy, that method that is the matrix and the mechanism of his constitutive materialism [...]. In the *Grundrisse* he deals with something else. In particular, it is an extraordinary theoretical anticipation of the mature capitalistic society" (Negri, 1998: 7).

According to both Panzieri (1961 and 1964) and early *Operaism*, machinery affects not only production as such but also productive relationships; the productive relationship is a relationship between those who command and those who are exploited. Thus, not only is machinery a productive tool, but it also embodies a structure of domination and command. Machinery, the system of machines, not only is the form that allows the exploitation of the labour force, but also, and above all, is the form in which the latter is ordered, commanded, and hierachised.

"When you analyze the development of the system of machinery, you will see that machineries 'run', as the old Marx were used to say, exactly where is the fight, the machinery intervenes to control the fight, the machinery is always subordinated. To say machinery has little sense; to say machinery means to say a series of material mechanisms organized and structured by knowledge. Hence, to say machinery or system of machineries means to refer to the organization of knowledge around it ..., we are referring to the organization of command obviously functional to such a process" (Negri, 2005).

Essentially, this understanding of Marxism is based upon the idea that capital is not a substance, but rather a relationship. Firstly, this means that capital is always something that establishes a relationship between a *command power* and an exploited subject; and, secondly, it is reaffirmed that such a relationship is necessary, namely that capital cannot avoid the subjectivity of the exploited. There is neither a history of capital, nor of capitalist development; what exists is only the history of the conflictual capital-labour relationship of strength that cannot be traced back to a mere *physical* relationship, but rather it organizes itself within structures that take the shape of industrial, institutional, or political machineries.

3. Bioeconomics and cognitive capitalism

With the shift from Fordism to cognitive capitalism[15], the social relationship embodied by capital shifts from being a relationship between labour-force and machineries and becomes a relationship between body and mind, brain and heart, unfolding itself within human beings. But, far from being the capital that becomes human, it is an individual's life, with its multiple singularities and differences, which becomes capital.

The relevance of the role of knowledge and general intellect in the accumulation process becomes its tangible outcome. It is not accidental that the productivity of bodies and the value of affections assume a central role and manifest themselves in three principal aspects characterising work activity (Fumagalli, 2007): communicative work, related to industrial production, more and more connected to the information net; work related to the interaction of symbolic analysis and solving-problem; and work related to the production and manipulation of affections and [collective] imaginaries. This last aspect, focalizing upon corporal production, becomes extremely important within contemporary networks of biopolitical production. It is precisely through comparing in a coherent fashion the

15 For a discussion on cognitive capitalism hypothesis, see Vercellone (2007), in Croatian.

different characteristics that define the bio-political context, and reconnecting these to the productive ontology, that it becomes possible to identify the new body of the bio-political collective. This body becomes structure not via a negation of the original vital force that animates it, but acknowledging it; it is language that animates a multitude of singular bodies connected by dynamic relationships. It is, also, a mix of production and reproduction, structure and suprastructure, as it is life in the fullest sense. The critical analysis of cognitive capitalism should concern the jungle of productive and conflictual determinations offered by the collective body bio-political.

In mere economic terms, the body bio-political upon which is exerted on the one side, Foucault's bio-power and, on the other, Deleuze's social control, is defined by the notion of human capital. However, human capital is still an insufficient concept, as it risks contributing to the mystification of the relationships of exploitation that pervade contemporary capitalism and are amplified within it[16]. We should then unveil the contradictions hidden by the notion of human capital: between living and dead labour, between concrete and abstract labour, between machinery and man.

4. The problematic nodes of bio-economics and cognitive capitalism

With regard to the critical analysis of capitalism deriving from Marx's reflections, the problematic related to bio-economics might initially be summarized in the redefinition of the relationship between living and dead labour and between concrete and abstract labour. Below, we attempt to re-interpret such relationships vis a vis bio-economic production characterizing cognitive capitalism.

4.1. The nexus between living and dead labour, namely word and language

One of the essential characteristics related to the bio-economic production is the dematerialization of fixed capital and the transfer of its productive and organizational functions into the living body of the labour force (Marazzi, 2005). This process represents one of the most glaring paradoxes of contemporary capitalism, namely, the contradiction between the increased importance of cognitive labour as a tool for wealth creation and, concomitantly, its devaluation both in

16 In economic science, the concept of *human capital* is developed inside the neoclassical paradigm, thanks to Robert Lucas (see Lucas, 1988). Lucas realizes that each worker more is productive, higher is the degree of education in his environment. In Lucas's model, the economic growth is strongly influenced by the dynamics of human capital. Nevertheless, Lucas's framework does not take in account structural changes in capitalistic accumulation process and the role played by intellectual property rights on knowledge diffusion (see Herrera and Vercellone, 2002).

terms of wages and occupational status. Such a paradox lies within what Marazzi (2005: 109) defined as

> "the anthropogenic character of contemporary capitalistic production: a model of production of men via men, where the opportunity of an endogenous and cumulative growth is given above all by the development of the educational (investment in human capital), health (demographic evolution, biotechnologies) and cultural (innovation, communication, and creativity) sectors)"

In the context of cognitive capitalism, human beings combine the functions of both fixed and variable capital, namely, the tools deriving from past and present (living) labour: the *bios*. The distinction between fixed and variable capital, namely between living labour incorporated in the labour-force and the dead labour incorporated in machinery, typical of the Fordist capitalist industrial model, loses its importance. The body of the labour force, as a sedimentation of past labour, namely codified, historically acquired knowledge and experiences, more than merely containing the faculty of labour, also contains functions typical of fixed capital, the means of production. In this new context, the relationship between living and dead labour becomes a new relationship that identifies the present forms of both of variable and fixed capital. It is a matter of identifying, within human beings and their relational, affective, and communicative practices, the components of living labour that can assume the form of fixed capital and those that instead constitute variable capital. As Rifkin puts it:

> "The economy, at least in physical terms, is shrinking. If the industrial era was characterized by the accumulation of physical capital and property, the new age privileges intangible forms of power bound up in bundles of information and intellectual capital. It is by now an established fact that material goods are progressively dematerializing" (Rifkin, 2000: 41).

Fixed capital is not undermined by the downsizing of physical capital. If during the phase of industrial capitalism this latter tends to coincide with physical capital, in cognitive capitalism, knowledge – as it is separated from any products in which it has been, is, or will be incorporated, namely when it is mere information and standardized communicative practice – exerts *in se* and *per se* a productive action, taking the form of standardized language, namely, software. It could, in other words, assume the role of fixed capital (Marazzi, 2005: 108), becoming in this way a sort of "cognitive machinery", substituting stored labour for simple or complex living labour (Stewart, 2002).

Similarly to language, the construction of software rests upon the allocation of living labour that, precisely when it transforms itself into a tool of language codification (cognitive machinery), assumes the semblance of dead labour, fixed capital. The function of words is different, intended as the art of communication.

Words, in fact, enable us to analyze the relationship among individuals not only as a means in itself, but rather as a social productive process.

Words are the *becoming* of language, whilst *language* is the codification and systematization of this social production and, therefore, regulation and normalization of the linguistic creativity of the subjects[17]. Hence, the mechanical codification of the linguistic practice, intended as a convention, has become the mechanic element of the *bio-economic* production, the fixed capital necessary for the valorisation of living labour contained in the word as an instrument of communication, relation, affection. However, the dialectics between word and language, namely between dead and living labour incorporated within the human body, generates a further problem, the one concerning abstract and concrete labour.

4.2. The nexus between abstract and concrete labour, namely cerebral alienation

According to Marx, concrete labour, qualitatively defined, is labour aimed at producing use-value. On the contrary, abstract labour is the pure manifestation of the human labour force, which sets aside both its qualitative aspects and the specific determinations that refer to the utility of singular labour and whose quantity determines the value so generated. In a capitalistic system of production, abstract labour is the socially necessary labour to produce goods that are realized in the market, namely exchange value, on the basis of the available technologies.

During the Fordist period, it was the social relationship between humans and machinery that determined the immanent form of abstract labour, which was transposed into the exchange value of material goods. At present, we attest to the development of the hegemony of immaterial labour[18], namely

> "labour that creates immaterial goods: knowledge, information, communication, linguistic or emotional relationships" (Negri, 2006: 159).

This hegemony implies a twofold fracture. Differently from the previously established industrial paradigm, because the division between working time and free time is fading away, we are faced firstly with a redefinition of the working

---

17 The difference between word and language has been the focus of L. Bloomfield (1996) studies and of those concerning the ethnography of communication, discipline attentive to the priority of the contextual functions and problematic in the language *vis a vis* the structure of the codex.

18 We use here the expression *immaterial labour*, in the sense of *cognitive labour*, since labour, *strictu sensu*, can never be immaterial.

day. In the industrial phase of capitalism, workers produced mostly during their time spent within the firm, as a result of the need to conjoin the mechanical means of production with the labour force. In this way, the form of abstract labour is defined by a sharp separation from the concrete, reproductive type of labour. Secondly, the dematerialization of fixed capital emphasizes a new *human* relationship between the means of production and the labour-force.

In the context of immaterial production, in fact, the body of the labour-force, more than merely containing labour, also contains the typical functions of fixed capital, namely the means of production intended as the sedimentation of codified knowledge, historically acquired knowledge, experiences, etc., In a nutshell all that can be referred to is past labour.

Hence, the separation between abstract and concrete labour becomes no longer clear. Firstly, what Marx named concrete labour, the labour that produces use value, today could be renamed as *creative labour*. This definition allows to better understand the cerebral [plus] entailed in such an activity, whilst concrete labour, although conceptually a synonym, takes us back to the idea of *doing* rather than of *thinking* – with a more marked reference to the labour of the craftsman. Rather, within cognitive activities, it is possible to indifferently shift from abstract to concrete-cognitive labour, with the result of valorising both exchange values and the production of use value[19]. In these respects, Holloway writes:

"Here then is the core of class struggle: it is the struggle between creative doing and abstract labour. In the past it has been common to think of class struggle as the struggle between capital and labour, understanding labour as wage labour, abstract labour, and the working class has often been defined as the class of wage labourers. But this is quite wrong. Wage labour and capital complement each other, wage labour is a moment of capital. There is indeed a

19 Riccardo Bellofiore proposes a different reading of the category abstract labour. Cf. Bellofiore (1996): abstract labour is understood as a sequence ranging from the labour force sold in the labour market to the living labour produced by the waged workers in production, to the dead labour objectivated in commodities (potential money). Hence, according to Bellofiore, the way in which the capitalistic production organized is seen as the result of a consciousness separated from the will of the workers, although it also represents the place where class antagonism occurs. Bellofiore does not deny the centrality of living labour – intended as the ability to work in *actu* and as a value *in potentia* – but he considers pure post-industrial mythology the analyses on the cognitive dimension of labour (see Bellofiore and Halevi, 2006: 63). In my understanding, living labour, intended as creative-created labour, derives from a careful analysis of the (tendencial) structural changes characterizing contemporary capitalism. In the context of cognitive capitalism, living labour can indeed be captured by capital and reduced to mere commodity; however, the creative and innovative abilities of single individuals are always greater than productive labour in a capitalist sense.

conflict between wage labour and capital, but it is a relatively superficial conflict. It is a conflict over the level of wages, the length of the working day, the conditions of labour: all of these are important, but they presuppose the existence of capital. The real threat to capital comes not from abstract labour but from useful labour or creative doing, for it is creative doing that stands in radical opposition to capital, that is, to its own abstraction. It is creative doing that says 'no, we shall not do what capital commands, we shall do what we consider necessary or desirable'" (Holloway, 2006).

It is indeed in order to infer that "creative labour" gets the upper hand over abstract labour that in this phase becomes central to control both training and learning processes, exactly as it is central to take control of knowledge, via intellectual property rights. In fact, training and learning processes are intrinsically ambiguous: to what extent is it possible to distinguish between the learning process aimed at developing one's own culture according to an autonomously chosen logic and the process of training necessary to carry out the working activity aimed at capitalistic accumulation? To what extent is it possible to separate, within a working day, the time necessary to produce exchange value from the time necessary to produce use value? Obviously it is impossible to provide an adequate answer to these questions. Unless we do not hypothesize a real subsumption process of individuals entire life. This leads, on the one side, to the disappearance of use value and, on the other, to the absolute predominance of exchange value. This, evidently, would be a dreadful perspective as it would entail the cerebral subjugation of human beings.

However, the intrinsic difficulty of separating concrete labour from abstract labour is testified by the increasing importance given to the training processes of the labour force, intended as investment. Firstly, this depends upon the fact that labour and training coincide with the workers entire life-cycle. It is not a *una tantum* investment, occurring during the scholarisation period, but rather it has become a long term investment (it least the entire working life) and therefore it should entail an amortization, similarly as to when an entrepreneur, in order to start a productive process, invests in machinery already thinking that, at the end of their utilization, he will substitute them with new ones.

Living labour, reproductive of the labour force, allows capital to reduce the costs of the labour force and, therefore, to increase the surplus-value. It would be possible to argue that the quantity of reproductive living labour is what permits the amortization of fixed capital. In fact, reproducing the labour force's use value, it reproduces, at the same time, its ability to consume capital. Secondly, to consider training as investment, also means to underline the fact that, from the national budget point of view, training is a current management cost that depends upon the annual fiscal income, which, in turn is conditioned by the amortization of investments. In this way, an imbalance between investment policies inherited from Fordism (according to which infrastructure costs – in the public hardware – played a strategic role) and training expenditure policies occurs. The privatisation of training cycles is an attempt to solve such an imbalance, although its outcome tends to worsen a further imbalance: the one referring to the social nature of human capital and the exclusion of an increasing quantity of the labour force from life-long training processes. Training-learning-culture, is the triad around which the process of valorisation and alienation of cognitive labour unfolds. The accumulation regime entailed by cognitive capitalism rests upon three different levels: information, knowledge and systemic learning. Such a cognitive division of production is transformed into a cognitive division of labour, represented by *training*, *learning* and *culture*.

Today, *training* is essentially considered as professional training, and provides the information; dynamic *learning* in time (also named life-long learning and/or apprenticeship) produces knowledge; systemic knowledge presupposes culture. If training is finalized to the immaterial production of exchange value, as it is manipulated and subjected to the intrinsic mechanisms of the schooling organization via the neo-liberal restructuring of educational paths, learning – where the human component is the intermediary and produces the refashioning of the received training – represents the dynamic moment in which the exchange value of information is also mixed with the production of use value: in this context, learning activity can become potential creative labour.

Intended as personal growth leading to a maturation of one's "view of the world", *culture* becomes antithetic to training, becomes its negation, as a product of the relative doing and antithesis to abstract cognitive labour.

However, the relationship between these three levels is not linear: it presupposes and returns us to the dialectic between abstract labour, which is the exchange of labour, and concrete-creative labour, that is concrete-creative knowledge, because at present the exchange of labour has become more and more the exchange of knowledge.

And it is from the fact that the development of professional training and apprenticeship negates and obstacles the development of culture that arises the process of alienation intrinsic to cognitive labour. The more professional training and apprenticeship extend themselves, the more ignorance, in its ethimological sense, namely "non-knowledge" and "non-comprehension" becomes diffuse.

As it resides within the individual, alienation becomes cerebral alienation, between heart and hand, between left and right brain hemisphere, no longer between inside and outside, between participation to production and outcome of the productive process itself.

4.3. The nexus space, network and cooperative relationships: the molecular space

With the diffusion of flexible accumulation and subsequently of cognitive capitalism, we insist on an even more profound permeation between productive place and the formation of a productive network: space, intended in its geographical and virtual dimensions, becomes a place of production no longer characterized by a unique and self-centred presence, but rather by an ensemble of formal and informal polycentric networks. *Bio-economic* production becomes the result of a network structure, more and more immaterial, which assumes a net-shaped form even when it has to do with material production. A structure characterized by fluxes, presupposes [linguistic hubs] of communication and high levels of social cooperation. Such cooperation concerns both the transmission of symbols and the logistic transportation of goods and commodities. However, within such a space, cooperation, far from being horizontal, develops itself along new trajectories of the spatial division of production and the cognitive division of labour. The net-shaped production – the network – becomes a molecular space, individualized, characterized by individual relationships that most of the time produce cooperation but that are not, paradoxically, cooperative between them (Salvini, 2006).

4.4. From the fetishism of commodities to symbolic fetishism. The commodity as the final elucidation of the symbolic imaginary

Under cognitive capitalism, commodities assume new significance. For Marx, a commodity is a unit of use value and exchange value; namely, it is at the very same time an object of a specific sensible quality and a crystallization of the expense of the indistinct human labour force; namely it is the result of the allocation of physical and intellectual energy with no regard to the form and the modality with which such an allocation occurs (see Marx, 1906). According to Marx, the value of a commodity is given by the working time socially necessary to produce it. Being value is a common quality of all commodities, differently from use value, which is different for any kind of commodity, it is possible to exchange commodities in a way quantitatively proportionate to the expended working energy, objectified within each commodity We have already seen that under cognitive capitalism, use value and exchange value are intrinsically linked to the extent that it is difficult to identify a clear demarcation between them. This is something that Gorz underlines when he discusses the novelty introduced by cognitive capitalism:

"The immaterial dimension of products prevails over their material reality; their symbolic, aesthetic or social value over their practical value, and over their exchange value, which it erases" (Gorz, 2003: 35).

When Gorz refers to exchange value as something that erases itself, he refers to the fact that the value of a commodity is no longer merely definable by "the necessary working time"; to that value, that in any case cannot disappear[20], should be added the value deriving from the degree of social symbolic nature that it contains. When its immateriality increases, the symbolic value of commodity becomes even more apparent. It is on this edge that the relationship between production and realization (the consumption of goods) is played out. The valorisation of the commodity no longer occurs within the productive process alone, but, as immaterial production has became the production of imaginaries, it occurs when the imaginary realizes itself – that is, at the very point of consumption: it is the result of what we can define as the *brandization* process, which goes beyond the commodity as it concerns more and more the territory and the space (Arvidsson, 2006). It does not relate to the mere act of consumption. When the commodity becomes a symbol, there is no difference between production and consumption; namely, there is no clear cut distinction between production and realization. This is the result of the process of the valorisation of language, which is so only when language is expressed rather than when it is created. It is in this sense that in the context of cognitive capitalism occurs the shift from the Marxian fetishism of commodity to the so-called symbolic fetishism, fetishism of language and, finally, fetishism of the imaginary (Castoriadis, 1998). Not only does this occur in any economic phase, from financing to consumption, but it becomes pervasive in the life of individuals, beyond the codified working time.

4.5. The overcoming of gender and racial differences: towards the bionic being, the perfect machinery of the anthropogenic evolution

Under cognitive capitalism, it is life in itself that has become subjected to the valorisation process. This occurs via the valorisation of the differences that characterize each individual. In their singularity, these differences make possible the relational activity at the root of the social cooperation that produces *general intellect*. It is no longer possible to refer to racial or gender differences. What is valorised are the differences *tout court*, apart from the anthropological characteristics defining them. What is segmented and divided are cerebral differences, namely individualities. The natural differences, gender and race first of all, might constitute the immediate disciplinary tools of the body social but only under conditions of backwardness, where cognitive capitalism and immaterial pro-

20 In my opinion, the use of the term "delete" seems too extreme.

duction are not jet fully deployed. But they are destined to be partially overcome towards the constitution of a human subjectivity characterized by the contradictory conflict between the creativity of *doing* and cerebral homologation: a sort of bionic being, the only one able to manage the anthropogenic process of production; *a world in which individuality is denied in favour of individualism.*

5. Bio-economic value

According to Marx's methodology, in order to discuss the theory of value attached to the bio-economic process, it is necessary to begin with the redefinition of surplus-value within cognitive capitalism. In the shift from formal to real subsumption of labour to capital, the surplus-value, the function of surplus-labour, can no longer be considered as merely deriving from living labour intended as simple labour (or immediate labour)[21], as mere expenditure of muscular energy. Living labour depends not only upon the labour activity – defined at an individual level – but is also the result of the relational and cognitive connection of the *general intellect*. To explain this, it is useful to subdivide living labour into two components: the first one refers to that part of living labour intended as the expense of physical energy that is partially crystallized in the physical capital of machines that are at the very basis of the new cycle of cognitive accumulation (hardware); the second, instead, becomes, in all respects, immaterial labour activity (that is, it is not crystallized in physical capital) constituting a sort of means of production (human capital) active in the production of knowledge, innovation, *general intellect*. This second component is not always be reducible to an objective means of production – it becomes so only partially – as it structures itself as the production of living labour by means of living labour. It represents the abstract labour in cognitive capitalism, whose productive system is definable as the production of knowledge by means of knowledge: K-K.

"In this transformation, it is neither the direct human labour he himself performs, nor the time during which he works, but rather the appropriation of his own general productive power, his understanding of nature and his mastery over it by virtue of his presence as a social body – it is, in a word, the development of the social individual which appears as the great foundation-stone of production and of wealth. The *theft of alien labour time, on which the present wealth is based,* appears a miserable foundation in face of this new one, created by large-scale industry itself. As soon as labour in the direct form has ceased to be the great well-spring of wealth, labour time ceases and must cease to be its measure, and hence exchange value [must cease to be the measure] of use value. The *surplus labour of the mass* has ceased to be the condition for the development of general wealth, just as the *non-labour of the few,* for the development of the general powers of the human head. With that, production based on exchange value

21 In *Grundrisse*, Marx often refers to "immediate labour" in order to indicate the direct application of labour, both in terms of fatigue and intellectual effort. In this case, by simple labour we refer to the immediate labour of physical nature (see Marx, 1973).

breaks down, and the direct, material production process is stripped of the form of penury and antithesis. The free development of individualities, and hence not the reduction of necessary labour time so as to posit surplus labour, but rather the general reduction of the necessary labour of society to a minimum, which then corresponds to the artistic, scientific etc. development of the individuals in the time set free, and with the means created, for all of them. Capital itself is the moving contradiction, [in] that it presses to reduce labour time to a minimum, while it posits labour time, on the other side, as sole measure and source of wealth. Hence it diminishes labour time in the necessary form so as to increase it in the superfluous form; hence posits the superfluous in growing measure as a condition – question of life or death – for the necessary. On the one side, then, it calls to life all the powers of science and of nature, as of social combination and of social intercourse, in order to make the creation of wealth independent (relatively) of the labour time employed on it. On the other side, it wants to use labour time as the measuring rod for the giant social forces thereby created, and to confine them within the limits required to maintain the already created value as value. Forces of production and social relations – two different sides of the development of the social individual – appear to capital as mere means, and are merely means for it to produce on its limited foundation. In fact, however, they are the material conditions to blow this foundation sky-high (Marx, 1973: 705-706).

In the above section from *Grundrisse* the issue with which we are dealing is condensed. The genesis of surplus-value cannot be exclusively based upon the division of the working day between the part necessary to the reproduction of the labour force (necessary labour) and the exceeding part that produces surplus-labour that, if realized, creates plus-value. It is indeed the difficulty to distinguish and separate the component of use value from that of the exchange value of the labour force that does not allow us to measure the rate of exploitation and therefore the origin of surplus value. This is the result – as Marx itself recognised – of the shift from formal to real subsumption of labour to capital, a passage that, however, makes it difficult to distinguish between labour enslaved to machinery and labour that we might be said to be *enslaved to itself*, and that is given when abstract labour becomes capital. The contradiction around which capital is entrapped is that

"it presses to reduce labour time to a minimum, while it posits labour time, on the other side, as sole measure and source of wealth" (Marx, 1973: 706)[22].

However, such a contradiction is only apparent. Firstly, because today the temporal reference that should be utilized is no longer the working day, but rather the entire life-cycle, within which we can find different phases of apprenticeship, development of knowledge, evolution of intellectual abilities and, therefore, different levels of social productivity. Secondly, because the reference to the reduction of working time can be ascribed only to material production that, although it was a peculiarity of Fordist industrial capitalism, at present has be-

22 It is a part of above quotation.

come a limited portion of the overall working time (life). Otherwise, starting form the mid-1970s, working time *de facto* has been progressively stretched as a result of the increase of cognitive labour (For an in-depth analysis see Foti, 1998, and Bologna, 1995). This is a paradox that cannot be understood unless we take into account the intrinsic differences of work activity, above all between material production (*hardware*), linguistic production (*software*), knowledge (*wetware*) and network production (*netware*). Obviously, this creates much confusion, reflected in the following statements:

"The sphere of capitalist production employs an increasingly lower volume of labour to produce a growing volume of wealth" (Gorz, 1995: 7).

"Since the dawn of time, human civilization has been structured to a large extent around the concept of work. From the Palaeolithic hunters-gatherers to the Neolithic farmers, to the medieval artisans, to the assembly-line workers of the contemporary age, work has always been an integral part of everyday life. Today, for the first time, human labour has been systematically eliminated from the production process; within the next century, the "mass" work in the market economy of market will probably have been cancelled in almost all the industrialized nations of the world" (Rifkin, 1997: 23).

or:

"For an increasing number of individuals, work has ceased to be the locus of personal fulfilment, and it is lived increasingly less as the node of the social bond" (Gorz, 1995: 7).

Even supposing that Tayloristic waged labour would have been the path leading to self-realization and a tool for social bonding (as it might have been in the professional labour performed by factory workers), the above statements, which for a certain time represented a fashionable attraction for many intellectuals, refer quite exclusively to Fordist manual labour, and do not take into account the new forms of digital-cognitive labour that are the heart of cognitive capitalism.

The extension of digital work as a form of linguistic performance, the diffusion of cognitive labour as a mode of flexible production of knowledge, the deployment of the relational structure as collective and social space where working activity produces wealth via social cooperation: these are the elements that make the working activity, on the one side, no longer homogeneous and definable according to a unique typology, and on the other, pivot on those that are human faculties possessed by each individual.

It is individuals' life that today is put to work. It is the reaction to such a human condition to assume different forms, both negative and positive, according to the situation of each singular individual.

Indeed, it is considering this typology of working activity that we may evince that it is no longer the working time that capitalism is exploiting, but rather the entire life-time. With the term life-time, we are not only referring to the sum of different daily working times, as it might be imagined if we would consider life as a sum of a number of days. The idea of life time as a sum of daily times refers to the biological or physical evolution of the body that, with the passing of time, tends to consume itself to the point of declining. Foucault, analyzing this aspect, spoke of capitalism as characterized by techniques of power that he defined as "disciplinary" (Foucault, 1997: 157). The French philosopher referred to the birth of the institutions of disciplinary capitalism that would have reached their apex with the Tayloristic-Fordist organization, aimed at controlling and repressing the body intended as a productive biological entity. Foucault, furthermore, believed that the capitalist organization characterized itself via specific techniques of *bio-political* power. With this term he referred to man as specie and not to the control "of man as simple body physical". These *bio-political* techniques, in fact, refer "to the global mass affected by biological processes specific to life, like birth, death, health, production, sickness. ... [biopolitics] relocates bodies in biological processes as a whole" (Foucault, 1997: 162).

This is exactly what happens under cognitive capitalism. Indeed, the idea of life time materializes itself, beyond the simple mechanical significance, as a process of creation of what lives. If during the Fordist period, the (surplus) value of the accumulation process was linked to the life-cycle of commodities, daily produced by living labour, at present, the (surplus) value is more and more directly interrelated with humans' life-cycle. This creates a parallel between accumulation and labour, which defines a new relationship between capital and labour. If on the part of the cognitive accumulation it is possible to speak of the knowledge life-cycle, on the part of labour subjectivities it is possible to speak of the labour life-cycle.

The above leads to a preliminary conclusion; under cognitive capitalism, the impossibility to detach the use value of the labour force from exchange value with reference to the working day (as a result of the prevalence of non quantifiable immaterial labour upon quantifiable material labour), leads to a need to consider the entire life cycle, namely the overall life-time of the individual, as the unit of measurement of the working activity. From the above discussion, also a second preliminary conclusion might be drawn: cognitive workers, precisely when language and communication become the engine of valorisation, find themselves – because they are "really subsumed" – within a cooperation process that leads them to perform a working activity that is collective in kind. As Felix Guattari puts it: "The term *collective* is... understood in the sense of a multiplicity that unfolds both beyond the individual, on the side of the *socius*, and within the persona, on the side of pre-variable intensities emanating from a logic of the affections more than from a logic of circumscribed wholes" (Guattari, 1996: 18). "Life time" and collective labour refer to the idea of a social being predicted by Marx in the *Grundrisse*. These are the boundaries within which we should define the subjectivity of labour and from which it is necessary to start if we want to discuss concepts like exploitation and alienation within the context of cognitive capitalism.

As it is possible to note, these are the very same variables that define the process of accumulation. And this cannot be otherwise, as working and cognitive activities (production and transmission of knowledge) tend to coincide and to define a multitude (multiplicity) of subjectivity *in opus*, within which the *bios*, namely the affections, sociality, the body and the mind are the sources from which the capitalistic valorisation arises.

*****

To conclude, in the cognitive phase of capitalism, the creation of value rests upon the process of exploitation of the *general intellect* for the purpose of private accumulation. The *general intellect* is the result of social cooperation that lies at the very basis of the accumulation process and allows the passage from tacit to codified knowledge – a process that enables the production of value in capitalistic terms. Such a passage is regulated by the evolution of the juridical forms of intellectual property rights. This property, in conjunction with the control of the means of production allows *private property* to control the process of generation (intellectual property) and diffusion of knowledge (ownership of the means of production). Because the exploitation of the *general intellect* implies the valorisation of the individuals' entire life, the process of wealth creation is no longer limited to the [extraction of value from the] singular working day but is extended to the point of incorporating the entire life of human beings. In other words, the rate of exploitation should no longer be measured according to the length of the working day generating surplus-labour, but rather according to the time necessary to generate codified and, therefore, social knowledge, that is expropriated *by* and *in* the accumulation process.

The forms – both effective and direct – with which the exploitation of the *general intellect* creates value assume different typologies. Among them, the valorisation placed by the process of *brandization* upon commodity is particularly noteworthy. To the increase of its symbolic significance and to the capacity to generate a shared imaginary on the part of consumers corresponds an increase of the value of commodity (Arvidsson, 2006). Also in this case, the surplus-value originates from totally immaterial elements, created by behavioural conventions, namely by common relational activities, similarly to the functioning of the financial markets. If private ownership of the means of production implies the theft of a portion of the working day destined to the generation of surplus-value, intellectual ownership is the theft of social knowledge as common good. According to the rules informing cognitive capitalism, wealth creation derives from the exploitation of what is "common".

References

Arvidsson, A. (2006), *Brands: Meaning and Value in Media Culture*, Abingdon: Routledge.

Bellofiore, R. (1996), "Marx rivisitato: capitale, lavoro e sfruttamento", *Trimestre*, XXIX (1-2): 29-86.

Bellofiore, R. (2005), "Quale critica dell'economia politica?", *Alternative*, 1: 86-98.

Bellofiore, R. and J. Halevi (2006), "Tendenze del capitalismo contemporaneo, destrutturazione del lavoro e limiti del "keynesismo"", in S. Cesaratto and R. Realfonzo (a cura di), *Rive gauche*, Roma: Manifestolibri.

Bloomfield, L. (1996), *Il linguaggio*, Milano: Il Saggiatore.

Bologna, S. (1995), "Orari di lavoro e postfordismo", in Aa.Vv. (1995), *Il giusto lavoro per un mondo giusto. Dalle 35 ore alla qualità del tempo di vita*, Acts of the international conference, Milano: Ed. Punto Rosso.

Castoriadis, C. (1998), *L'enigma del soggetto. L'immaginario e le istituzioni*, Bari: Dedalo.

Foti, A. (1998), *Cronocrazie*, Milano: Etas-libri.

Foucault, M. (1997), *Il faut défendre la société, Cours au Collège de France (1976)*, Paris: Gallimard-Seuil (engl. transl. "Society must be defended", in P. Rabinow (ed), *The Essential Works of Foucault, vol. 1: "Ethics, Subjectivity and Truth"*, New York: New Press).

Foucault, M. (2004), *Naissance de la biopolitique. Cours au College de France. 1978-79*, Paris: Gallimard-Seuil.

Fumagalli, A. (2007), *Bioeconomia e Capitalismo Cognitivo. Verso un nuovo paradigma di accumulazione*, Roma: Carocci.

Gorz, A. (1995), "Dépasser la société salariale", *Trasversales*, (32).

Gorz, A. (2003), *L'immatériel – Connaissance, valeur et capital*, Paris: Galilée.

Guattari, F. (1996), *Caosmosi*, Genova: Costa&Nolan.

Herrera, R. and C. Vercellone (2002), "Transformations de la division du travail et endogénéisation du progrès technique", *Economie Appliquée*, 55(1): 63-78.

Holloway, J. (2006), "Noi siamo la crisi del lavoro astratto", paper presented at the seminar of UniNomade, Bologna.

Lucas, R. E. (1988), "On the mechanics of economic development", *Journal of Monetary Economics*, 22(1): 3-42.

Marazzi, C. (2005), "Capitalismo digitale e modello antropogenetico del lavoro. L'ammortamento del corpo macchina", in J. L. Laville, C. Marazzi, M. La Rosa and F. Chicchi (a cura di), *Reinventare il lavoro,* Roma: Sapere 2000, pp. 107-126.

Marx, K. (1906) [1867], *The Capital: A Critique of Political Economy, Vol. I. The Process of Capitalist Production*, Chicago: Charles H. Kerr and Co.

Marx, K. (1973), *Grundrisse, Outlines of the Critique of Political Economy*, translated by M. Nicolaus, London: Penguin.

Negri, A. (1979), *Marx oltre Marx. Quaderno di Lavoro sui Grundrisse*, Milano: Feltrinelli.

Negri, A. (2005), comment at a UniNomade seminar held in Padova, September.
Negri, A. (2006), *Movimenti nell'Impero. Passaggi e paesaggi*, Milano: Raffaelo Cortina Editore.
Panzieri, R. (1961), "Sull'uso capitalistico delle macchine", *Quaderni Rossi*, 1: 53-72.
Panzieri, R. (1964), "Plusvalore e Pianificazione", *Quaderni Rossi*, 1964 (eng. trans. "Surplus Value and Planning. The Labor Process & Class Strategies", *CSE Pamphlet* n. 1, London, 1976).
Rifkin, J. (1995), *The End of Work*, New York: G.B.Putnam's Son.
Rifkin, J. (2000), *The Age of Access,* New York: Tharcher.
Salvini, F. (2006), "La città linguistic", Graduation Thesis, Università L. Bocconi, Milano.
Smith, A. (1904) [1776], *An Inquiry into the Nature and the Cause of Wealth of Nations*, London: Methuen and Co., Ltd., ed. Edwin Cannan.
Sraffa, P. (1979), *Produzione di merci a mezzo di merci: Premesse a una critica della teoria economica*, Torino: Einaudi [1960].
Stewart, T. A. (2002), *The Wealth of Knowledge: Intellectual Capital and the Twenty-first Century Organization*, New York: Currency Books.
Vercellone, C. (ur.) (2007), *Kognitivni kapitalizam*, Zagreb: Politička kultura.

3. Values and capabilities as historical determinants of social development

Matko Meštrović

1. Individual, or total social capital?

The analytical framework for all the major problems of society that gradually reached modernity after 1492 is the world system and not the local and national formations that compose it. Underdevelopment is not a backward phase of development but a modern phenomenon of world-wide capitalist expansion initially polarizing centres and peripheries. The world system is based on the capitalist mode of production whose logic overturns the order of previous dispensations and is expressed in economistic alienation. The law of value dominates not only economic life (which becomes autonomous) but all other aspects of social life (which become subject to it). To advance the analysis of capitalist polarisation, Samir Amin (1994) firmly believes the distinction between the law of value in general and the law of world-wide value is fundamental (68-69).

As Kojin Karatani (2005) observes, classical economists conceptualized the labour value that exists beyond empirical prices, while neoclassical economists negated the value and sought to remain in the sphere of empirical prices. What they both overlooked is that price as well as labour-value are derivative variants of the form of value (qua relational system) (228-229).

To Marx, what distinguished industrial capital from merchant capital was, first and foremost, that the former discovered a "special commodity" that the latter had not known – the commodity of labour power, Karatani reminds us. Industrial capital purchases this most special commodity in human history – labour power – in order to produce products, and then sells those products to the commodity itself – labourers – in order to earn surplus value. For neoclassical economists, consumers and companies are the only economic subjects to them; labourers are deemed just wages as part of the costs of production.

Namely, Karatani explains, the surplus value of industrial capital is attained only in *a sort of* circulation process: capital purchases labour power from living labourers, who, in consequence, buy back what they produce from capital. It is not that individual workers buy the very same things they produce, but that *in totality* – and herein the concept *totality* intervenes as a sine qua non – labourers qua consumers buy what they produce. This further signifies that surplus value cannot be considered on the level of individual capital but strictly as *total social capital* (235). In this context, the level should be further upgraded from that of a nation-state to total world capital. Marx's *Capital* therefore is truly "A critique of political economy" because it sought to grasp capitalism from the stance of world capitalism beyond a polis (nation-state), Kojin Karatani concludes (263).

2. Total subsumption

If communication constitutes the fabric of production and the substance of the form of value (qua relational system), if capital has become therefore so permeable that it can filter every relation through the material thickness of production, if the labouring processes extend equally as far as the social extends, what then are the consequences that we can draw with the respect to the law of value? – Toni Negri (1996) is asking. And he gives precise answers:

- there is no possibility of anchoring a theory of measure on something extraneous to the universality of exchange;
- there is no longer any sense in a theory of measure with respect to the immeasurable quality of social accumulation;
- even the space for the development of the labouring relations, the interaction among labouring subjects, the productive routes within society, all this is immeasurable

But the immeasurability of the figures of value, he insists, does not deny the fact that labour is at the basis of any constitution of society. Exploitation is politically produced as a function of capitalist Power from which descends a system of matrices and limits adequate to the reproduction of the system (152-153). It is the political sign of domination above and against the human valorisation of the historical/natural world (157).

We are at the beginning of a new epoch and no longer simply within the phase of the completion of the process of abstraction of labour. Now cooperation is posed prior to the capitalist machine, as a condition independent of industry. New period of the capitalist mode of production, after manufacture and large-scale industry, after the phase of professional worker and of the mass worker, is presented as the period of "social worker", which vindicates the real mass autonomy, the real capacity of collective auto-valorisation with respect to capital. In a contrast to this, Negri argues, the fundamental function of Power is that of stripping from the social process of productive cooperation the command over its own functioning. The labour-time of full, whole social cooperation is submitted to the law of the maintenance of domination (156; 154).

The intellectual and scientific forces which have gradually become central in production are nonetheless powers of labour. The growing immateriality does not eliminate the creative function of labour, but rather exalts it in its abstraction and its productivity. Only the creativity of labour (living labour in the power of its expression) is commensurate with the dimension of value (152).

Capital, however reformist it may be, never willingly passes to a subsequent or superior phase of the mode of production. The more radical the innovation is, the more profound and powerful were the antagonistic forces which have determined it.

Every innovation is a revolution which failed – but also one which was attempted. Within the process of socialization of the form of value it becomes evident that the dialectical process, which modifies the capitalist ordering and determines the sense of its innovations, attacks capitalist Power and it hegemony on the socio-political transformation of society to a continually greater degree. The motor force which constitutes the form of value, the antagonistic expression of the productive force of living labour, is simultaneously the motor of the deconstruction of the form of value. In the phase of the total subsumption of society and the complete multi-nationalization of the productive process, what alternative does it have left? – Toni Negri is asking again. Everyone is waiting, he says, to see to what extent the malaise of capitalist civilization is really the anarchy of meaning and the emptiness of its soul (158-159).

3. Focus and scope

Since people use ethical ideas in orienting their behaviour, explanatory economics must understand those ideas and their roles; they are part of human and societal reality. Ignorance of and segregation from ethics as a subject profoundly damages economics, Des Gasper (2007) points out as a principal topics of Amartya Sen's famous lectures *On Ethics and Economics* (1987).

Sen has always aimed to influence mainstream economics from within, with no offence or confrontation. As Gasper remarks, he has evolved a powerful form of policy analysis guided by humanist values. The methodology moves away from and far beyond the economic cost-benefit analysis where he began. A wider range of values is employed in valuation, far beyond willingness-(backed by ability)-to-pay. It brings a focus on core human realities, not on slices of experience selected according to commercial significance and/or convenience for measurement. Central attention goes to how do, and can, people live. That is a scope of Sen's conceptual and theoretical investigation (7).

Amartya Sen responds to such issues in his form of value-oriented reality-driven economics, and shows how it is value-guided as well as value-conscious. It discusses both the capability approach and entitlement approach, and their integration (8). His insights are deep and valuable but not sufficient as a full theoretical and methodological basis for a Human Development Approach, Des Gasper comments.

Value-laden does not mean fact-empty. The methodological injunction – to look always for the value inputs that underlie prescriptions, or, by extension, evaluations – is not tied to one ontology, and leads in the opposite direction from the attempted epistemological proscription: it encourages examination of and engagement with values (9).

Values always are involved in the allocation of attention (11). Cost-benefit analysis treats only monetizable aspects, treats people overwhelmingly as individuals in a market, weighs people's wishes in proportion to their purchasing power and ignores people without money. These are not choices openly made at a stage of setting policy objectives. They are instead built into the method, as part of a worldview that values monetized economic production (13). So we require not the "fundamental theorems of welfare economics" but assessment of the full range of human functionings that generate and are generated by a system of production, exchange and consumption, a system of human living (15).

Entitlements analysis, used as a generative schema, has lost prominence as a separate approach but has been absorbed into the Sustainable Livelihoods Approach (SLA), the Human Development and capability approaches, and rights-based approaches. SLA, in its assets analysis makes a useful breakdown of the "endowments" category into five (or more) categories of capital – natural, social, human, physical, financial (and sometimes cultural and political) – and in its attention to diverse forms of claiming-capacity. It also deals with "capabilities", as skills, agency and assets, not only Sen's sense of attainable valued functionings (18).

An approach cannot do everything required but should do something useful and not undermine what else is required. The long used language of class does not bring such widespread and fine-tuned attention to effective acquirement capacities and their determinants as do the languages of entitlements, rights and livelihoods, Gasper remarks. In any case, he argues, Sen's framework does not preclude or dissuade but rather induces attention to meso-and macrodeterminants (22).

A principle that all those affected by a decision should be able to influence it might only be operationalizable via allocation of certain rights. At the same time rights-based approaches highlight that empowerment, not merely legislation, is the path to entitlement, Gasper explains quoting Watts (1991). Namely, the empowerment presupposes increasing of the spiritual, political, social and economic strengths of individuals and communities, the empowered developing confidence in their own capacities.

Real operationalization of value alternatives in policy analysis means comprehensive incorporation into methodology, Gasper continues. The rights-based approaches represent a partial move, which needs to be taken further in methods of policy analysis – in concept formation, situation analysis, options analysis, appraisal and evaluation – especially in reframing issues, reallocation of onuses of proof, and (re)allocation of responsibilities.

These are issues of politics, values and social theory not only of technique, Des Gasper points out, referring to Korten's question what is the Human Development Approach's underlying political and economic theory; and to his warning that in the absence of any conscious theory it slid back to liberal presumptions and became merely a human face of the Washington consensus (26-27).

4. "Global market forces"

As Amartya Sen (1999) argues the value of democracy includes its *intrinsic importance* in human life, its *instrumental role* in generating political incentives, and its *constructive function* in the formation of values. Nonetheless, he gives no real argument for the force of the claim that democracy is a universal value. It seems that this winner of the 1998 Nobel Prize for Economics lacks a more profound insight of the multiple levels inter-relational value dependencies (16).

In *Economics for Humans,* Julie A. Nelson (2006) discredits the deeply-embedded idea that our economic world should somehow be separate from our concerns for ethics and personal relationships. We can wed our desire for profits with our justifiable concerns for the environment and general social welfare. But we can only do so if we begin to think of economics not as a robot-like machine, but a living, beating heart that keeps the body running, while serving as an emblem of compassion and care. Simply put, an economy that values human capital as much as it does monetary capital is in the best interest of everyone, Julie Nelson believes.

A break must be made from contemporary mainstream economics at the level of ontology, or the study of the nature of reality, she firmly emphasizes. Ample historical precedent and intellectual argument exist for a view of the world as open, evolving, and permeated with value. Because in this view knowledge is not merely reflective of reality, but rather helps to create it, the issue of "value" becomes central to discussions of "science" (Nelson, 2000).

The ontology behind science/value split familiar in modernism is one in which mind and matter are considered to be separate "things". There is a given reality "out there", it is assumed, waiting to be known. While values and purposes are something that humans have and sometimes try to impose, external reality is bereft of intrinsic value, subjectivity, or purpose (7). Hence this strain of scientific thought – expanded to technical and economic thought – purports to objectively describe the world as it is. Our attempts to find religious, moral, and aesthetic meaning in the universe, in this view, are epiphenomenal and quixotic, if not downright delusional, Julie Nelson argues (8).

The assumption that matter is senseless seems so tied up in our notions of science that it may be hard to see that this ontological view is not required by science itself, she observes. Science conceived of as methodical inquiry, as openness to new evidence, as experimentalism – such a definition does not rely on a mechanistic or reductionist worldview. Such a conception of science is quite consistent with a view of experience itself as holistic. Scientific thought, as inquiry, involves extending our perceptions and refining our powers of reflection, and as such is both a part of experience, and a purposive seeking to understand and better our lives through (extended) experiences (10-11).

The notion of values, however, must be carefully redefined, Nelson warns. The tendency in the Western world since the time of Plato has been to think of the actual world going through time as being a corrupted reflection of ideal forms, which themselves are universal and time-invariant. We see such thinking in neoclassical economic thought which finds "behind" the actions of individuals a pure problem in rational choice, and "behind" actual markets the laws of The Market, impersonal and competitive. In this way of thinking, if values objectively exist, they must exist as universals as theoretical invariants, lying out there somewhere waiting to be discovered (11).

The reductionist worldview has been characterized as tough, hard-nosed, realistic, and leading towards clarity, precision, certainty and real objective knowledge and control, while the process, pragmatist and institutionalist views were dismissed as, by comparison, soft, sentimental, sullied by the acknowledgment of interests, muddy, contingent, and ineffective, Nelson reminds us, quoting ironically Steven Weinberg (1992). Any attempt to include purpose and values could be labelled as inferior in rigor, and reminiscent of an "old-fashioned" naive, holistic, religious and/or magical worldview, such as that associated with pre-scientific, medieval alchemy and witchcraft (13).

The social structure of modernist, "value-free" science is grounded in a cultural belief that matter is purposeless and has no intrinsic value. It follows that a new understanding of value in the economic and social realms is on weak ground unless it also is grounded in a legitimizing metaphor, one that sees the natural world also as potentially purposive and meaningful, Julie Nelson suggests (17).

For the believers in ideal and inexorable principles of Market as an expression of the deepest truth about human nature, free-market economics is in touch with the real underlying "stuff", while views that see anything else as important are merely "ideology". Therefore, Nelson underlines, politics, nation-states, inequities, concerns for local communities, ecological implications, an ethos of corporate responsibility (or irresponsibility), compassion, ambition, discrimination, religious interests, cultural norms and practices, history and institutions, corruption, and all other factors that might shape economic relations within and between nations, all fall away into insignificance before the abstract "global market forces" (21).

5. The overall pattern

Brian Holmes (2003) thinks that the real subsumption of traditional culture by capitalist relations of production almost immediately creates an imperious need to invent new forms of non-monetary exchange, so as to escape from the constrictive and sterile realm of pure commodity relations. He believes that the continuing imposition of networked capitalism is backed up increasingly by military force as the symbolic language of money loses its ability to integrate the world system. This is going to bring up waves of violent resistance whose nature we cannot really understand from our positions here in the Western world.

Namely, as Holmes put it in a recent discussion (2008) there is no inherently progressive aspect to immaterial labour, and "Empire" is still driven and piloted by imperialist nation-states, above all Britain and the USA. But still there is a deep ambiguity in the practice of immaterial labour, to the extent that it too is subject to a double movement – or in other words, to the extent that we too can recoil from the pressure of total commodification of ourselves.

It is tremendously important, Holmes remind us, to understand the degree to which all forms of cultural and scientific production are increasingly being functionalized for market exchange, whose quintessence is the trading of immaterial goods on Wall Street.

The point is to see how specific social institutions impress upon us the basic underlying procedure of neoliberal subjectivity, which consists in understanding yourself, your accomplishments and your own creativity, indeed your own desire, as *human capital*, to be nourished and cherished in terms of its potential returns on the market, and to be used as a measurement of the value of any kind of experience whatsoever. To explore how neoliberal subjectivation takes place in the knowledge society, and look at a deliberate attempt to escape this form of subjectivation (6).

China's transformation is becoming the central phenomenon in the emergence of a new, complex and in many ways threatening world society, Holmes (2008a) observes. The global extension of the Anglo-American technological and organizational toolkit has given rise to a world civilization, what Félix Guattari called "integrated world capitalism". This overall pattern of world civilization can only be governed and normed at a regional or continental scale, using cultural and political resources that are specific to that scale, Holmes arhues. The continental scale – whether a nation-state like India or China, or a regional bloc like the Russian Federation or the EU – has become decisive in the world today, because only that scale can fully internalize, but also *resist* global forces. An entire political economy lodges in the tension of these intersections. The unanswered question is how those tensions are expressed and elaborated by individuals: how the emergence of a world society is tangled up with the production of new subjectivities.

Global individualism, Holmes explains, results from the monetization and contractualization of social relations, which is an essential part of the neoliberal economic order. What you feel in urban China today is an extraordinary productive energy, which corresponds to a tremendous achievement: an exit from hunger and poverty for hundreds of millions of people, and the invention of a new development path promising equality with the Western nations. But the same social reality has a much crueller side, which few of its proponents care to mention.

Brian Holmes points to the development of a global division of labour, and indeed, of a global society, which is now coming concretely into being. The availability of the China price depends in its turn on the capacity of the urban white-collar worker to extract tremendous amounts of underpaid labour from his other half, the peasant arriving to toil in the factories. The communist version of the *hukou* or household registration system, which served to immobilize people in their locality of origin, the very system that denies peasant populations their full urban citizenship is also at the basis of the incredible engine of wealth-production that attracts them to the city in the first place. The *hukou* system allows rural labour to play the same role in China that transnational migrant labour does in the European or North American economies, furnishing human fuel to sweatshops and low-end service industries while exerting downward pressure on the wages of more established workers. The evolution of the hukou system over the

the next ten years, Holmes remarks, may be the most precise barometer for registering the inevitable changes in the class structure, not just of China, but of the world.

Critical interpretations of the new cultural forms, and of the social and political frames in which they create their effects and meanings, will be crucial in opening the imaginary space where people can gain some kind of relative autonomy, some capacity to be their own steersman. Today it is the economic imperative, not the state, that commands in detail what should or should not be represented by the creative industries. The result has been a gradual neutralization of ethical and political speech. This gap at the heart of self-expression is now being exported across the earth. What's missing in all our societies are the psychic and social resources for resistance to the present.

This seems to be the most relevant insight from Brian Holmes in his personal witnessing of contemporary China and its significance for the world of today.

References

Amin, S. (1994), *Re-Reding the Postwar Period: An Intellectual Itinerary*, New York: Monthly Review Press.

Gasper, D. (2007), "Problem – and policy-analysis for human development – Sen in the light of Dewey, Myrdal, Streeten, Stretton and Haq", *ISS Working Paper* N. 451.

Holmes, B. (2003), Revenge of the Concept, available at http://www.mail-archive.com/nettime-l@bbs.thing.net/msg00280.html.

Holmes, B. (2008), "Articulating the Cracks in the Worlds of Power", *16 Beaver Group talking with Brian Holmes*, available at

Holmes, B. (2008), "One World, One Dream", available at
http://brianholmes.wordpress.com/2008/01/08/one-world-one-dream/.
http://www.16beavergroup.org/drift/readings/16b_bh_articulatingcracks.pdf.
http://www.pcdf.org/1994/CONFEREN.htm.

Karatani, K. (2005), *Transcritique – On Kant and Marx*, The MIT Press.

Korten, D. C. (1994), "Sustainable development strategies: the people-centered consensus - reflections on SID's 21st World Conference", available at

Negri, T. (1996), "Twenty theses on Marx – interpretation of the class situation today", in S. Makdisi, C. Casarino and R. Karl (eds), *Marxism Beyond Marxism*, London: Routledge, pp. 149-180.

Nelson, J. A. (2000), "Confronting the Science/Value Split: Notes on Feminist Economics, Institutionalism, Pragmatism and Process Thought", *paper presented at EAEPE Conference*, Berlin, November, 2-4 2000, Economics and social Sciences: Complements, Competitors, Accomplices, Program and Abstracts, Session S2A: Conceptual Frameworks.

Nelson, J.A. (2006), *Economics for Humans*, Chicago: The University of Chicago Press.

Sen, A. (1999), "Democracy as a Universal Value", *Journal of Democracy,* 10(3): 3-17.

Watts, M. (1991), "Entitlements or Empowerment? Famine and Starvation in Africa", *Review of African Political Economy*, 5: 9-26.

Weinberg, S. (1992), *Dreams of a Final Theory: The Search for the Fundamental Laws of Nature*, New York: Pantheon.

4. Labour and welfare state in the transition to cognitive capitalism

Jean-Marie Monnier and Carlo Vercellone

Introduction

There is general agreement today that capitalism's current transformation, characterized by the rise of a knowledge-based economy, is responsible for a far-reaching change in labour and work relations that undermines the foundation of the previous Fordist system of social welfare. Most analysis, however, attempts to understand this crisis by treating the social welfare system simply as a dependent variable in relation to changes in the accumulation of capital. In our view, this approach is too reductive. In particular, it obscures the crucial role of the welfare state, understood both as a system of distribution and a system of production, in the process that led from the crisis of Fordist industrial capitalism to the emergence of "cognitive capitalism".

In recent years, a significant body of work has developed on the various models and main functions of the welfare state. Often separating the welfare state from the capitalist logic of accumulation, this literature attempts to present a comprehensive analysis of public policy in the sphere of social welfare[23]. Esping-Andersen (1990) in particular has described the institutional relationships between the private sphere, the market, and the state according to three models: free market, social-democratic, and corporatist-conservative (with which France is associated). This taxonomic approach causes Esping-Andersen to take an essentially static perspective of the economy (Barbier and Théret, 2004). In effect, even if the various models of the welfare state are put into historical perspective, comparative analysis (such as that employed by Esping-Andersen) tends to oversimplify particular contexts and minimize the dynamics of current transformations, however large or small, by focusing on a system that "crystallized" after the second world war. If, as Esping-Andersen points out, a "theory that seeks to explain welfare-state growth should also be able to understand its solidification or decline" (Esping-Andersen, 1990: 32), then his own analysis of the welfare-state depends strongly on its stability as a system. This is particularly true for the "corporatist-conservative" model, whose defining characteristic is the preservation of existing rights and benefits. Furthermore, the feminist critique of Esping Andersen points out that he ignores the importance of gender in his analysis of the transformations of the welfare state. For example, he neglects the role of unpaid work by women in considering the question of welfare. Understanding the current crisis of the social welfare

23 See Merrien, Parchet, and Kernen (2005).

system as well as the various proposals for its reform, therefore, will only be possible through a complete analysis of the dynamics of capitalist transformation itself. In the article the study of the historical dynamic of capitalism is divided in two parts.

The first part of the article is devoted to an analysis of the welfare system development. We describe its role in the process that led from industrial capitalism to the fordist model and its eventual colapse, and we emphasize three fundamental characteristics of this model. Fordism hinges upon a precise regulation of wage and gender relations and upon a standard for productivity derived from the "scientific" organization of labour. Finally, it depends on a static conceptualization of the intersection of different uses of social times.

The second part of the paper is devoted to the transition to cognitive capitalism. We demonstrate how the autonomous dynamic of the institutions of social welfare set in motion a break from the logic of industrial capitalist development, but also created the subjective conditions and structural basis for the rise of a knowledge-based economy. Cognitive capitalism has grown out of four main processes and has affected the ensemble of Fordist norms regarding productive labour, the articulation of social times, the division of labour, the measure and source of value.

1. Labour and social welfare in the Fordist model

The current social welfare system in France was created during the period of Fordist growth according to a complex dialectic between conflict and innovation.

The Fordist model itself results directly from the developmental logic of industrial capitalism and in many ways represents its culmination. Fordism depends upon a precise regulation of the wage relation and a strict technical, social, and sexual division of labour. To fully grasp the meaning of the radical changes in labour currently underway, as well as the present crisis of the social welfare system, it is crucial to understand three fundamental characteristics of the Fordist model.

1.1 Gender and access to social welfare in the Fordist model

First, the gradual expansion of the labour force took place throughout industrialized countries but was institutionalized in differing ways. In this regard, men - the labourers of big industry - were the primary breadwinners, and their function was to guarantee the livelihood and reproduction of the family through their income[24]. This system experienced its apex during the period after the second world war, in allowing "a greater number of men than before to support a wife at home who in turn would look after the children and other dependents" (Orloff, 2006: 14). From this perspective, the development of the welfare state and in particular the French system, relied upon two factors: the wage labourer, who held a stable job that provided employment benefits; and his dependents, who benefited from so-called "derived" rights (Belorgey, 2000). As such, women's relationship to employment and social welfare was defined largely by family ties (Daune-Richard, 2004). This traditional form of gender relations[25] no doubt helped to alleviate much of the poverty that had previously afflicted a great number of women. However, the system of derived rights associated with the sexual division of labour, in which child care was left entirely to women, generated a relationship of strict dependence on the breadwinner. Finally, compulsory payroll taxes have made possible the progressive coverage of the entire population. This has also been caused by policies favoring full employment and by the actions of large corporations in establishing employment and salary standards.

1.2 Labour time and the measure of value

In extending an old tendency of the first industrial revolution, Fordism adopted a standard for productivity whereby *direct labour time spent in production* became the measure of and primary factor in the creation of value. During this process, a central role was assigned to mass production by large industry, which had at its core the separation of intellectual and manual labour. This separation reflected the incorporation of knowledge within the managerial structure and fixed capital of the enterprise. In effect, the "scientific" organization of labour in terms of prescribed tasks in a given time frame presupposed a separation between a worker's labour and his subjectivity. In other words, this process represented the objectification of labour through an array of finite and quantifiable tasks, all of which were supposed to be established and measured within the chronometer watch norm. A clear distinction emerged, therefore, between the labourer's educational time and his productive working time, which is typically organized by management in such a way as to ensure his silent cooperation and seamless integration into the workflow. Accordingly, the main criterion of economic efficiency and productivity becomes the search for homogenous economies of

24 According to the model of the "male breadwinner" developed in the feminist literature in which gender relations confront welfare state institutions (Sainsbury, 1999: 254).

25 In the contemporary feminist literature, the distinction between sex and gender is a distinction between "the biological differences between men and women" and "the social construction of sexual identity that assigns roles, rights, and opportunities to people based on their sex" (Barker, 1999: 390).

time and the principle of productivity-yield[26] (Veltz, 2000). These criteria directly linked a standard measure for produced value and productivity with remuneration for work according to two complementary factors: 1) the direct labour time spent in production; and 2) the growth of real *wages* parallel to gains in *productivity* stemming from the mechanization and Taylorist rationalization of the production process.

1.3 Productive and unproductive labour in Fordism

Within the Fordist regime of accumulation, the ensemble of norms regulating the technical, social, and sexual division of labour also resulted in a static conceptualization of the connection of different uses of social times. This took the form of a split opposing direct wage labour time, seen as the sole form of productive time, and other activities, such as domestic labour, education, and the reproduction of the labour force, which were viewed as essentially unproductive. This divide, which led in a more general manner to the relegation of all non-commodified and non-monetary activities to unproductive status, was apparent at several levels:

(a) In the dual, synchronic opposition between "labour time" as a period of subordination and "free time" as removed from the imposition of the workplace.

(b) In the distinction between wage labour and unpaid domestic labour, providing the foundation for much of the inequality that existed between men and women. Although men worked primarily in the first register (paid wage labour), women carried out their work activities (paid wage labour[27] and unpaid domestic labour) where they suffered various forms of discrimination (Daune-Richard, 1983).

(c) In the opposition between the sphere of production and the sphere of consumption, in which Fordist consumer goods (especially household items) served to reduce the time and cost of reproducing the labour force.

(d) In the standardized and diachronic organization of the life cycle into three distinct phases: education, professional life, and retirement (Vallade, 2002).

---

26 That is to say, an essentially quantitative conventional determination of productivity, founded on the relationship between the quantities produced and the volume of labor employed measured in hours of work.

27 Let us note in passing that for a long time in France many types of unpaid labor carried out by women constituted familial forms of production of goods to be sold. That said, immediately after the second world war, salary inequalities and the system of social welfare for families, in particular the "single-salary allowance" (*allocation de salaire unique-ASU*), tended to discourage women to engage in paid wage labour, despite the fact that the ASU was intended as a compensation for a "lack in earning potential" (Daune-Richard, 2004). Women continued to enter the workplace, however, and by the early 1970s the percentage of women at work surpassed 50%.

This framework (upon which mainstream economic theory is largely built and its conception of the "work/leisure" trade-off), excludes from view a range of activities and uses of time that cannot be incorporated into the universe of wage labour and value creation. Furthermore, it ignores unpaid labour time (Gauvin and Jacot, 1999) and stigmatized any other social times devoted to the formation and reproduction of labour power considered as unproductive.

The social welfare system, therefore, was established within the conventions of Fordism and relied upon a dual model of masculine work. First, this model held the man as primary breadwinner for the family and the woman as responsible for child care[28] and housekeeping. Second, this model was connected with a specific norm of employment taking the form of a stable job, particularly a job for life in a large company. The stability of this system and the financing of social welfare itself, therefore, depended upon steady growth at close to full employment, the gradual integration of the entire labour force into secure, Fordist-style employment, as well as the closing of the circle between production and mass consumption.

With Fordist growth, the creation of the social welfare system was closely related to a culmination of the tendencies of industrial capitalism, and to what Marx called the logic of the real subsumption of labour to capital. Thus, we can begin to see the ambiguous nature of the social welfare system during the growth of the *Trente Glorieuses* (1945-1975).

In effect, although the institutions of social welfare were at first powerful regulatory elements of the Fordist wage relation and gender norms, the system resulting from the expansion of public spending and services and of social security by the welfare state ultimately expressed its own autonomous dynamic, which prompted a departure from the developmental logic of industrial capitalism. This explains why the solution to the current crisis of the social welfare system cannot simply be conceived of as a return to the neo-Fordist model of full employment.

2. Welfare state in the transition from industrial capitalism to cognitive capitalism: tensions, ambiguities, alternatives

The concept of cognitive capitalism can be understood from two points of view. First, from a methodological and critical perspective the two terms warrant separate examination: a) the term "capitalism" underlines the permanence of the

28 Here we see one of the two traditional models of gender that, according to Pfau-Effinger (1999: 62-63) have been dominant since the Second World War.

structural constants of the capitalist mode of production, such as the driving role of profit and the wage relation or more precisely the different forms of dependent labour upon which the extraction of surplus labour rests; b) the term "cognitive" emphasizes the changing nature of the division of labour as well as the forms of property now essential for capital accumulation. The combination of these two terms, therefore, underlines both the conflicts and contradictions brought about by the shift towards the current phase of capitalism.

Second, from an historical perspective, cognitive capitalism is a "new historical system of accumulation"[29], in which the cognitive and intellectual dimensions of labour take on an increasingly important role and displace the previous centrality of fixed capital and material labour. With this shift, the valorization of capital is directly related to the control and to the transformation of knowledge into a fictitious commodity (in the sense of Polyani).

The defining characteristic of this evolution is the role of knowledge as the main economic driving force. This change was brought about by a substantial increase in the average level of education of the labour force. Thus, the new hegemony of the knowledge incorporated into living labour, over *dead knowledge*, incorporated in fixed capital and the managerial firm organisation, represents the main feature of Cognitive Capitalism (Vercellone, 2003).

Today, we see a reversal of the capital/labour relation, which is comparable in importance but opposite to that anticipated by Gramsci during the 1930s in "Americanism and Fordism". Knowledge, which is increasingly shared collectively and more widely distributed, progressively overturns the ways that labour is organized within corporations, as well as its relationship to society as a whole. Cognitive capitalism has grown out of four main processes that have become visible since the end of the 1960s. These processes were behind crisis in the Fordist wage relation and the social welfare system, which, in exceeding the traditional formulations of Fordist regulation, laid the groundwork for an economy based on the production of knowledge. This transition has affected the ensemble of Fordist norms regarding productive labour, the articulation of social times, the division of labour, and the measure and source of value.

---

29 This intermediate category, absent from theories of regulation, is defined as the association of the capitalist mode of production with a dominant logic of accumulation. An historical system of accumulation orients itself over the long term towards the valorization of capital and the reproduction of the most fundamental social relations: thus, industrial capitalism succeeded mercantile capitalism, and then gave rise to a new historical system of accumulation called cognitive capitalism.

2.1 The elevation of the general level of education and the constitution of a diffuse intellectuality

The increase in the educational and skill level of the labour force led to the rise of immaterial and intellectual labour. But it also led to question the industrial capitalism's division of labour and system of technical change. This transformation is visible throughout the entire economy, as evidenced by the importance given to knowledge related externalities as well as the diffusion of knowledge and information intensive tasks in all sectors of the economy, including many low-tech industries (Eliasson, 1996; Lojkine, 1992 and 2006).

In a growing number of activities, education and the exchange of information have begun to determine labour time, which corresponds less and less to the regimented and regularized nature of collective labour under Fordism. Direct labour time spent in production has come to represent only a fraction of overall labour time; with the development of the immaterial and intellectual dimensions of labour, total labour time is determined by the complex combination of a variety of activities, including reflection, communication, sharing, and the development of knowledge. These activities occur as much outside as within the bounds of direct labour time. Here, the precise delineation and synchronic unity of time and workplace, which provided the basis for the Fordist wage relation, is substantially altered. In this way, the traditional division between labour and non-labour has become less clear. Thus, the effective labour time expended by the labour force often exceeds that accounted for by the traditional work day, and increasingly subsumes all of social time. This produces a contradictory result: corporations, while assigning a greater autonomy to labour in terms of its organization, also exercise an intense pressure over the subjectivity of workers, in order to guarantee their complete involvement and internalization of the goals defined by management. What results is a new sort of productivism, which encroaches upon fundamental areas of an individual's personal life and is in large part responsible for the recent appearance of a new kind of "work-related illness" (Askenazy, 2004; Askenazy and Caroli, 2006). Taken together, these changes translate to an increase in the amount of nontraditional labour that goes unmeasured due to the difficulty of quantifying it with traditional criteria. Today, this is a key reason to comprehensively rethink the notion of productive labour and the connection between different social times in respect to the Fordist model.

2.2 The rise of cognitive labour and the destabilization of the sexual division of labour

One of the most striking features of the diffusion of knowledge and the restructuring of the division of labour is the increased access of women to secondary and higher education, which in some disciplines now surpasses that of men. This change goes hand in hand with the rise of labour force participation rate of women and the general feminization of the labour force[30]. In addition, it is often the relational and emotive qualities of reproductive labour, traditionally carried out by women, which are now considered, albeit ambivalently, to be fundamental characteristics in the new paradigm of cognitive labour.

The rise of women paid labour participation has also its origin in a host of factors both demographic and political: "the decline of fertility rates, the aging of the population, the crises with regard to retirement, and the movements for gender equality have all come together to destabilize the old balance of gender relations within the family and in the workplace" (Orloff, 2006: 14). These changes call into question the very foundation of the patriarchal family model[31], upon which rested the reproduction of the labour force, the sexual division of labour, and the social welfare system.

This process of emancipation, however, remains largely unfinished with respect to certain forms of employment, the regulation of the labour market, and the adaptation of the social welfare system. Thus, despite the setting up of policies favoring women's access to employment, the system remains fundamentally based on a masculine model[32]. The development (in the 1980s) of part-time and temp work, in particular, facilitated the access of women to the labour market but accentuated the separation between skilled and unskilled women. Many part-time and temp jobs, for example, offer short term contracts, low pay, and unfavorable work hours, especially with regard to family life. In other words, women's access to employment represented only a partial break with the inequality of the patriarchal model. Moreover, the recent changes in benefits

30 Between 1970 and 2006 the labor force participation rate of women between the ages of 15 and 64 went from 47,6% to 63,9% in France.

31 In the old model of French patriarchy, behind the apparent neutrality of the state towards the employment of women, they depend on their family position for access to a salary and to societal rights, while the husband is the person who controls "by law" their possessions (Daune-Richard, 2004: 73).

32 Thus, as Anne-Marie Daune-Richard (2003: 146) explains, equally in terms of skills as in terms of remuneration, the feminine shrinks before the masculine: "the social hierarchy of masculine and feminine causes women's skills to disappear from the scale of values at work".

provided to families in France, notably the extension in 1994 of the "parental education allowance" (*allocation parentale d'education, APE*) to couples with two or more children (instead of three or more previously), the setting up in 2001 and the increasing importance of the French income tax credit (*prime pour emploi, PPE*), have caused poorly paid women with families to remove themselves from the labour market (Afsa, 1998; Piketty, 1998; Concialdi and Monnier, 2002: 138).

As for the duties traditionally performed by women, there has been a "defamilialization" of dependent care in the developed world and a consequent growth in the number of dependent elderly persons who must be supported. In this regard, since the 1950s France has build up a model for meeting in different ways and in different contexts the consequences of child care services needs and of an increasing proportion of population growing older than ever before: childcare services, for example, are highly defamilialized, whereas care for dependent elderly people comes down largely upon families (Sainsbury, 1999: 246-247).

In summary, we can recall a proposition made by Crompton (1999: 204-205) with respect to the examination of national systems of gender relations. These systems can be situated between two poles: the "traditional pole", which takes men as the principle breadwinners and women as charged with dependent care (male breadwinner/female carer), and the "egalitarian" pole (dual earner, dual carer), which Crompton sees as an unrealized ideal. Between these two poles we find the "less traditional models", in which each member of a couple contributes resources (dual earner), and in which dependent care is partially or completely defamilialized, either through institutional systems (state carer) or paid services (market carer). In these intermediate models, gender inequalities can remain very strong. Thus conceived, the French system is still very unequal, as much between men and women as among women themselves (Daune-Richard, 2004: 79). The contradictions resulting from this conflict between emancipation and inequality threaten to become still more heated in the future, as it is the younger generations of women who will suffer most directly in terms of access to social rights and disrupted professional careers[33]. This will, in turn, have a negative effect on the collective mobilization of knowledge.

---

33 Today, inequalities in the area of retirement reflect these contradictions. In effect, even if the labor force participation rate of women has continuously grown in France since the Second World War, disparities between the sexes with respect to retirement often result from preexisting differences in work status and inequalities on the job market (more frequent interruptions of careers for women than for men, unequal salaries, etc) (see Bonnet, Buffeteau, and Godefroy, 2004).

2.3 The driving role of the welfare state in the rise of a knowledge based economy

From the end of the 1960s, there was a substantial expansion in the public services and benefits provided by the welfare state. This increase contributed to the crisis of Fordism by reversing the "long tendency towards reducing the social costs of the reproduction of the labour force" (Aglietta, 1976: 326). In hindsight, the expansion of social welfare provided the foundation for a knowledge based economy in two central ways:

- The first of these is directly linked to the rise of a diffuse intellectuality. This goes back to the historical process in which the portion of capital invested in people (R&D and above all training, education, health) has surpassed the portion of material capital in the stock of total capital (Kendrick, 1994). In this way, intangible capital, actually embodied for the most part in human beings, has become the main driving factor of economic growth. The shift towards intangible capital illustrates the extent to which the education and reproduction of the labour force has become directly productive. In addition, it illustrates the idea that the "wealth of nations" depends more and more on productive cooperation taking place outside of the corporate realm. In the end, this indicates that the driving sectors of the new, knowledge based capitalism increasingly depend upon the public services historically provided by the welfare state. In other words, the economy is defined more and more by the growth of activities with dominant intellectual, communicational, and affective dimensions. It is the growth of these aspects of labour that could also support a mode of development based on the *production of man for and by man*[34] (health, education), and on the central role of universal services provided according to a non-commodified logic.
- The second reason has to do with the way by which the expansion of the "socialized income" have induced a decrease of the constraint to the wage relation. It implied an increase of free time, which, in the context of a knowledge based economy, constitutes an "immediately productive force". We must, in this regard, highlight a central but often neglected point. The "liberation of free time", of time removed from the direct control of capital and the constraint of subordinated labour, is not simply a positive effect of growing productivity in the "official economy", but instead is one of the explanations of this growth because of its direct and indirect effects on the diffusion and cumulative production of knowledge. In so far as immaterial and intellectual labour predominates, free time ceases to be in immediate opposition to direct labour time (Vercellone, 2007). In the same way, the liberation of free time is

34 This notion is also used by Robert Boyer (2002) as defining the possible long run emergence of what he called an *antropogenetical* model.

also responsible for the creation of alternative forms of social and productive cooperation, of a "free labour" of self-production, which represents a source of wealth that escapes the narrow criteria of national accounting. Free time is no longer reducible to its individualized, cathartic function; or, in other words, to its effect on the reproduction and reinvigoration of the labour force. Instead, free time also makes learning, self-education, and knowledge sharing possible. Each of these activities constitute different human experiences and work to weaken temporal boundaries; individuals carries their knowledge with them from one time to another, elevating the use value of different social times and the cumulative process of knowledge production along the way (Vallade, 2002).

In this sense, the importance of lengthening the workday or of paying years of taxes to qualify for a full retirement is not only outdated but also contrary to the tendency for labour time to decrease over the long term. These measures, like all attempts to increase the precariousness of the labour force, also threaten to weaken the most fundamental mechanisms of growth, productivity, and innovation.

2.4 The crisis of Fordist employment and the question of flexibility

Many factors have contributed to shake the logic of subordination in exchange for security that provided the foundation of the Fordist compromise. Foremost is the refusal of compartmentalized work, the increase in workers' desire for autonomy, the rejection of patriarchal gender inequalities at the workplace, and opposition to the institutions of a disciplinary society.

These actions correspond in many ways to what Boltanski and Chiappello (1999) have called the association of social and artistic critique. They have contributed to two processes that are crucial to understanding the current changes in labour and the social welfare system.

First, since the 1970s a new cultural model has emerged that rejects the association between stable employment and subordinated labour as the path par excellence to social recognition and self worth. This attitude is apparent in the desire for alternative forms of productive social cooperation outside the system of wage labour (Zoll, 1992). In other words, the crisis of the Fordist system of employment resulted not only from policies favoring the flexibilization and deregulation of the labour market, but also from the subjective behaviors of the labour force. This observation allows us to rethink potential reforms of the social welfare system. The desires of younger generations are not a return to the "old model" of stable, lifelong wage labour (Paugam, 2000).

Instead, they desire social welfare programs providing income maintenance while adapting itself to employment discontinuities and the development of individual lifestyles. These include experiences such as volunteer work, sports and leisure activities, and educational endeavors that do not necessarily lead to professional advancement.

Second, the new cultural and intellectual composition of work has rendered traditional industrial forms of labour less practical. In many areas of production, these changes have favored the passage from a Taylorist to a cognitive division of labour. By this we mean that efficiency no longer depends on reducing the operating time necessary for individual tasks, but instead on the knowledge, capacity for training, and adaptability of the labour force within a constantly changing work environment (Mouhoud, 2003; Lebert and Vercellone, 2004).

In this respect, we begin to understand why *flexibility* and *knowledge* have become the operative terms in describing the changing regulation of the wage relation. Flexibility itself, however, is an extremely ambiguous concept and can be interpreted in two different and potentially contradictory ways[35].

On the one hand, flexibility could bring about policies that favor the learning ability of the labour force, including higher training levels and privileging mobility, creativity, adaptability and reactivity to the unforeseen.
From a neoliberal viewpoint, however, flexibility implies a reassessment of the labour market "rigidities" that theoretically prevent wages and employment from adjusting to fluctuations in economic activity. In this sense, flexibility is synonymous with policies generalizing precariousness of labour force. This second type of flexibility is, therefore, quite different from the first and could have a catastrophic effect on the mobilization of knowledge. In fact, the production of knowledge requires a long term approach, which associates income and social rights with individual people and not particular jobs. This guarantee would also give workers the opportunity to pursue educational activities throughout their lives and provide stability while transitioning between different occupations.

Lastly, the relative priority given to these two meanings of flexibility, as well as other institutional factors, will go a long way in determining the evolution of the new capitalism towards disparate modes of regulating the wage relation.

35 On this point the distinction between the concepts of defensive flexibility and offensive flexibility established by Boyer (1986b) is extremely useful.

3. Concluding remarks

In several respects, Fordism crisis is unique in relation to previous crises in capitalism that have taken place since the first industrial revolution. Our thesis is that the "nature" of the Fordist crisis is not simply one of a "great crisis" of *transformation* internal to industrial capitalism.

Its historical significance is related not only to the structures breakdown of a particular mode of development (Fordism). It also relates to the end of industrial capitalism itself as an *historical system of accumulation*. The crisis in Fordism indicates a higher level of "great crisis", midway between regulationist notions of a "crisis in the mode of development" and a "crisis in the mode of production itself"[36]. The crisis in Fordism, therefore, called into question a number of tendencies that had previously defined the logic of industrial capitalism, while also establishing the subjective conditions and structural basis for the creation of a post-industrial, knowledge-based economy.

Cognitive capitalism is the result of a restructuring process through which capital attempts to control collective conditions of knowledge production and tends to absorb and redirect its energy towards a new logic of capital accumulation.

This perspective allows us to see more clearly the importance and specificity of the problems posed by the current transformation of capitalism. In effect, cognitive capitalism has been unable to achieve a coherent recomposition of the institutions necessary to set a *new order* (in the sense of Gramsci). By this concept we mean a new system of accumulation the viability of which depends upon the elements of "hegemony", both social and cultural, that incorporate subaltern classes' particular claims and interests into its reproduction logic. In reality, the transition to cognitive capitalism is a complex and contradictory process, which could lead in opposing directions, as shows by the size and the gravity of the current systemic crisis. In this sense, the transition to cognitive capitalism is far from complete and still runs up against powerful social resistance and structural contradictions. These conflicting forces represent the few remaining obstacles that capital must confront in its attempt to privatize the commons, to commodify knowledge and to comply its production with the short term logic of the finance and capital accumulation.

---

36 In the terminology of the French regulation school (Aglietta, Amable, Boyer, Coriat, Lipietz, Petit), the notion of crisis in "the mode of development" indicates a great crisis in the transformation and dynamic of industrial capitalism. The theory of regulation has not, however, considered the possibility of a higher level crisis, which we could define as a "great crisis in the historical system of accumulation of industrial capitalism".

References

Afsa, C. (1998), "L'allocation parentale d'éducation: entre politique familiale et politique pour l'emploi", *INSEE Première*, (569): 1-4.

Aglietta, M. (1976), *Régulation et crises du capitalisme*, Paris: Calmann-Lévy.

Amable, B. (2005), *Les Cinq capitalismes*, Paris: Le Seuil.

Askenazy, P. (2004), *Les désordres du travail*, Paris: Le Seuil.

Askenazy, P. and E. Caroli (2006), "Innovative work practices, information technologies and working conditions: evidence for France", *Economix Working paper* 2006-02, available at http://economix.u-paris10.fr/pdf/dt/2006/WP_EcoX_2006-2.pdf.

Barbier, J. and B. C. Théret (2004), *Le nouveau système français de protection sociale*, Paris: La Découverte.

Barker, D. K. (1999), "Gender", in J. Peterson and M. Lewis (eds), *The Elgar Companion to Feminist Economics*, Cheltenham, Northampton: Edward Elgar, pp. 390-396.

Bélorgey, J.-M. (2000), *Minima sociaux, revenus d'activité, précarité*, Paris: Commissariat Général du Plan et La Documentation française.

Boltanski, L. and E. Chiappello (1999), *Le nouvel esprit du capitalisme*, Paris: Gallimard.

Bonnet, C., S. Buffeteau, and P. Godefroy (2004), "Retraites: vers moins d'inégalités entre hommes et femmes?", *Population et sociétés*, (401): 1-4.

Boyer, R. (1986a), *La théorie de la régulation: une analyse critique*, Paris: La Découverte.

Boyer, R. (2002), *La croissance, début de siècle*, Paris: Albin Michel.

Boyer, R. (ed) (1986b), *La flexibilité du travail en Europe*, Paris: La Découverte.

Concialdi, P. and J.-M. Monnier (2002), "Scénarios de réforme de la CSG", *Revue Française de Finances Publiques*, (78): 113-138.

Crompton, R. (1999), "Discussion and conclusion", in R. Crompton (ed), *Restructuring Gender Relations and Employment*, Oxford: Oxford University Press, pp. 201-214.

Daune-Richard, A.-M. (1983), "Travail professionnel et travail domestique: le travail et ses représentations au sein de lignées féminines", *Travail et emploi*, (17): 49-55.

Daune-Richard, A.-M. (2003), "La qualification dans la sociologie française: en quête des femmes", in J. Laufer, C. Marry, and M. Maruani (eds), *Le travail du genre. Les sciences sociales du travail à l'épreuve des différences de sexe*, Paris: La Découverte/MAGE, pp. 138-150.

Daune-Richard, A.-M. (2004), "Les femmes et la société salariale: France, Royaume-Uni, Suède", *Travail et emploi*, (100): 69-84.

Eliasson, G. (1996), *Firm Objectives, Controls and Organization: The Use of Information and the Transfer of Knowledge Within the Firm*, Dordrecht: Kluwer Academic Publishers.

Esping-Andersen, G. (1990), *The Three Worlds of Welfare Capitalism*, Cambridge: Polity Press.

Gauvin, A. and H. Jacot (eds) (1999), *Temps de travail, temps sociaux, pour une approche globale*, Paris: Editions Liaisons.

Gramsci, A. (1977), *Quaderni del carcere*, Tomes I-II-III-IV, Turin: Ed. Einaudi.

Kendrick, J. W. (1994), "Total capital and economic growth", *Atlantic Economic Journal*, 22(1): 1-18.

Lebert, D. and C. Vercellone (2004), "L'économie de la connaissance entre économie et histoire", *Cahiers lillois d'économie et de sociologie*: 17-39.

Lojkine, J. (1992), *La révolution informationnelle*, Paris: PUF.

Lojkine, J. (2006), "Nouveaux rapports de classe et crise du politique dans le capitalisme informationnel", in P. Cours-Salies, J. Lojkine, and M. Vakaloulis (eds), *Nouvelles luttes de classe*, Paris: PUF, pp. 15-27.
Merrien, F.-X., R. Parchet, and A. Kernen, (2005), *L'Etat social*, Paris: Armand Colin.
Mouhoud, E. (2003), "Division internationale du travail et économie de la connaissance", in C. Vercellone (ed), *Sommes-nous sortis du capitalisme industriel?*, Paris: La Dispute, pp. 121-136.
Orloff, A. S. (2006), "L'adieu au maternalisme?", *Recherches et Prévisions*, (83): 9-28.
Palme, J., (2002), "Protection sociale et lutte contre les inégalités: le modèle scandinave", *L'économie Politique*, (13): 103-112.
Paugam, S. (2000), *Le salarié de la précarité*, Paris: PUF.
Pfau-Effinger, B. (1999), "The modernization of family and motherhood in Western Europe", in R. Crompton (ed), *Restructuring Gender Relations and Employment*, Oxford: Oxford University Press, pp. 60-79.
Piketty, T. (1998), "L'impact des incitations financières au travail sur les comportements individuels: une estimation pour le cas français", *Economie et Prévision*, (132-133): 1-29.
Sainsbury, D. (1999), "Gender, policy regimes, and politics", in D. Sainsbury (ed), *Gender and Welfare State Regime*, Oxford: Oxford University Press, pp. 245-275.
Vallade, D. (2002), "La dynamique du temps libre: un vecteur de recomposition des temps sociaux. Une analyse de long terme, 19ème et 20ème siècles", Thèse de doctorat en Sciences Economiques, University of Montpellier I.
Veltz, P. (2000), *Le nouveau monde industriel*, Paris: Gallimard.
Vercellone, C. (2003), "Mutations du concept de travail productif et nouvelles normes de repartition", in C. Vercellone (ed), *Sommes-nous sortis du capitalisme industriel?*, Paris: La Dispute, pp. 249-272.
Vercellone, C. (2007), "From formal subsumption to general intellect: elements for a Marxist reading of the thesis of cognitive capitalism", *Historical Materialism*, 15(1): 13-36.
Zoll, R. (1992), *Nouvel individualisme et solidarité quotidienne*, Paris: Kimé.

5. Common good in the age of knowledge? Arguing for a radical political economy

Cosma Orsi*

1. Post-Fordism and the political economy of freedom

The recent debate on the socio-economic transformation of Western countries emphasizes the crisis of the Fordist model[37]. In order to define the current evolutionary stage of capitalism, most scholars utilize the term post-Fordism (see Lipietz, 1997 and Fumagalli, 2007) intended as "a social model in which production is no longer dominated by hierarchically organized forms of communication or by the negotiation of wealth distribution carried out by representatives of collective bodies and supervised by the State. On the contrary, the post-Fordist model is characterized by forms of flexible accumulation that can integrate and connect highly diversified modes, times and places of production" (Zanini and Fadini, 2001). At the root of the Fordist crisis is the resurgence of the laissez-faire doctrine in its neo-liberal form. At its heart is the belief that because the market is the best form of socio-economic organization (it is supposed to restrain totalitarian impulses[38] whilst providing well-being for all) any attempt to

* I am grateful to my colleagues who have been kind enough to read this article at different stages providing valuable comments and suggestions for improvement: Prof. Andrea Fumagalli, University of Pavia; Prof. Duccio Cavalieri, University of Florence, Prof. Piero Roggi, University of Florence, Dr. Stefano Lucarelli, University of Bergamo; Dr. Marika Macchi, University of Florence. Special mention goes to Dr. Francesco Cattabrini (University of Florence) with whom I discussed several times aspects of this work. As usual, warm thanks are due to Miss Samantha Ball who has carefully proofread the manuscript and imputing meaning.

37 Based on increased mechanization and the consequent automation of productive processes, Fordism provided the basis for a historically unprecedented increase of productivity. Roughly speaking, the four pillars upon which the Fordist paradigm was based were i) a Taylorist division of labour between creative and manual (repetitive) work governed by hierarchical procedures aimed at ii) producing mass material goods iii) whose effective demand was guaranteed by a distribution of the gain of productivity via wages and iv) by a social regulation aimed at guaranteeing a further re-distribution via collective arrangements and welfare policies. In that phase of capitalist development, whilst the duty to guarantee the well-being of its citizens fell upon the State, the responsibility to make production effectual fell upon capitalists.

38 The most influential scholar advocating such an idea has been the Austrian economist von Hayek, who argued that even milder economic planning inevitably tends towards totalitarianism because it allows the collection of economic information only by the state rather than by impersonal market forces (Hayek, 1935). Following this train of thought, his normative horizon has always been that of enhancing a model of social coordination in which individual autonomy is maximized (see Hayek, 1960: 13).

alter its course would not only be economically disastrous but also morally unacceptable.
Because it calls for the absence of compulsory control over personal conduct by society interfering with economic agents doing as they like and associating on terms initially agreed upon, contemporary *mainstream* economics will be here referred to as the *political economy of freedom*. At the basis of the *political economy of freedom* lies the idea of a general economic equilibrium achieved via the play of supply and demand. If this mechanism is allowed to work properly, then all resources (labour included) will be fully utilized. As a market economy can only be sustained within a market society, not only should this mechanism inform the economic domain but also society at large. To enable such a mechanism to work properly, government should not intervene in economic matters: namely, the less the State intervenes, especially through taxation, the wider will be the so-called *trickle-down* effect[39].

From the beginning of the 1980s, in order to establish an economy that increasingly relies upon the use of ideas rather than physical abilities and upon the application of technology rather than the transformation of raw materials, its advocates have unilaterally promoted a formidable world-wide socio-economic reengineering (see Offe, 1985; Lash and Urry, 1994; Harvey, 1989). In Europe, the support from workers, trade unions, and the general public was gained by convincing them (fraudulently, we shall see!) that the hyper-technological nature of such a reshaping would free them from heavy and risky duties; release a considerable portion of their time as a result of a diminished working schedule, and that with the introduction of a flexible system of production even the weakest and marginalized strata of the population would be involved in the growth process and share in its benefits (see Amoroso, 2005; Amoroso and Orsi, 2006). With the general support banked, organizational changes such as forms of subcontracting and/or outsourcing, "just-in-time" production, individual bargaining and crowdsourcing (Howe, 2008) and the like have been introduced (Lash and Urry, 1994: 56; see also Boyer, 2004; Bardhan and Kroll, 2003; Mann, 2006).
However, looking at the most recent data offered by international organizations such as EuroStat, ILO, and OECD, many scholars highlight that in spite of the magniloquent rhetoric characterizing the *political economy of freedom*, the

39 The trickle-down assumption aims to justify an economic system within which there is no significant barrier to the accumulation of wealth by individuals. If the rich are allowed to increase their profit without limitations, benefits will trickle down upon the whole population. Within this framework, lower taxes on high income or capital gains will benefit most of the population because if more is given to those at the top, they will start and expand new business and provide jobs and income for all. In what follows, we shall see that at the burden of proof this sounds more like propaganda rather than scientific theory.

promise of a better life for a large number of European citizens went unmet, showing how far from reality is the assumption that growth and competitiveness generate societal well-being. Unable to bring about the promised results, the introduction of these changes whilst have significantly reduced both stock inventories and turn-over times, have created the conditions for the precarization of millions of low and middle-skilled workers whose entire labour process "has become subject to increasing intensification as well as to acceleration in the transformation of .... [their] skills" (see Smart, 2003: 153). Accordingly, they concluded that although the promise of social justice is the most important inducement for the European population to support an economically competitive EU, a policy orientation overly geared towards improving the competitive position of the European economy by privileging labour market flexibility, deregulation, and privatization of public welfare leaves behind vast sectors of the population to struggle with the dynamism of contemporary societies – especially precarious low and mid-skilled workers, migrants, disabled, and women (see Capecchi and Gallina, 2006; Zupi, 2006).

Refusing to take for granted the patterns of economic relations endorsed by the *political economy of freedom*, the approach to political economy that we shall develop here, and which we shall refer to as the *political economy of reciprocity*, stresses the normative aspect of the discipline, namely that relating to the "ideal form of social organization". The emphasis is placed upon the normative aspect because *mainstream* economic doctrine fails to give an account of the true extent to which the majority of ordinary people are pitted against a socio-economic order that favours an over-privileged minority that is free to impose, more or less at will, socio-economic arrangements that undermine both autonomy and well-being of a powerless multitude.

As a social science that studies humans in their associative life, such an approach to political economy is intended both as historical and ethical: historical because its attempt to find interpretative schema aimed at explaining *classes of phenomena belonging to the practical dimension of human action* occurs within a complex reality in constant transformation. If so, these schemas cannot hold a general validity, immutable in time and space, but rather, should *be evaluated in terms of their relevance in relation to a particular institutional context and its evolution*. In other words, as its outcomes depend upon specific and unique circumstances, the entire economic process can only be conceived as intrinsically historical (see Cavalieri, 2007: 1). However, political economy is also an ethical enterprise as it is for ethical reasons that we are preoccupied by phenomena such as poverty, unemployment, exploitation, etc. Economic reasoning comes to the stage as we need economic tools in order to defeat such plagues that we perceive as immoral.

In order to challenge the methodological assumptions upon which *mainstream* economics is construed, it adopts a radically different approach to the understanding of socio-economic phenomena. Such an approach fulfils specific conditions: a) economic theory should concern reality rather than abstract rationality; b) the economic logic should not only have formal rigour but also internal consistency; c) since most economic problems are extremely complex, a multiple approach to economics should be implemented; d) as many fundamental problems are located at the boundaries of the economic discipline, the border between economics and other social sciences must be kept open; e) allowance must be made for the complexity of human behaviour and culture; f) a strongly and deeply felt social concern (for point a, b, and f see Pasinetti, 2005: 841-842; for point c, d, and e see Swedberg, 1991: 30-31).

The *political economy of reciprocity's* main critique of prevailing economic doctrine is that, taking the market both as an analytical assumption and as a normative ideal of which should be demonstrated its optimality *vis a vis* other ways of organizing the economic activity, not only conceals the extent to which within our societies the autonomous action of the majority of members is virtually denied, but also, and more importantly, it is incapable of crediting that when a tiny minority, by virtue of its economic power, is allowed to decide upon economic matters just as their own whim or judgement leads them, and when the implementation of these decisions impedes a vast number of members from developing, exercising, or expressing their full potentiality, then forms of domination and oppression are at work[40].

More or less explicitly, any approach to political economy grounds its analysis upon pre-economic assumptions concerning the agents involved in the economic process and the principle of justice guiding their actions. These assumptions, in turn, shape the institutional setting of the system of social cooperation. In this respect, we shall see that, building upon a relational understanding of humans encapsulated by the notion of *person-in-community*, the *political economy of reciprocity* conceptualises a *well-functioning community*[41] – intended as the

40 In what follows we shall understand domination and oppression in Young's terms. Namely, the former will be conceived of as institutional constraints on self-determination and the latter as institutional constraints on self-development (Young, 2000: 34; see also Young, 1990).

41 We shall refer to the notion of community as a socio-economic unit that its members recognize as their living space (namely, that territory across which people develop their social relationships, work, spare time, and so on), and *where social and systemic problems are felt.* Conceived as a lived, affective bond, it captures the idea that it is something about the relationship among its members, rather than merely their propinquity. And, indeed,

common good *par excellence* – as a social order characterized by a very high level of social cohesion. On this account, social cohesion refers to the capacity of socio-economic institutions to maintain the harmonious coexistence and cooperation among all the social strata so as to allow all members to contribute to the prosperity and management of the system itself.

The *political economy of reciprocity's* critical dimension emerges from its focus on how best to create economic institutions that allow each person to reach their full potential. Inspired by the idea that productive and distributive processes occur *within* the broader social reality and that they are not guided by "natural laws" but rather, are products of a particular social context, it aims to identify the conditions for the establishment of an empowering and enabling system of social cooperation. In doing so, it entails a reflection upon the end of the economic process rather than the means to achieve the maximization of profit(s). It also entails both the identification of the limits inherent to the current model of economic growth and the normative horizon informing institutions and the strategies needed to achieve the desired form of social organization. Thus, within the parameters of this framework, political economy ceases to be the study of optimal allocation of scarce resources via the mechanism of the invisible hand. Rather, starting from the analysis of the relationship between the process of wealth creation (economic growth) and the social transformations (social evolution) that accompany it, the *political economy of reciprocity* aspires to provide a sufficiently robust normative basis to arrive at a theory of economic change.

2. Neo-liberal knowledge-based societies

It is well-known that the theory of general economic equilibrium, the yardstick of the *political economy of freedom,* aims to show how voluntary exchanges between well-informed individuals (each is perfectly aware of their choices), self-interested, and rational (each behaves in a way that maximises their utility) inevitably leads to a societal organization of production that is efficient and beneficial to all. Saturated with this normative apparatus, the European Commission has put forward the model of the Knowledge-Based Economy and Society as the scaffold for synchronizing the EU effort to meet the challenges posed by the post-Fordist revolution whilst maintaining the inclusive character of the European Social Model (ESM). According to the socio-economic model entailed by the Lisbon strategy, the EU objective for the first decade of the XXI Century is to become "the most dynamic and competitive knowledge-based economy in the world

---

this is what makes their association a community rather than just social grouping (see Kukathas, 1996: 85).

capable of sustainable economic growth with more and better jobs and social cohesion, and respect for the environment" (European Commission, 2004).

However, scholars from different disciplines have found that, since the inception of such an economic course, the effort to meet the needs of the newly established accumulation paradigm has reinforced the power of the business sector, whilst undermining people's basic needs as well as minimal requirements of justice and social cohesion (Bessis, 1995; see also Hutton, 2003). More specifically, their analyses show that as a result of the implementation of policies asserting the centrality, if not the dominance, of the needs of powerful economic actors competing in the global *marketplace,* European societies are enduring a stark socio-economic polarization that sees, on the one hand, a multitude that having lost much of its social and economic power, has become powerless and, on the other, an over-privileged tiny minority that enjoying virtually unlimited power, is allowed to implement social, economic and political arrangements that favour only their economic appetites.

There is no need to provide in-depth philosophical reasoning to understand that when conflicting interests arise between powerful and powerless actors, as the former do not have to seek anyone's leave, they are always in the position to impose their decisions upon the latter. Acknowledging the imbalance of power pervading the existing economic decision-making structure, the *political economy of reciprocity* finds the explanation that unequal income distribution, labour market precariousness, and the dismantling of previously established systems of social protection are the result of unintended and unpredictable market outcomes unconvincing and misled: such an explanation, in fact, assumes an abstract world where unbalanced power relations do not exist. In the real world, market outcomes are the result of conscious decisions of a few powerful actors who have little interests in the wealth of the nation but rather in their own[42].

a) Income distribution and labour market precariousness

According to the *political economy of freedom*, human needs and expectations are better served within a well-functioning market mechanism. Such a mechanism, in fact, would guarantee an increasing growth whose benefit would even-

---

42 According to the *political economy of reciprocity*, what makes these decisions arbitrary, and thus illegitimate, is that they systematically reject representative democracy involving civil society organizations, trade unions, users, consumers, community association, and the like. As Young pointed out, this can be defined as *external exclusion*: it occurs when persons or groups of persons, who ought to be included in decision-making processes, are left - purposely or inadvertently – out of the *forum* of discussion and decision-making (Young, 2000: 53-55).

tually relapse upon the poorer strata of society – the much prised *trickle-down* economics. However, on closer view, the divorce between theory and reality has never been wider: the claim that, in the long run, the implementation of the *trickle-down* approach is likely to bring about more opportunities and higher standards of living for all is simply untenable.

The competition triggered by the actual cycle of economic growth based upon technological innovations, markets, deregulation, and multinational corporations has definitively altered the old socio-economic *status quo*: especially in Europe, it has rendered obsolete entire productive sectors, firms have been obliged to reduce costs and to pursue the maximum possible efficiency, unemployment rate increased in traditional sectors, and the immigration labour – often of high quality – has helped in the fight to reduce wages. Whilst innovative sectors are still able to retain their niche of rent, the well-being of the middle classes is seriously threatened (see Fassina and Visco, 2007: 220-221). Nobody could be surprised if, under these circumstances, the unfailingly positive claims about the ability of the market to redistribute the social product become particularly disenchanting when income and wealth distribution are examined (Stiglitz, 2002). The patterns of economic development occurring in recent decades show that, rather than shrinking, the gap between rich and poor countries, has widened. However, since the early 1980s, evidence is mounting that the rise in inequality has become a permanent feature, not only in underdeveloped and developing countries, but also within the most developed ones (Guio, 2005).

Growth of inequality on income distribution can be mainly attributed to the reduced access to work activity for low and middle-skilled workers. Within contemporary societies, the message sent to millions of workers is crystal-clear: for a hyper-technological, knowledge-based labour market, they have become virtually redundant. There is an abundance of literature produced by labour market analysts, which underlines the fact that unemployment has become the instrument for achieving economic prosperity (Zamani, 2003). It is not the enterprise in crisis that dismisses workers, but rather the healthy one that strives to increase its own competitiveness. Under this light, unemployment cannot be seen as the inevitable outcome deriving from a situation of crisis, "but rather as a strategy in order to compete successfully in the global market" (Zamagni, 2003).

Another factor leading to the increase of social inequality is represented by the fact that when the wealthiest entrepreneurs have money to invest generated either by their profitable activities or obtained through tax cuts dispensed by market-friendly governments, the money is likely to go directly into the their savings account rather than be reinvested in new business, and by this process creating new jobs. If it is invested, most of the time these savings go directly into the financial market, which produces nothing other than more money for the shareholders. Naturally the more entrepreneurs invest in the financial market, the less they invest in productive sectors, with the result that both ordinary people's job opportunities and income are not increased but rather diminished.

For those who still maintain a job, the labour market is not a piece of cake: the likelihood of holding a decent, full-time, life-long work activity is a dwindling option. This latter claim rests on the simple observation that, as a result of the introduction of new labour-saving technologies and electronic devices within productive processes, an increasing number of workers are more likely to face the precariousness of casual and/or temporary jobs[43]. According to the German sociologist Ulrich Beck (2004), flexible work is urged everywhere: "*Flexibility* means redistribution of risks from the state and the economy to individuals. Available jobs become *renewable*, that is short-term and more easily terminable. *Flexibility* means ultimately: Rejoice, your knowledge and ability are antiquated and no one can tell you what you must learn to be needed in the future" (Beck, 2004). In a similar vein, Gorz argues that the central figure of our society is that "of the insecure worker, who at times 'works' and at times does not 'work', practices many different trades without any of them actually being a trade, has no identifiable profession … and cannot therefore identify with his/her work" (Gorz, 1999: 53).

In practical terms, this is the result of the neo-liberal labour market regulation, whose primary objective has been the artificial segmentation of *cognitive* labour. The first sector is made of a specialized intellectual elite that dominates the most profitable economic activities – especially financial services for enterprises, applied research, patents, and the like. In the second sector is concentrated the less skilful workforce, whose qualification is not recognized. Whilst highly skilled workers and employers see their remunerations recognized according to their competences and enjoy protective schemes such as integrative pension funds and private health insurances, the same cannot be said for unskilled workers. With their bargaining power drastically diminished, their wages fall even further.

It is apparent that, under these circumstances, the contract offered to low – and mid-skilled workers becomes *an offer that cannot be refused*: that is, employees have no possibility of negotiating the terms of their contracts offered. In the majority of cases these jobs pay an exploitative wage. Moreover, to accept a job on

43 That the model of economic growth presupposes a typology of employment based upon short-term contracts has been advanced by authors such as Bertola and Boeri (2002); see also Boyer (2004).

a *take-or-leave* basis, usually implies submitting to the employer's will, even if this means working extended and exhausting working-days often in hazardous and disease-causing conditions[44]. As Miller explains, ordinary people's powerlessness in bargaining for both their wages and working conditions is due to the fact that in the real world the contract stipulated between workers and capitalists cannot be compared with a mutual contract between buyers and sellers negotiating from an equal standing in the competitive market. Rather, it is an unbalanced pact between two parties having very different contractual power.

b) The dismantling of the welfare system

Borne out of Keynes' idea that the market could not be the sole regulatory mechanism of our societies, the mission of welfare systems has been to redistribute more equitably the fruits of economic growth. Until the 1980s, government activity was characterised by the extension of fully developed welfare schemes such as retirement pensions, housing benefits and health insurance plans for trade unions members, financed from taxes and by employer and State contributions. At the same time, other social policies such as education and public health were financed by general taxation. In promoting these policies, central governments created a sufficient – albeit fragmented and stratified – level of social cohesion. This suggests that, from the aftermath of World War II to the mid-1970s, social cohesion and security was maintained thanks to a political regulation geared around the strategic idea of a social contract between the fundamental subjects of modern production, namely labour and capital. In this context, "the function of labour, fully recognized in its explicit social character as the bedrock of citizenship, was incorporated in the public sphere via an articulated system of normative guarantees [...] and a variety of public institutions aimed at safeguarding social rights" (Revelli, 1997).

However, from the mid-'70s the political climate changed dramatically. In their attempt to guarantee the reproduction of the post-Fordist regime, the majority of Western governments began favouring socio-economic processes aimed at implementing flexibility and competitiveness on a global scale (Jessop, 1982 and Jessop, 1993) – a goal that has replaced the previously established Keynesian redistributive policy architecture. The rationale inspiring neo-liberal's formidable attack on the system of social protection is that a welfare architecture thought and developed in the aftermath of World War II, when the economic trend was in constant augment whilst the rate of unemployment was low, has become too generous and, therefore, no longer competitive (Alesina and Perotti,

44 According to ILO (2003), 270 million people are victims of industrial injuries, 160 million are affected with work-related illnesses, and almost 2 million die.

1997). As a result of this trend, what is emerging "is a new regime which could be termed, albeit rather inelegantly, the *Schumpeterian Workfare State*. Its distinctive economic and social objectives can be summarized in abstract terms as: to promote product, process, organizational and market innovation and enhance the structural competitiveness of open economies mainly through supply-side intervention; and to subordinate social policy to the demands of labour market flexibility and structural competitiveness" (Jessop, 1993: 4).

In the 1980s and 1990s an increase in the number of welfare beneficiaries in Europe resulted in the introduction of a principle whereby, in order for citizens to have full access to unemployment welfare benefits they had to be willing to accept any form of gainful employment. Failure to do so could mean a drastic curtailing of benefits in the sense that beneficiaries would only be guaranteed a limited access to services – generally of a low quality – tailored to their bare subsistence. In addition to the productive requisite, a temporal limit concerning the length of time beneficiaries were given access to benefits was also introduced.

Another aspect of the *workfare* model is its compatibility with a variety of policy initiatives promoting "the sale of nationalized industries and contracting out of public service provision to private agencies" (Smart, 2003: 45). The rationale underpinning the shift from public to private management is inspired by public choice theory assumptions. Public choice theorists perceive public services as an *integral part of the global marketplace*. First of all, their analyses seek to prove that bureaucracy is bad and, secondly, that public is less efficient than private. Such a negative vision of the State has been assumed by European policy-makers for, at least, the last three decades, spreading the idea that States are inherently inefficient; state officials always act in their own self-interest and that State intervention has to be limited to market-friendly action such as investments in education and training creating a competitive climate for business and maintaining a stable macro economy.

Sadly, once private companies have replaced the State in running welfare services they tend to ensure the primacy of business needs, objectives, interests, and values. What is worth noticing is that the business agenda requires that both the power of labour and civil society organizations be marginalized. This is "accomplished by further centralization of decision-making, reduced accountability, less transparency under the guise of 'modernization'. On this ground, Dexter Whitfield concludes that 'the primary reason for Public-Private Partnership (PPPs) – the private sector designs, builds, finances and operates public buildings and transport systems – is not a short-term financial assistance to help states out of temporary fiscal crisis or to demonstrate 'business in the community' but to create new forms of capital accumulation through private ownership and control of national and global infrastructure" (Whithfield, 2001: 3).

Further than the replacement of the State by big corporations in providing welfare services another important feature concerning the intrusion of market mechanisms in the social protection system is the privatization of pension funds. This practice has a double effect: on the one hand, it links to the positive performance of the financial market increased quotas of postponed salary (namely, the amount of money that workers do not receive directly in cash but that is put aside against the risk attached to health and unemployment), so as to spread financial risk upon the collectivity, and on the other, to enlarge participation in the financial market. The financialization of postponed salary has allowed business and corporate interests to extend even deeper into our daily lives. As Fumagalli cogently said, at present, it is the most sophisticated form of *bio*-power (Fumagalli, 2007: 30).

Drawing from the above, it is possible to evince the extent to which the societies in which we live, being geared around the idea that the control of hyper-technological economic processes and means of production is in the hands of one set of individuals while work is produced by another, allow "a continual net transfer of part of the power of some men to others" (Macpherson, 1973: 10-11). However, it is not difficult to see that when power is unequally distributed in society between two parties, it is synonymous with domination and oppression, since such unequal distribution covers relations of autonomy and dependence between the two parties (Giddens, 1979). From the unequal distribution of power, wealth and resources derives the dependency of ordinary people on those who produce profit out of their work[45].

Furthermore, we have seen that, as *mainstream* economics fails to perceive such an outcome as morally questionable, it considers any previously established and/or future implementation of re-balancing mechanisms specifically designed at reducing the imbalance of power characterizing contemporary society as illegitimate. Transformed into a powerless mass of precarious wage-earners, to the majority of ordinary people is given only the possibility of signing a pact of surrender to the accumulation of capital. The promised achievement in terms of an equal redistribution of the wealth produced is, in reality, nothing but the com-

45 In a similar vein, Udehn argued that the control over economic resources "gives sanctioning power to the owner [...]. The sanctioning power of [...] A over [...] B increases to the extent that B depends upon A for the satisfaction of his/her needs or desires. In general, then, control over economic resources gives, to owners of capital, a considerable power over everything that money can buy, including people" (Udehn, 1996: 205).

pulsory liquidation of the vast majority of ordinary peoples' patrimony (of their forms of life, production, and knowledge). As a result, contemporary societies no longer guarantee *well-being* and emancipation for all but sacrifices and submission.

3. In search of the well-functioning community

It seems rather apparent that the societal vision enhanced by the *political economy of freedom* is unable to contemplate the hypothesis of a system of social cooperation where the opportunity to participate on equal terms in the active life of community is given to all; where redistributive strategies could be grounded in an explicit theory of justice aimed at redressing the imbalance of power, and where social solidarity is triggered by a sense of recognition and belonging.

In its attempt to carve out a sufficiently robust argument able to sustain the reason for a shift towards a more balanced system of social cooperation, the *political economy of reciprocity* sizes the problem of how to organize the economic activity within a broader issue of how to organize the wider community. Following this path, it starts from the acknowledgment of the complexity of a social reality where the information technology revolution (ITR) has expanded well beyond the high-tech sector. It recognizes the extent to which such a revolution – in Europe, as well as the rest of the world – has shaken the very foundations of the old industrial and occupational structure, redefining the rules of entrepreneurship and competition – and the fact that, although knowledge – and its diffusion – has been the key driver of economic growth for centuries, today knowledge-based firms gain competitive advantages by their ability to use process, analyze and share on an unprecedented scale and speed powerful information and communication technologies.

In this context, the paradigm of reciprocity recognizes the relevance of the reflection proposed by some heterodox economists who, departing from the notion of *knowledge-based economy* that they find rather mild, if not incapable of grasping the true nature of the transformation that contemporary societies undergo, advance the idea of *cognitive capitalism* (see Vercellone, 2008; Fumagalli, 2007; Boutang, 2008) – definition that emphasizes both the historical dimension and the conflictual relationship between the two terms[46]. On this ac-

46 As Vercellone puts it, "The term *capitalism* reaffirms the presence, within the process of change, of the fundamental invariance entailed by the capitalistic system, such as the primary role of profit-making and the centrality of the wage relationship, or more precisely of the different forms of dependent labour upon which the extraction of plus-value rests. The term *cognitive* specifies the new nature of labour, of the sources of value, and of the forms of property upon which the accumulation of capital rests along with the

count, within cognitive societies we assist the establishment of what Fumagalli names *bio-economy* intended as the development of forms of social control necessary to favour the economic valorisation of human life; in a nutshell, "*bio-economy* means the totalizing and pervasive power of the capitalist accumulation process upon human beings' lives. More specifically, *bio-economic* accumulation means the attempt to exploit humans' abilities, primarily the language and the rational ability to generate knowledge via the dynamic of social relationships" (Fumagalli, 2007: 10).

The paradigm of reciprocity assumes that a renewed economic vision cannot but derive from the way in which we conceive the social reality surrounding us. This, in turn, is derived from the way in which we understand human beings and from how they relate one another. Their relationships depend upon the values (freedom, equality, reciprocity, and mutual solidarity) that they believe to be the most fundamental. The recovery of the social (relational) dimension is unavoidable as the individualist assumptions that inform the *political economy of freedom* have for too long prevented "complete understanding of how the economy really functions [...] leading to a whole set of questionable assertions and findings" (Lutz, 1999: 7). The neglect of the social perspective has seriously impeded mainstream economics understanding that many of the problems pervading contemporary societies – be they individual or territorial inequalities, growth without employment, increased GDP with no improvement of the quality of life for the many – have much to do with social rather than economic scarcity.

To those who will contest such an approach on the grounds that it takes into consideration non-economic factors (laws, customs, institutional and social structure, are conceived of as irrelevant for a proper economic investigation), it is possible to counter that the economic performance of a productive system is deeply affected (either positively or negatively) by the quality of the functioning of the mechanisms that regulate the inter-subjective and inter-collective relationships within a given social order. Apropos, it holds that in determining the growth expectations of any economy, perhaps even more important than the intensity of the accumulation of capital, is the "social capability": namely, an ability attached to the internal relationships occurring within the social, political, and institutional structure (Abramowitz, 1986). According to this perspective, the institutional architecture of society directly affects (negatively or positively) the ability to dispose of human and natural resources in a way that trigger virtuous processes of wealth creation.

---

contradictions that they generate. These contradictions manifest themselves both in the relationship capital labour and in the increased antagonism between the social character of production and the private character of appropriation" (Vercellone, 2008: 2).

a) Human nature

The general equilibrium theory upon which *mainstream* economics is based, produces mathematical models where the economic agent, although interdependent, still remains a solitary and atomized individual. To put it simply, but not simplistically, its advocates see human beings as individuals unable to take part in social relationships, devoid of any form of social reflexivity, incapable of comprehending others' situation as well as the consequences of their actions (Udehn, 1996: 363). As the above characteristics pertain to all human beings, at any time and place, then they should be universally applied. Given these assumptions, economic actors exist autonomously and independently from each other and are related only via external relations. It follows that the only possible interaction among them must assume the feature of impersonal exchanges between free and equal independent producers knowing perfectly what they want. In such a social context, economic activity does not take place according to social requirements established by the broader society. Rather, it is regulated by economic contracts, the sole bond that links otherwise independent producers.

This framework impedes seeing that what may be true of the individual taken in isolation is not necessarily true of all individuals taken together. Namely, what is true for a singular individual, a firm, or an industry, might not be true for the entire socio-economic order. This is commonly known as the *fallacy of composition*. Yet in 1936, Lord Keynes discussing the *paradox of savings* claimed attention upon the existence of such a shortcoming afflicting mainstream economics. Although individual savings may increase a person's wealth, they do not necessarily increase the wealth of the community as a whole (Keynes, 1971). As cogently noted by Hodgson, Keynes' aggregate savings "meant a reduction in effective demand and could lead to a reduction in business expectations and a general contraction of the economic activity" (Hodgson, 1988: 233). This line of argument has been taken up by Joan Robinson, who protested against the absurdity of applying microeconomic relationships to the economy as a whole. Invoking Keynes, she argued that "It is true for any one employer, or for any one industry – to a lesser extent for any one country in international trade – that a cut in wages, by lowering the price of the commodity produced, will increase its sales, and so lead to an increase of employment in making it. But if all wages are cut, all prices fall, all money incomes fall, and demand is reduced as much as costs. No one employer that has any motive to take on more man. In a crowd, anyone can get a better view of the procession if he stands on a chair. But if they all get up on chairs no one has a better view" (Robinson, 1951: 135).

Taking on board the shortcoming of the individualistic approach to economics, the first step towards conceptualizing the organization of the economic activity of a well-functioning social order should involve the scrutiny of the conception of human nature underpinning mainstream economic doctrine (*Homo Oeconomicus),* and to evaluate the extent to which this account of human nature is correct. Many scholars warn us against applying such an understanding of human nature when we try to explain human action in the economic life. At present the most influential figure endorsing such a position is Amartya Sen, who plainly compared *Homo Oeconomicus* to a *social moron* (Sen, 1977: 336), and argued that "economic theory has been much preoccupied with this rational fool decked in the glory of his one all-purpose preference ordering" (Sen, 1977: 335).

Other critiques come from authors that move from the assumption of a socially embedded individual. For example Hodgson refers to a notion of "institutionalised individual" (Hodgson, 2000), and Mayhew to an "enculturated individual" (Mayhew, 2000). In the field of socio-economics, Lutz refers to humans as social individuals "embedded in a web of constitutive social relations" (Lutz, 1999). Daly and Cobb speak of *person-in-community* (Daly and Cobb, 1994). To end this rather brief list, the republican philosopher Pettit cannot be forgotten. He emphasises that persons are situated in and attached to their community via the social relations they develop and maintain with others (Pettit, 1997: 275; see also Taylor, 1989). What these authors are trying to tell us is that, although undeniably present, the characteristics attached to *Homo Oeconomicus* are not universal. The individual as maximizer of his/her utility can be applied only to a restricted group of people, who are subjected to particular forms of socialization via their exposure to a set of institutionalized social norms (Watson, 2005). In light of the above, the first undertaking of the *political economy of reciprocity* is that of identifying a richer understanding of human nature.

Moving from the sociological evidence that real people are constantly interrelated by virtue of their living and dwelling together, it might well inspire the idea that people become who they are via the social relations they establish within their communities. Beautifully captured by Daly and Cobb (1994: 161-165), this understanding of human nature is embodied by their notion of *person-in-community.* According to these authors, as relatedness is the natural condition of human existence, it follows that the idea of a separated and solipsistic individual becomes simply a myth. If the community is made of and shaped by the relationships occurring among its members it cannot be conceptualised as merely made up of numerous separated individuals living together, as orthodox economic doctrine depicts. Rather, it becomes the place where those practical and moral relations between persons occur. The individual as a social atom has no meaning except for statistical purpose, for example, *ad hoc* explanations of societal facts, or to enable the use of census and electoral lists. Hence, according to this account social relations are the means to the enhancement of the primary human experience of coexistence, constitutive of each human being. Since *persons-in-community* are inherently part of a web of moral and practical relations that enable them to form and express their potential as human beings, it is correct to claim that they are moral agents *constantly and inextricably affected by the fate of others*[47].

b) The contract of reciprocal solidarity

It is at this point that the endeavour of the *political economy of reciprocity* becomes irreducibly ethical because, before advancing any policy prescription, it should firstly identify a sufficiently robust notion of justice that informs the envisaged form of social organization. On these grounds, we have to ask what kind of social contract would be the most suitable in order to bind together *persons inextricably affected by the fate of others*? As partners of equal dignity constantly interrelated with and affected by others, it is reasonable to imagine that *persons-in-community* may favour a model of communal living intended as a cooperative enterprise for the achievement of the common good. Such a tall order calls for an institutional architecture designed to ensure that all members of the community would be enabled to benefit from the system of social cooperation according to their needs whilst enabling them to voluntary contribute according to their ability[48]. Because this societal architecture rests on the double assumption that each person owes something to the wider community as well as that the community owes something to each of its members, the notion of justice that underpins it can be rightly defined as *justice as reciprocity.*

The claim that each person owes something to the wider community within which he lives is sustained by the fact that real persons live together with others in the wider social context, and perform their activities within institutions (such as communities, families, associations, political parties, trade unions, circles of friends, schools, universities, clubs, etc.) within which they constantly establish more or less stable social relationships. Without these relations to bond and affect their lives, it is difficult to imagine that they can lead a meaningful life. Individuals can exist and flourish only if we postulate a vital community, and within it, smaller communities and social groups forming and nurturing historical memory, upon which the web of social relationships is constructed. It may

47 As we shall see, only by embracing such a wider perspective might we come to explain why – within the envisaged form of social organization – instead of trying to evade anything more than the *minimal demands of social life*, people could be motivated to discharge their obligations towards society *as wholeheartedly as possible* (see Skinner, 1990: 308).

48 Elsewhere I named such an institutional "agreement" *Contract of Reciprocal Solidarity* (Orsi, 2006).

be further added that real persons owe something to the community because it provides things like protection, education, nurture, comfort, equipment, opportunities, and a variety of services and goods. Hence, the claim that each person owes something to the wider community resides in the fact that each of them depends on it for both their social heritage and well-being. This said, it becomes clear why the well-functioning of the community as a whole may be recognized as the *common good* to be pursued through the mutual co-operation of all actors involved: in production for use rather than exchange, in distribution according to need, rather than according to productive input.

The claim according to which the wider community owes something to each of its members is supported by the fact that they are central for both productive processes (as producers and consumers), and for the process of social reproduction. If so, it follows that if the main institutions of the community do not take responsibility for providing, to the greatest possible extent, the objective conditions to retain their centrality in both productive and reproductive processes then it would collapse. This is even truer within *cognitive* societies. In fact, if the process of wealth creation rests upon the valorisation of knowledge, and if knowledge is, by definition, a social (common) resource, (it is the result of past and present social cooperation, Marx would have said *general intellect*) then it becomes apparent why the community as a whole owes something to each of its members. The above reflections lead to the conclusion that the current model of economic growth that tends to reduce the overall societal well-being via forms of economic domination and oppression, is doomed to impoverish its main resource, running the risk of endangering the entire socio-economic system.

4. A well-functioning economy

A system of social cooperation which no longer requires that part of the immense *surplus* of wealth generated – either by the increase of productivity or financial investments – be reinvested in strategies aimed at redressing social and economic polarization, is unable to maintain an harmonic coexistence among its members. A more balanced way of organizing economic activity, further than being inspired by the idea that the criteria for evaluating economic success is the expansion of everyone's autonomy and well-being, calls for a wider participation both at decision-making level and in the active life of the community. This is even more important within an economic context in which all crucial decisions are taken by entrepreneurs (the owners), managers, or big retailers who, for example, determine what kind of goods should be produced and/or distributed. If so it is evident that ordinary people can only choose among a predetermined set of goods, rather than asking for what they really want and/or need (see Gorz, 1973: 195-197).

Evidently, such an argument poses the issue of the democratic structure of the economy. The most general ground that the *political economy of reciprocity* can advance in support of such a thesis can be found in the ideal of democracy. If there exists a commitment to such an ideal, it follows that its importance should be recognized not only in political life but in the economic domain as well. Apropos, Dahl convincingly wrote that if "democracy is justified in governing the state, then it is also justified in governing economic enterprises. What is more, if it cannot be justified in governing economic enterprises, we do not quite see how it can be justified in governing the state. Members of any association for whom the assumption of democratic processes are valid have a right to govern themselves by means of the democratic processes. If, as we believe, these assumptions hold among us, not only for the government of the state but also for the internal government of economic enterprises, then we have a right to govern ourselves democratically within our economic enterprises" (Dahl, 1985: 134-135). Following this train of thought, a model of economic development can only be successful within a society where participation is not merely formal, but effective and fully recognised. This would not only legitimize the social order, but would also represent a potential vehicle for strengthening the social alliance between different sectors of civil society in the attempt to face the challenges characterizing present days. In other words, only an inclusive and pluralist model of development could lead to the implementation of a renewed way of organizing economic activity designed with the precise intention of revitalizing a worn-out and over-exploited civil society.

Obviously, a more participatory system of social cooperation needs to be informed by a multidimensional and dynamic socio-economic process that, without denying the importance of the profit-seeking rationale, will leave enough room for mutual cooperation for the common good. In other words, as without the effective participation of all the members of the community, "those who have the exclusive right to shape all the key-decisions will unavoidably neglect others in society" what is called for is a way of organizing the economy "wherein citizens and the many communities to which they belong can feed their input into a collective decision-making process" (Tam, 1998: 93). On these premises, the *political economy of reciprocity* endorses a model of economic development that further than comprising a market economy – within which profit-oriented enterprises operate – and a non-market economy – within which governmental agencies have the mandate to *re*distribute fairly both social power and material resources – should also comprise a fully independent *for-benefit* economic domain formed by membership associations "that are open and egalitarian enough to permit voluntary participation" (Barber, 1998: 34-35) having equal dignity and status.

Within a socio-economic order geared around the normative ideal of inclusion and participation, for the *for-benefit* economic domain a wider field of intervention should be identified. Its field of intervention, in fact, ought not to be confined to voluntary activities having high social content but low remunerative returns excluding civil society from the participation in economic activities having not only high social content but also high remunerative returns (high social content infrastructures such as motorways, railways, universities, schools, asylums, urban renewal, parks, libraries, cinemas, hospitals, museums, social centres, gyms, recreational spaces, etc.).

Traditionally, most of these fields of intervention have been managed principally by the State allowing mainly private enterprises to participate (the earlier mentioned Public-Private Partnership). The State, thus, should be engaged in a delicate intervention aimed at establishing clear boundaries between the market and the *for-benefit* domain. Only in this way might a virtuous mechanism be primed, one which would enable economic activities having high social content but low rate of remuneration to be financed by those economic activities having both high social content but also highly remunerative rates of return. It is apparent that to take this path will require a redefinition of the modality of access to credit, which should take into consideration not merely the financial situation of the recipient, but also the social relevance of those interventions for which access to credit is required. In the long term perspective the strategy of organizing the economic process welcoming civil society to collaborate in designing the socio-economic landscape rather than simply entrusting it with "mere interstitial functions", seems to be not only morally sound but also more rational.

Under this light, it is not surprisingly that at the heart of this way of organizing the economic activity there is the belief that the theory of value informing *mainstream* economics is fairly inaccurate as it explains the process of wealth creation without taking into consideration to what extent relational factors influence economic activity. In a relational context, value can be seen as a symbolic mediation between powerful and powerless economic actors. Evidently, such mediation does not occur in a vacuum: the value assigned to a produced object reflects the relationships of the subject with others. Only via these relationships, can the subject have an idea of the value of the things she happens to deal with (see Vanin, 2000). Recognizing the extent to which the process of wealth creation is constrained and shaped by the myriad of human interactions occurring within the system of social cooperation[49], it becomes necessary to depart from

49 If wealth creation is generated by the *encounter* of real, rather than anonymous agents, it follows that it cannot be conceived other than as a social rather than an economic phenomena.

the dominant idea which holds that supply and demand under conditions of free competition determine the value of goods and services, and maintains that the creation of value depends upon the degree to which the system of social cooperation favours or restrains a kind of social interaction which allows each person to fully express their potentialities.

5. The partner state and universal basic income

Recognizing that within *cognitive* societies the vast majority of people are dominated and oppressed by tiny economic elite, the *political economy of reciprocity*, firstly, advocates that a kind of autonomy according to which each person could have an active role to play not only in the political, but also in the economic and social arena should be actively promoted. Secondly, it advocates forms of redistribution of power and resources aimed at enabling all *person-in-community* to be protected from forms of domination and oppression on the part of the powerful in economic terms. From a normative point of view this means that – in order to feel part of, and not hostile towards their community – each member of the community should be enabled to choose the course of their life independently (*self-determination*) and to develop and exercise their capacities and abilities (*self-development*) (see Young, 2000: 35)[50].

In a nutshell, the promotion of an empowering and enabling system of social co-operation able to generate a virtuous socio-economic circle specifically designed to facilitate the inclusion (active participation) of all its members in both market and non-market (*for-benefit*) activities requires that the role of the State can no longer be restrained to that of countering market failure, but rather it should be expanded to the transformation of actually existing unbalanced social relations (Panitch and Gindin, 2000). However, this reasoning begs a major question: what sort of State architecture is the most appropriate to deal with ill-outcome generated by the maintenance and perpetration of unbalanced social relations within *cognitive* societies? The achievement of a socio-economic order able to generate virtuous mechanisms aimed at facilitating the inclusion of all of its members in the social, political, and economic life of their respective communities calls for a substantial transformation of the State into what can be defined a *Partner State.*

In order to fulfil its mandate, the *Partner State* should be engaged in the maximization of citizens' opportunities, autonomy, and well-being. The approach to

50 The normative basis upon which the set of equal positive rights to *self-determination* and *self-development* rests, is that since all *persons-in-community* have equal moral worth, then there is no reason for anyone to have more rights than others to such opportunities and conditions.

power characterizing the *Partner State* is *responsiveness*; not only should it be accountable towards those who give it mandate, but, in order to rebalance power in society, it should also empower those social forces that are not directly subordinate to the profit-oriented, market-mediated logic of capital accumulation. Obviously, such an attitude towards power cannot be merely reduced to an executive or procedural role. Accordingly, amongst the duties of the *Partner State* will be that of enabling its members to be better equipped to face the challenges attached to the dynamism of contemporary societies. If so, rather than being concerned with securing the conditions for international competitiveness and innovation in relatively open economies, its primary concern would be to put in place mechanisms and policies aimed at bringing about a societal context within which social and economic power is distributed in a way that would enable all its members to participate on equal grounds in the active life of the wider society. But, we might ask, what structural policies might trigger the shift from actually existing polarized societies into more fair and just ones?

It is obvious that in order to establish a system of social cooperation where participation is open to all and where cooperation for the common good is preferred by the vast majority, if not by all, among others macroeconomic changes it will be necessary to reverse the ill-outcome deriving from the redistributive patterns informing the existing accumulation paradigm. As we have seen, in spite of the ill-distribution of income, the spread of social insecurity as a result of the fragmentation of the labour market along with the drastic cut to public spending, neo-liberals still uphold a *re*distributive pattern according to which those who have more than enough power and resources to satisfy their wants and desires have no positive duties or obligations to use their additional resources in order to sustain those who are struggling with the dynamicity of *cognitive* societies. Conversely, they have the right to utilise their additional resources in order to lead a luxurious lifestyle, if they wish to do so.

However, there is a widespread agreement among scholars concerning the fact that to occupy the former or the latter social category plays a fundamental role in the access to, or enjoyment of opportunities and privileges that will shape the rest of a person's life. If so, the implementation of a conception of justice entailing the reduction, if not the elimination, of transfers of basic resources from the *well-off* to those who cannot even meet their basic needs, simply means undermining ordinary people's right to *self-determination* and *self-development*. As we have seen, those at greatest risk are poor, ill, disabled, women, elderly, unemployed, underemployed or precarious workers who, living in an inferior socio-economic condition, marginalized and excluded from the main body of society, can not only be said to lack freedom – as in the attempt not to exacerbate their already precarious living conditions, they are *obliged* to act in a submissive manner, even if no form of direct coercion is at work – but also, and perhaps more importantly, are rendered unable to contribute to the system of social cooperation. If so, we cannot hope that an *ex-post* approach alone, although obviously necessary, would be sufficient to reverse such an unbalanced societal situation. Rather, what is needed is a precautionary approach, *ex-ante*, that places the emphasis upon the flourishing of people via the implementation of structural policies that would have as their primary objective that of combating the *social heredity of disadvantage* (Esping Andersen, 2003).

Such a long term strategy is particularly needed within contemporary societies geared around a paradigm of *flexible accumulation*: in fact, short-term policies aimed at implementing safety nets for the worst-off have been proven insufficient to bring about an inclusive and enabling model of communal living. This is because short-term policies are generally designed to protect the worst-off from shocks that are temporary, but are inadequate for dealing with problems such as permanent poverty, long-term unemployment or work precariousness (Ravenga, 2003). Thus, amongst possible options the first step towards a community within which the *social heredity of disadvantage* would be drastically reduced, might be that of introducing structural policies aimed at providing all its members with an appropriate degree of *socio-economic independence,* intended as "the wherewithal to operate normally and properly in … society without having to beg or borrow from others, and without having to depend on their beneficence" (Pettit, 1997: 158).

If we really want the ideal of providing the maximum possible degree of *socio-economic independence to* all to descend from the sphere of dreams to reality, then further than guaranteeing access to fundamental public services, it will be necessary for the *Partner State* to introduce structural policies, such as universal basic income (*UBI*) fixed at a level sufficient to guarantee the material subsistence (Gorz, 1999; Van Parijs, 1996; Offe, 1996), the reduction of the working time within the formal labour market (Laville, 1999; Mazzetti, 1997; Aznar, 1994), active labour policies, wider access to credit, training and life-long learning policies. Given the length and space of this article, we shall discuss only the introduction of UBI, although it should be said that it cannot be detached from the other.

UBI should be understood as the allocation of a regular and perpetual monetary sum to all the members of a given community. It should have the following fundamental characteristics: a) it has to be universal, that is non-discriminatory – it must be given to all human beings regardless of their sex, race, social, economic and marital status, religion, and age; b) unconditional, that is, paid irrespective of one's income, or ones' willingness to accept a job if offered; c) Cumulative to other forms of income already existing or yet to come; d) Paid on an individual basis and not to households.

By at least partly resolving the problems related to the material subsistence, *UBI* would noticeably increase people's degree of autonomy. In the formal labour market, not being forced by hardship into precarious, meaningless, unpleasant or hazardous work, workers would be able to better negotiate their wages, working conditions and contracts with an increased bargaining power. In addition, as *UBI* would be provided regardless of the recipient's willingness to undertake any effective employment, it would allow the full enjoyment of economic citizenship without forcing the recipients to enter into the hierarchized process of material/immaterial production. Thus, it is fair to say that if *UBI* were to be institutionalised, all beneficiaries would see their *self-determination* (namely, the freedom to choose the course of their lives) dramatically increased.

The claim that *UBI* should be paid to all, raises the question of whether or not minors should also have an entitlement to it. Within the envisaged socio-economic order, *UBI* should be seen as an inclusive policy whose primary scope is that of reducing the social risks of exclusion and marginalization to the largest possible extent. In order to be successful, any structural policy aimed at fighting social exclusion should be informed by the richest notion of membership possible: to be explicit, one that includes minors. Indeed, to connect citizenship with the status of minors may give shape to a *contradictio in adjectio.* The first term of this approach presupposes precisely that emancipation of the person that is obviously denied by the second one.

Nonetheless, *UBI* should be provided independent of age. The normative basis upon which this claim rests derives from the necessity to provide an adequate response to the exigencies of minors in an equitable way, at least comparable with the way in which the wider society responds to the exigencies of all other adult members. This argument, in turn, is grounded on the belief that today's young generations represent a fundamental resource for the future *well-being* of the community. Hence, since the pact of solidarity among different generations upon which most of the social fabric rests would be strengthened, it would be in the general interest to preserve minors' substantial equality of treatment. Conversely, any infringement of this pact would risk weakening the ability of the community as a whole to deal with its future tasks.

Indeed for these reasons, *UBI* can be rightly conceived as a powerful tool for the realization of the potentialities of each member of society, contributing significantly to the creation of their positive liberty. In this sense, *UBI* overcomes the negative definition of human liberty as simple absence of coercion. In light of what we have said, it is not difficult to understand why such a structural policy has been perceived as dangerous by those who control and shape current economic processes – and who consequently dismiss it as undesirable. In their eyes, the provision of *UBI de facto* represents a *counterpower* measure to the rules imposed by market-oriented processes and the derived social polarization. Having more bargaining power both within society and the economic realm, ordinary people would enjoy the possibility of opting out of the imbalanced power relations pervading contemporary knowledge-based societies. If this happened, one of the main disciplinary tools of social control would vanish.

Within the parameters of the above framework, the introduction of UBI – obviously along with other structural policies such as a drastic reduction of working time in the formal labour market with no loss in earning, active labour policies, wider access to credit, training and life-long learning policies – might indeed represent a structural policy that, if implemented, would represent the first significant step towards the possibility of turning into reality a never realized promise: that a flexible socio-economic order freeing the vast majority of the population from the heaviest duties would also render all the members of society freer as they would be enabled to fully develop their potentialities.

References

Abramowitz, M. (1986), "Catching up, foreign ahead, and falling behind", *Journal of Economics History*, 46(2): 385-406.

Alesina, A. and R. Perotti (1997), "The Welfare State and Competitiveness", *American Economic Review* 87(5): 921-939.

Amoroso, B and C. Orsi (2006), "Il sogno di Keynes e il contratto di reciproca solidarietà", *3rd STOREP Conference*, Bari.

Amoroso, B. (2005), "Le vie del denaro", *Interculture*, (6).

Aznar, G. (1994), *Lavorare tutti per lavorare meno*, Torino: Bollati-Boringhieri.

Barber, B. R. (1998), *A Place For Us. How to Make Society Civil and Democracy Strong*, New York: Hill and Wang.

Bardhan, A. D. and C. Kroll (2003), "The new wave of outsourcing", *Fisher Center Research Reports:* Report (1103), available at *http://repositories.cdlib.org/iber/fcreue/reports/1103.*

Beck, U. (2004), "Brave new world of work: the political economy of insecurity", available at http://chicago.indymedia.org/newswire/display/42516/index.php.

Bertola, G. and T. Boeri (2002), "EMU labour markets two years on: microeconomics tensions and institutional evolution", in M. Buti and A. Sapir (eds), *EMU and Economic Policy in Europe*, Cheltenham: Edward Elgar.

Bessis, S. (1995), "From social exclusion to social cohesion. Towards a policy agenda", *Management of Social Transformation Policy Paper*, (2), available at http://www.unesco.org/ most/besseng.htm.

Boutang, Y. M. (2008), *Le Capitalisme Cognitif: La Nouvelle Grande Transformation*, Broché.

Boyer, R. (2004), *The Future of Economic Growth*, Cheltenham: Edward Elgar.

Capecchi, V. and A. Gallina (2006), *Towards a Balanced Development in Europe: Experiences From the Application of the ESDP*, Copenhagen: Federico Caffè Centre, Roskilde University.
Cavalieri, D. (2007), *Teoria economica*, Giuffrè.
Dahl, R. (1985), *A Preface to Economic Democracy*, Cambridge: Polity Press.
Daly, H. E. and J.-B. Cobb (1989), *For The Common Good, Redirecting The Economy Toward Community, the Environment, and the Sustainable Future*, Boston, MA: Beacon Press.
Esping Andersen, G. (2003), *Why We Need a New Welfare State*, Oxford: Oxford University Press.
European Commission (2004), *Facing the Challenge, The Lisbon strategy for Growth and Employment*, Luxembourg: Office for Official Publications of the European Communities.
Fassina, S. and V. Visco (2007), *Governare il mercato. Le culture economiche del partito democratico*, Roma: Donzelli.
Fumagalli, A. (2007), *Bioeconomia e capitalismo cognitivo. Verso un nuovo paradigma accumulativo*, Milano: Carocci Editore.
Giddens, A. (1979), *Central Problems in Social Theory. Action, Structure and Contradictions in Social Analysis*, London: Macmillan.
Gorz, A. (1973), *Socialism and Revolution*, New York: Garden City.
Gorz, A. (1999), *Reclaiming Work. Beyond the Wage-Based Society*, Cambridge: Polity Press.
Guio, A.-C. (2005), "Income poverty and social exclusion in the EU25", *Statistics in Focus: Population and Social Conditions*, 13: 1-7.
Harvey, D. (1989), *The Condition of Postmodernity*, Oxford: Blackwell.
Hayek, F. A. (1935), *Collectivist Economic Planning*, London: Routledge.
Hayek, F. A. (1960) [1976], *The Constitution of Liberty*, Chicago: University Press.
Hodgson, G. (2000), "What is the essence of institutional economics?", *Journal of Economic Issues*, 34(2): 317-329.
Hodgson, G. M. (1988), *Economics and Institutions*, Cambridge: Polity Press.
Howe, J. (2008), *Crowdsourcing: Why the Power of the Crowd Is Driving the Future of Business*, New York: Crown Business.
Hutton, W. (2003), *The World We're in*, London: Abacus Book.
ILO (2003), *La Sicurezza in Cifre. Indicazioni per una Cultura Mondiale della Sicurezza sul Lavoro*, Ginevra: ILO
Jessop, B. (1982), *The Capitalist State*, New York: New York University Press.
Jessop, B. (1993), "Towards a Schumpeterian workfare state? Preliminary remarks on Post-Fordist political economy". *Studies in Political Economy*, (40): 7-40.
Keynes, J. M. (1971), *The Collected Writings of John Maynard Keynes, 7, The General Theory of Employment, Interests and Money* [1936], London: Macmillan.
Kukathas, C. (1996), "Liberalism, communitarianism, and political community", *Social Philosophy and Policy*, 13(1): 80-104.
Lash, S. and J. Urry (1994), *Economies of Signs and Space*, London: Sage.
Laville, J.-L. (1999), *L'economia solidale*, Torino: Bollati Boringhieri.
Lipietz, A. (1997), "The Post-Fordist world: labour relations, international hierarchy and global ecology", *Review of International Political Economy*, 4(1): 1-41.
Lutz, M. A. (1999), *Economic for the Common Good. Two Centuries of Social Economic Thought in the Humanistic Tradition*, London: Routledge.

Macpherson, C. B. (1973), *Democratic Theory; Essay in Retrieval*, Oxford: Oxford University Press.
Mann, C. (2006), *Accelerating the Globalization of America: The Role for Information Technology*, Washington D.C.: Institute for International Economics.
Mayhew, A. (2000), "Comments on papers presented at the "Institutional economics at the millennium: its past and future"", *Journal of Economic Issues*, 34(2): 331-333.
Mazzetti, G. (1997), *Quel pane da spartire. Teoria generale della necessità di ridistribuire il lavoro*, Torino: Bollati Boringhieri.
Offe, C. (1985), *Disorganized Capitalism: Contemporary Transformation of Work and Politics*, Cambridge: Polity Press.
Offe, C. (1996), *Modernity and the State: East, West*, Cambridge: Polity Press.
Orsi, C. (2006), *The Value of Reciprocity. Arguing for a Plural Political Economy*, Copenhagen: Federico Caffè Centre, Roskilde University.
Panitch, L. and S. Gindin (1999), "Transcending pessimism: rekindling socialist imagination", *Socialist Register 2000*, (36): 1-29.
Pasinetti, L. L. (2005), "The Cambridge School of Keynesian Economics", *Cambridge Journal of Economics*, 29(6): 837-848.
Pettit, P. (1997), *Republicanism: A Theory of Freedom and Government*, Oxford: Oxford University Press.
Ravenga, A. (2003), "Unemployment, poverty, and social exclusion in Central and Eastern Europe", in B. Funck and L. Pizzati (eds), *Labor, Employment, and Social Policies in the EU Enlargement Process. Changing Perspectives and Policy Options*, Washington D.C.: The World Bank.
Revelli, M. (1997), *La sinistra sociale. Oltre la civiltà del lavoro*, Torino: Bollati Boringhieri.
Robinson, J. (1951), *Collected Economic Papers,*Vol. 1, Oxford: Basil Blackwell.
Sen, A. (1977), "Rational fools: a critique of the behavioral foundations of economic theory", *Philosophy and Public Affairs*, 6(4): 317-344.
Skinner, Q. (1990), "The republican ideal of political freedom", in G. Bock, Q. Skinner, and M. Viroli (eds), *Machiavelli and Republicanism*, Cambridge: Cambridge University Press.
Smart, B. (2003), *Economy, Culture, and Society*, Buckingham and Philadelphia: Open University Press.
Stiglitz, J. (2002), *Globalization and Its Discontents*, New York: W.W. Norton.
Swedberg, R. M. (1991), "Toward a paradigm shift?", in A. Etzioni and P. R. Lawrence (eds), *Socio-Economics: Toward a New Synthesis*, New York & London: M. E. Shape. Inc.
Tam, H. (1998), *Communitarianism: A New Agenda for Politics and Citizenship*, London: MacMillan.
Taylor, C. (1989), *The Source of the Self*, Cambridge, MA: Harvard University Press.
Udehn, L. (1996), *The Limits of Public Choice. A Sociological Critique of Economic Theory of Politics*, London and New York: Routledge.
Van Parijs, P. (1995), *Real Freedom For All. What (If Anything) Can Justify Capitalism?,* Oxford: Oxford University Press.
Vanin, P. (2000), "Valore, relazioni e ragionamento simbolico", unpublished paper.
Vercellone, C. (2008), "Lavoro, distribuzione del reddito e valore nel capitalismo cognitivo", *Posse*.
Watson, M. (2005), *Foundations of International Political Economy*, London and New York: Palgrave.
Whithfield, D. (2001), *Public Services or Corporate Welfare. Rethinking the Nation State in the Global Economy*, London: Pluto Press.

Young, I. M. (1990), *Justice and the Politics of Difference*, Princeton, NJ: Princeton University Press.
Young, I. M. (2000), *Inclusion and Democracy*, Oxford: Oxford University Press.
Zamagni, S. (2003), "Per un'economia civile nonostante Hobbes e Mendeville", available at http://www.pust.edu/oikonomia/pages/2003/2003_ottobre/studi_2.htm.
Zanini, A. and U. Fadini (eds) (2001), *Lessico postfordista*, Milano: Feltrinelli.
Zupi, M. (2006), "Mutamenti delle politiche nazionali europee per combattere la povertà", in G. Vacca and J. L. Rhi-Sausi (eds), *I Dilemmi dell'integrazione Il futuro del modello sociale europeo*, Rapporto 2006 sull'integrazione europea, Bologna: Fondazione Istituto Gramsci, CeSPI Centro Studi di Politica Internazionale, Il Mulino.

6. The challenges of the new millennium and the specific properties of knowledge require a new understanding of knowledge

Aleksandar Keševlić

1. Introduction

The expression "knowledge revolution" denotes the fundamental shift that is occurring from the economy based on physical resources to the one based on knowledge. The emergence of wealth and power will in the future mainly derive from intangible resources. In its background lies the problem of knowledge, which has become one of the most important production factors. It is becoming apparent that ownership of the means of production in the knowledge economy will be less straightforward than in the past because the most valuable assets reside in the brains of knowledge workers. Hence the conventional wisdom concerning the organization is challenged by the knowledge organization. Knowledge capitalism is a new, generic variant of capitalism based more on the accumulation of knowledge than on the monetary and physical forms of wealth. It seems that among the various factors causing change in the economy none is more important today than the role of knowledge.

Knowledge is not a conventional commodity, because it is never lost upon sale of purchase; each transaction only increases it, leading to increasing returns. The law of diminishing returns does not apply to knowledge; on the contrary, the value of knowledge increases with its use. Therefore, the characteristics of knowledge overturn the traditional theoretical views on the economy. Nevertheless, knowledge is paradoxically the least understood and the most undervalued of all economic resources. Owing to these specific properties of knowledge, and in order do demonstrate the inadequacy of understanding about knowledge, we need a new definition of it. I believe that we need new lenses through which to view knowledge in a completely different way. Hence, the main intent of this paper is to define knowledge in terms of its content (substance view), in relation to all major agents of knowledge (subjective-market view), and from the perspective of different scientific communities (holistic view).

2. Knowledge in terms of substance

Knowledge is a whole comprising experience, and in which information, based on combinations of data, is sorted by cognitive processes into patterns of thought. The view of knowledge as capital entails, that knowledge is ascribed a certain economic value define in accordance with the supply and demand for it on the market. From the perspective of substance, therefore I shall treat knowledge as information, cognitive process, and capital.

Knowledge can be understood as information based on rational combinations and relations among data acquired by observation. Information is produced by the combination and classification of data. The understating of information is of key importance for the definition of knowledge, because information is important in decision-making by individuals or entities (Schwalbe, 1999) and in establishing their equilibria (Machlup, 1984). Regardless of the type of equilibrium (partial/general, static/dynamic), the market is at the centre of this type of analysis, as the occurrence of equilibria is ensured by the market's allocative efficiency, which thus becomes synonymous with information efficiency. Rationality and utility maximization lead, through the price mechanism, to a partial or general equilibrium.

However, the information function of the market and equilibrium cannot yield satisfactory insights into the understanding of knowledge. Knowledge should not be equated with information, because it is a set of experiences whereby information is classified into patterns of thought through cognitive processes. This means that knowledge, through cognitive processes, also involves the capacity to interpret information and to solve problems (Dosi, 1998). The following section examines the cognitive processes most frequently studied by psychology.

The cognitive process has three aspects: perception, learning and thinking (Pečjak, 1975). Simon (1955, 1959) links the aspect of learning and thinking with the question of "what is rational". Blaug (1992) defines rationality as an approach where individual economic agents maximize their utility, subject to given constraints, by choosing among alternatives in accordance with their preferences; furthermore, complete and free information is available to all agents. The desire for rationality is understandable, because it employs deduction to lead to elegant models.

Economic theory has reduced the entire cognitive process to rationality and the mechanics of processes whereby an individual's conduct is subject to objectively calculated laws. Owing to perfect information and unlimited cognitive capacity, individuals have no problems in comparing and choosing among the alternatives (unbounded rationality). Socio-cultural considerations do not influence the choice (universal rationality), and subjective knowledge is – owing to perfect information – not relevant in decision-making (objective rationality). However, a completely rational and quantitatively utilitarian "homo oeconomicus" does not have any psychological cognitive characteristics:

- Unbounded rationality requires mutual comparison and selection of the best possibility. However, the complexity of this task prevents the human mind from accomplishing the operation in a rational manner, because its cognitive capacity is bounded (Simon, 1955, 1979);
- The sociologization of economics has shown that an individual is not merely "homo oeconomicus" but primarily a social and cultural being. Cyert and March (1963), Sen (1977), and Fukuyama (1995) call attention to the fact that the inclusion of an individual in society has an impact on his cognitive processes;
- The rationality of "homo oeconomicus" stands in relation to an external observer who evaluates the conduct of the subjects studied. According to the assumption of neoclassical theory, future changes are known to economic agents with certainty. This is consequently also called the "single outcome theory" because it only offers one *a priori* solution. However, subjects act according to their own knowledge, not according to the knowledge of an external observer. Penrose (1980) and Machlup (1984) believe that rationality is subjective because it depends on the individual's perception.

The above-cited contributions point to the fact that human cognitive capacity is bounded. Knowledge as a cognitive process is essentially related to the individual, since only subjective knowledge can provide the basis for decision-making. With the inclusion of individuals in society, cognitive processes become socially contingent. Nevertheless, the subject to whom the capacity of cognition is ascribed may use knowledge and exchange it through the system of property rights for other rights in the market. The market becomes a value-adding process through which knowledge turns into capital.

Characterizing knowledge as capital brings economic returns to its owners. I believe that the cohabitation of human, social, and intellectual capital enables an understanding of knowledge as capital in its full meaning. The value of knowledge was defined for the first time by the neoclassical theory of human capital (Mincer, 1958; Becker, 1964; Schultz, 1961). Knowledge represents an investment by an individual who forgoes part of his or her income during education, trading it for a higher income in the future. However, the failure of human capital theory to comprehend relations adequately prevents it from accounting for problems related to the transfer of knowledge and returns:

- Coleman (2000), for example, argues that the quality of knowledge transmission from parents to children depends on the education of the parents and the time that they devote to their children. A lack of human capital may motivate parents to spend much more time with their children, thus generating a higher level of social capital between them, and consequently a lower percentage of school dropouts;

- Sawyer (1978) finds that diminishing returns to human capital result from the separation of an individual from the environment, given that individuals are bounded in their capacity to employ their knowledge efficiently.

Human capital theory does not account for sociological factors, mostly because they are strongly subjective, and because the theory does not wish to threaten the position of the individual as the fundamental unit of analysis; hence, society is understood as a group of atomized individuals (Sawyer, 1978). Considering these shortcomings, the only sensible appraisal of the theory is one made from the viewpoint of an alternative theory. Since human capital theory has simply no competitor of a comparable scope in the field of economics, while the new theories (e.g. segmented markets theory, signal theory) mostly supplement it, it may be sensible to look for solutions in closer cooperation with other scientific disciplines.

Upgrading the concept of human capital with that of social capital requires an interdisciplinary approach reflected in the tradition of economic sociology. Economics and sociology are connected through their treatment of knowledge as capital, which appears in the form of human capital in economics, and in the form of social capital and its impact on knowledge in sociology. The emphasis on the word "capital" indicates that the value component of relations is expressed, and that this component may become a source of competitive advantage (Nahapiet and Ghoshal, 2000; Adler and Kwon, 2002). Human capital theory underlines that knowledge is basically a personalized process. On the other hand, through learning, values, and communication, knowledge becomes more sociologically contingent; hence, the failure properly to grasp the notion of social capital will prevent any adequate understanding of knowledge as a factor of production.

The key inadequacies of such a socio-economic approach are manifest when the external effects of knowledge are measured. Without measurement, there can be no efficient knowledge management. Measuring human capital is not straightforward because its effect is not easily measurable (Machlup, 1984; Adler and Kwon, 2002). Moreover, there is no consensus on the method with which to measure social capital with the consequence that authors reach opposite conclusions (e.g. Putnam, 1995 versus Paxton, 1999). Hence, the solution is sought in closer cooperation with the managerial theory that stresses the measurement and management of knowledge. Knowledge management is becoming a tool to boost intellectual capital. Wiig (1997) and Edvinsson (1997) understand intellectual capital as a broader phenomenon; knowledge management is focused on the processes related to knowledge (e.g. Roos et al., 1997; Edvinsson, 1997; Jones and Jordan, 1997; Edvinsson and Malone, 1997).

Knowledge is today becoming the core of the new managerial paradigm and a new way to manage business changes. Knowledge management must ensure that knowledge is translated into action with the maximum permanent effect. The ability to measure the externalities of knowledge is gaining importance because only what is measurable can be efficiently managed. New approaches to measurement are devised at the intersection between the traditional approach, which relies on the recognition and management of knowledge, and accounting techniques. Kaplan and Norton (2000) build a "balanced scorecard", system of indicators which highlights the non-financial performance indicators that are strongly related to knowledge.

The soundness of seeking solutions in closer cooperation with managerial theory, and upgrading the understanding of knowledge in terms of human and social capital with intellectual capital, is further corroborated by the fact that most definitions of intellectual capital emphasize the importance of human and social capital:

- Edvinsson (1997) divides intellectual capital into human and structural capital. Structural capital is divided into partnership and organizational capital, where the former is related to the company's external environment and the second to its internal one;
- Roos and Roos (1997) divide intellectual capital into human, organizational, and relational-consumer capital;
- Sveiby (1997) divides intellectual capital into the capacities or capabilities of the employees, external relations, and internal relations.

Authors foreground human capital either directly (e.g. Edvinsson; Roos and Roos) or indirectly through the understanding of capabilities (e.g. Sveiby). Highlighting relational capital (e.g. Roos), structural capital (e.g. Edvinsson, Saint-Onge), and external or internal relations (e.g. Sveiby) certainly indicates an understanding of social capital.

Human capital theory emphasizes that knowledge is related to the individual. Through the processes of socialization, knowledge becomes increasingly socially contingent. Hence, an adequate grasp of knowledge requires that closer attention be paid to social capital. However, the main difficulty of the socio-economic approach is the immeasurability of the externalities of knowledge. Without measuring knowledge and its market evaluation there can be no economic decision-making and rational management of knowledge. The understanding of knowledge within human and social capital theory should therefore be upgraded through the intellectual capital. This definition represents a conception of knowledge as capital in the full meaning.

3. Knowledge from the subjective-market view

Knowledge requires a carrier (e.g. an individual, an organization) in which it is to a certain extent institutionalized, and which uses this knowledge is the market and exchanges it for other entitlements. Therefore, from a subjective-market perspective, I understand knowledge in relation to the individual, the organization, and the market.

Individuals are among the main carriers of knowledge because cognitive processes are basically related to the individual. Acquiring knowledge is an individual process, so that the individual can acquire knowledge only through individual education. Nonaka (1994) and Grant (1997) emphasize that individual knowledge is stored in physical skills and in the brain, and can therefore only be transferred with the person that possesses it. Consequently, an organization can only learn from the learning of its members or by accepting new ones (Senge, 1990). The contemporary business literature lists knowledge managers, knowledge engineers, and knowledge producers as the main agents of knowledge (Nonaka and Takeuchi, 1995; Davenport, 1997; Jones, 1999). Accordingly, the creation of new posts has become a quite common practice in many organizations. Apostolou and Mentzas (1999) warn of the danger of the "knowledge bureaucracy" which may occur as a result of excessive zeal in establishing new functions. Hansen et al. (1999) maintain that knowledge-related processes should not become ends-in-themselves. Lank (1997) argues that agents of knowledge should only be focused on as long as the importance of knowledge management is not strongly "anchored" in the organization.

Viewing individuals as the sole agents of knowledge is in part appropriate, since cognitive processes are primarily related to the individual. By means of individual learning, individuals upgrade their experience into individual knowledge. However, knowledge in an organization is transferred through relations, and it is often materialized in machinery, teamwork, and in production-organizational processes. As a result, organizations may also be important agents of knowledge, besides individuals.

Organizations should be viewed as consisting in a lot more than a group of individuals. Numerous authors acknowledge the capacity of organization to create, learn, and store knowledge:

- Nelson and Winter (1973, 1982) stress that an organization creates its own organizational knowledge through its operations, learning, and experience;
- Penrose (1980) and Nelson and Winter (1982) relate rational capacities to individuals, and "organizational routine" to the organization. Routine is a form of organizational memory, and the way in which the organizational knowledge is stored;

- Ule (1996) uses the metaphor of "collective brains" to point out that an organization can "know" by itself, independently of the individuals;
- Holzner and Marx (1979) assert that an organization, as a "collective agent of knowledge", has the capacity to learn;
- Nonaka (1994) and Jones (1999) highlight that, owing to the increased scale and complexity of interconnectedness, organizations are gaining significance as agents of knowledge.

From a subjective view, this concerns the individual knowledge possessed by the individual, and the socially contingent knowledge held by the organization. An individual can never appropriate knowledge in its entirety because some knowledge is necessarily dispersed and not given completely to anyone. Organizational learning, organizational routines, and collective brains are notions that point to a conception of the organization as an agent of knowledge. Thus, for instance, Senge (1990) speaks of a "learning organization", Quinn (1992) of an "intelligent organization", and Nonaka and Takeuchi (1995) of a "knowledge enterprise". The process of acquiring knowledge fundamentally related to the individual apparently generates externalities manifest at the organizational level. Accordingly, contemporary organizations are now realizing that organizational knowledge is an important factor in business performance and competitiveness, and consequently devote more attention to its management.

Like any other commodity in the market, knowledge requires a carrier, an agent, who understands it as a property right. However, there are certain types of knowledge that can never be owned by a single subject (e.g. an individual, an organization). Hence, knowledge can never be appreciated entirely through individual subjects, but only through a more profound understanding of the market mechanism. Various school of economics thought have developed different ideas of the market, consistently with changes in the way economic theory has viewed the importance and role of the market throughout history and its evolution. I strongly believe that these changes have also affected the capacity of economic theory to understand knowledge itself. From the perspective of knowledge, it makes sense to restrict the treatment to three periods in the development of economic thought that have contributed differing views on the operation and role of the market mechanism to better comprehension of knowledge itself: 1) the (neo)classical school, 2) the Marxist school, and 3) the Austrian school.

In classical political economy, Smith's metaphor's of the "invisible hand" referred to the attainment of broader social interests through the maximization of individual benefit, the importance of freedom of choice, the division of labour, and the competitive mechanism of market prices. Marginalists upgraded the ideas of the classical economists with methodological individualism, rationality, maximization of benefit, and the price mechanism that leads to market equilibria. In that period, the market was an abstract notion as the main mechanism of allocation which employed the informational mechanism of price to provide for the efficient allocation of the production factors, and brought social needs and preferences in line with productive capacity. Kaldor (1972) and Swedberg (1994) maintained that such a narrow understanding of the market mechanism "only" concerned the allocative function of the market. It soon became clear that (neo)classical theory was unable satisfactory to grasp knowledge by only focusing on allocation and human capital, and by interpreting knowledge as information.

The Marxist school developed somewhat different approaches to the understanding of the market mechanism. With its theory of "commodity fetishism", it pointed out that market commodity relations actually conceal broader social relations (Swedberg, 1994). Knowledge is a commodity with both use and exchange value. Knowledge is essentially a private commodity because its acquisition pertains to individuals who appropriate the majority of the benefit derived from the investment in knowledge. Since individual knowledge cannot be appropriated, only contractual relations are possible between employer and employee. However, such relations also generate externalities, because knowledge increasingly spills over to other users, and thus becomes a public commodity (World Report, 1999). Thus, social relations appear in the background of knowledge as a commodity, so that knowledge is not only embodied in individuals but also resides in the relations between them.

Unlike the (neo)classical and Marxist schools, the Austrian school was considerably more successful in understanding the relation between knowledge and the market. By viewing the market as an economic system of knowledge, the Austrian school highlighted two aspects:

- Hayek (1945) maintained that the market is a means to convey knowledge among various subjects in the market. The information function of prices enables individuals to learn from each other. Hence, learning is not based merely on the individual's own experience but also takes place through the market. It is in the rational interest of an individual to take others into account, which is how the market becomes a mode of social learning that emphasizes relations between individuals;
- Schumpeter's business cycle theory called attention to the meaning of knowledge at the entrepreneurial level. Innovations implemented by the most daring entrepreneurs generate dynamic disequilibria and development.

The views of various schools of economics have clearly shown that concentrating solely on the market's allocative function does not yield a satisfactory understanding of knowledge. It is obvious that the (neo)classical conception of the market was too narrow, and that the contributions of the Marxist and especially the Austrian schools furnished a deeper notion of knowledge. An important contribution by the Austrian school was its emphasis on the importance of entrepreneurial innovation and its conception of the market as resulting from spontaneous action by subjects who possess partial knowledge. The market mechanism of social learning leads to the transfer of knowledge between individuals in the market. Hence, viewing the market as "only" providing for the efficient allocation of the production factors does not suffice if we are to understand the knowledge inscribed in the relations among individual subjects in the market. Consequently, knowledge only "fully comes to life" with the Austrian school and its understanding of the market mechanism.

4. Holistic view of knowledge

Knowledge has been the subject of research in many scientific disciplines. There is almost no scientific discipline in which "knowledge" or terms closely related to it are not mentioned. Different definitions of knowledge proposed by individual authors indicate the breadth of the notion of knowledge. The history of science testifies that individual authors have defined knowledge in very different ways, and mainly from the perspective of the scientific communities to which they belong:

- Psychology deals predominantly with the cognitive process of knowledge. Authors hold that the capacity of the human mind is relatively small compared to the scale of the problems that individuals face (e.g. Simon, 1979, 1955; Pečjak, 1975);
- Sociology studies the effect of relations on the transfer and understanding of knowledge, which thus becomes increasingly sociologically contingent (e.g. Fukuyama, 1995; Granovetter, 1985; Etzioni, 1990);
- Managerial theory has foregrounded the categorization of various types of knowledge in order to generate sound business performance (e.g. individual/social, explicit/tacit). Business theories point out the problem of knowledge management and the evaluation of knowledge within the framework of intellectual capital theory (e.g. Roos and Roos, 1997; Nahapiet and Ghoshal, 2000; Edvinsson and Malone, 1997; Jones and Jordan, 1997);
- Economic theory equates knowledge with information (e.g. Stigler, 1961; Hirshleifer, 1973; Schwalbe, 1999), human capital (e.g. Walsch, 1935; Schultz, 1960, 1961, 1962; Becker, 1964; Mincer, 1958), production factors and technological progress (e.g. Solow, 1956, 1957; Romer, 1990, 1994; Lucas, 1988). This understanding of knowledge within the economic scientific community is also supported by the Machlup trilogy (1980, 1982, 1984) which is one of the most complete classifications of knowledge.

It seems that the scientific community of economists only devotes attention to particular dimensions of knowledge. As a result, the comprehension of knowledge is inadequate and deficient. Analysis from the perspective of substance has shown the following:

- Economic theory relates knowledge to information and rationality (unbounded, universal, objective). The distinctive reductionism of economic theory precludes it from full comprehension of cognitive processes. To be encouraged, therefore, is cooperation of economics primarily with those scientific communities that devote more attention to cognitive processes (e.g. psychology);
- With human capital theory, economic theory underlines that an individual's capacities are not inherited by birth but must be acquired through education. Investments in human capital bring yield diminishing returns if the individual is separated from the environment. Without a grasp of the social inclusion of the individual, it is impossible to understand the increasing returns of knowledge. Hence, economics should work closely with those sciences that study relations (e.g. sociology);
- Without closer collaboration with business sciences (e.g. managerial theory), economics will remain unable to efficiently specify the various forms of knowledge, their management, and the market evaluation of the knowledge thus recognized.

Analysis in light of substance has shown that if economics does not cooperate more closely with psychology, sociology, and business sciences, it will not be able to define knowledge adequately. The holistic perspective underlines that only greater scientific interdisciplinarity will make it possible to supersede the derogatory attitude towards knowledge assumed by economic scientific community.

The institutionalization of science impedes efficient communication among different scientific communities, thus precluding the possibility of a more profound understanding of knowledge. Results are interpreted within the frameworks of individual scientific communities, so that divisions in scientific communities become synonymous with partial analyses of knowledge. Burell and Morgan (1979) have shown that more intense collaboration between economics, sociology, and managerial theory is impossible because of the mutual exclusion of their respective paradigms and the lack of consensus in scientific communities on the fundamental starting-points for dialogue with the others. Kuhn (1998) stresses that paradigms are not mutually comparable because they are derived from different assumptions; hence, they are in a state of "paradigmatic war". This implies a competitive battle between particular paradigms in which there can be no real winner, because it is impossible to determine whether, for example, neoclassical theory has the edge over the institutionalist theory. The problem becomes even more acute when attempts are made to evaluate why a theoretical achievement of, say, an economist would be superior to that of a sociologist.

The divisions in the scientific-research community and the desire for universal domination cause increasingly more aggressive "invasions" by economics into traditionally non-economic fields of study. Economic imperialism is based on the idea that rationality can be applied to all fields of human life where resources are finite, or limited, and where the problem of choice arises (Becker, 1976). Owing to the application of economics in new fields, many commentators have recognized it as the universal science (Eichner, 1983; Fukuyama, 1995).

The foregoing holistic analysis has shown that a deeper understanding of knowledge requires superseding the traditional divisions in the scientific community, because this is the only way to go beyond the derogatory attitude towards knowledge shown by particular scientific communities. In a way, economics with its partial analyses, and relentless invasion to other scientific fields undermines the foundations of a more fruitful cooperation with other scientific communities which would yield a deeper grasp of knowledge. Because of its unwillingness to work with other scientific communities and its desire for universal domination, economic theory has lost its capacity to take an "anthropocentric" view of the world, which in turn prevents it from independently addressing the contemporary challenges that require a deeper comprehension of knowledge.

5. Concluding remarks

By constructing a theoretical model, the paper has defined knowledge from three perspectives. From the perspective of substance, or content, knowledge should be understood as information, cognitive process, and capital. From a subjective-market perspective knowledge is defined in relation to the individual, organization and market. From the holistic perspective knowledge can be understood only through greater scientific interdisciplinarity. These three perspectives are interrelated.

Knowledge is, from perspective of substance, a whole comprising experience and in which information based on rational combinations of data is sorted through cognitive process into patterns of thought. Human cognitive capacity is bounded owing to imperfect information and the limits of the human mind. Knowledge as a cognitive process and the conception of knowledge as human capital highlight that knowledge is a process related mainly to the individual. Acquiring knowledge is in essence a process that pertains chiefly to the individual, since new knowledge is generated primarily through processes of individual education.

With the individual's inclusion in the organization, and through the socialization process, knowledge becomes increasingly socially contingent. Hence, an adequate grasp of knowledge transfer and increasing returns to knowledge requires that closer attention be paid to relations (social capital) in organizations. On taking the perspective of the subject, it is possible to explain that some forms of knowledge are socially contingent because they can be possessed by an organization. Knowledge, that is to say, is materialized in machinery, teamwork and the production process.

However, there are also some forms of knowledge that cannot be appropriated by single subjects (individuals, organizations) because they are inscribed in the relations among these individual subjects in the market, and as such they are dispersed and not appropriable by any single entity. Hence, knowledge cannot be entirely understood through the prism of an individual or an organization, but only through more profound insight into the market mechanism. Knowledge enters the market through the system of property rights, where knowledge can be exchanged for other entitlements. Through the market, knowledge becomes capital, since knowledge is ascribed a certain economic value that is defined in accordance with the supply and demand for it on the market. I believe that the cohabitation of human, social, and intellectual capital enables the understanding of knowledge as capital in its fullest meaning. Through Hayek's conception of social learning, the market mechanism also becomes an important way to transmit knowledge, as a specific type of commodity with increasing returns, among individual subjects in the market. In the background, social capital emerges through the market as a process of social learning. Through these relations, and through the materialization of knowledge, knowledge is increasingly becoming a public commodity. Knowledge ceases to be a private commodity where individual subjects appropriate the majority of the benefit deriving from investment in it, since knowledge increasingly spills over to other users through the market, and thus becomes a public commodity.

This conception of knowledge requires an entirely different approach to be taken at the epistemological level. Analysis from the substance and subjective-market perspectives clearly indicates that the partial analysis and institutionalization of knowledge within the framework of individual scientific communities does not yield an adequate understanding of knowledge. For economic theory to fully understand knowledge and overcome the derogatory attitude towards knowledge held within its own scientific community, it will have to devote less attention to its own partial analyses, expansion and desire for universal domination, and more to cooperation with other scientific disciplines.

References

Adler, P. and W. S. Kwon (2002), "Social capital: prospects for a new concept", *Academy of Management Review,* 27(1): 17-40.

Apostolou, D. and G. Mentzas (1999), "Managing corporate knowledge: a comparative analysis of experiences in consulting firms", *Knowledge and Process Management,* 6(3): 129-138.

Becker, S. G. (1964), *Human Capital: A Theoretical and Empirical Analysis with Special Reference to Education*, New York: National Bureau of Economic Research.

Becker, S. G. (1976), *The Economic Approach to Human Behaviour,* Chicago: Chicago University Press.

Blaug, M. (1992), *The Methodology of Economics,* Cambridge: Cambridge University Press.

Burell, G. and G. Morgan (1979), *Sociological Paradigmas and Organisational Analysis*, London: Heineman.

Coleman, S. J. (2000), "Social capital in the creation of human capital", in E. Lesser (ed), *Knowledge and Social Capital*, Boston: Butterworth, pp. 17-41.

Cyert, M. R. and G. J. March (1963), *A Behavioral Theory of the Firm,* New Jersey: Prentice Hall Inc.

Davenport, T. (1997), "Ten principles of knowledge management and four case studies", *Knowledge and Process Management,* 4(3): 187-208.

Dosi, G. (1998), "The contribution of economic theory to the understanding of a knowledge based economy", in D. Neef (ed), *The Economic Impact of Knowledge*, Boston: Buttenworth Heinemann, pp. 123-129.

Edvinsson, L. (1997), "Developing intellectual capital at SKANDIA", *Long Range Planning,* 30(3): 366-373.

Edvinsson, L. and M. Malone (1997), *Intellectual Capital*, New York: HarperBusiness.

Eichner, A. (1983), *Why Economics is not yet a Science?*, New York: M.E. Sharpe.

Etzioni, A. (1990), *The Moral Dimension,* New York: The Free Press.

Fukuyama, F. (1995), *Trust*, New York: Simon&Schuster.

Granovetter, M. (1958), "Economic action and social structure: the problem of embeddedness", *American Journal of Sociology,* (91): 481-510.

Grant, M. R. (1997), "The knowledge based view of the firm: implications for management practice", *Long Range Planning,* 30(3): 450-454.

Hansen, M., N. Nohria, and T. Tierney (1999), "What is your strategy for managing knowledge", *Harvard Business Review*, 77(2): 106-116.

Hayek, F. A. (1945), "The use of knowledge in society", *The American Economic Review,* 35(4): 519-530.

Hirshleifer, J. (1973), "Where are we in the theory of information", *The American Economic Review,* 63(2): 1-39.

Holzner, B. and J. Marx (1979), *Knowledge Application: The Knowledge System in Society*, Boston: Allyn&Bacon.

Jones, A. B. (1999), *Knowledge Capitalism*, Oxford: Oxford University Press.

Jones, P. and J. Jordan (1997), "Assessing your company's knowledge management style", *Long Range Planning*, 30(3): 392-398.

Kaldor, N. (1972), "The irrelevance of equilibrium economics", *The Economic Journal,* 82(328): 1237-1255.

Kaplan, R. and D. Norton (2000), *Uravnotežen sistem kazalnikov*, Ljubljana: GV.

Kuhn, T. (1998), *Struktura znanstvenih revolucij,* Ljubljana: Krtina.

Lank, E. (1997), "Leveraging invisible assets: the human factor", *Long Range Planning,* 30(3): 406-412.

Lucas, R. E. (1988), "On the mechanics of economic development", *Journal of Monetary Economics*, 22(1): 3-42.

Machlup, F. (1946), "Marginal analysis and empirical research", *The American Economic Review,* 36(4): 519-554.

Machlup, F. (1980), *Knowledge: Its Creation, Distribution and Economic Significance,* Volume I, Princeton: Princeton University Press.

Machlup, F. (1982), *Knowledge: Its Creation, Distribution and Economic Significance: The Branches of Learning,* Volume II, Princeton: Princeton University Press.

Machlup, F. (1984), *Knowledge: Its Creation, Distribution and Economic Significance: The Economics of Information and Human Capital,* Volume III, Princeton: Princeton University Press.

Mincer, J. (1958), "Investment in human capital and personal income distribution", *The Journal of Political Economy,* 66(4): 281-302.

Nahapiet, J. and S. Ghoshal (2000), "Social capital, intellectual capital and the organizational advantage", in E. L. Lesser (ed), *Knowledge and Social Capital*, Boston: Butterworth, pp. 119-157.

Nelson, R. and S. Winter (1973), "Toward evolutionary theory of economic capabilities", *The American Economic Review*, 63(2): 440-449.

Nelson, R. and S. Winter (1982), *An Evolutionary Theory of Economic Change,* Cambridge: Belknap Press.

Nonaka, I. (1994), "A dynamic theory of organizational knowledge creation", *Organization Science,* 5(1): 14-37.

Nonaka, I. and H. Takeuchi (1995), *The Knowledge Creating Company,* New York: Oxford University Press.

Paxton, P. (1999), "Is social capital declining in the USA?", *American Journal of Sociology,* 105(1): 88-127.

Pečjak, V. (1975), *Psihologija spoznavanja*, Ljubljana: Državna založba.

Penrose, E. (1980), *The Growth of the Firm,* New York: M.E. Sharpe.

Putnam, R. (1995), "Bowling alone: America's declining social capital", *Journal of Democracy,* 6(1): 65-78.

Quinn, J. (1992), *Intelligent Enterprise*, New York: The Free Press.

Romer, P. (1990), "Endogenous technological change", *Journal of Political Economy,* 98(5): 71-102.

Romer, P. (1994), "The origins of endogenus growth", *Journal of Economic Perspectives,* 8(1): 3-22.

Roos, G. and J. Roos (1997), "Measuring your company's intellectual performance", *Long Range Planning*, 30(3): 413-426.

Roos, J., G. Ross, N. Dragonetti, and L. Edvinsson (1997), *Intellectual Capital,* London: MacMillan Press.

Saint-Onge, H. (1996), "Tacit knowledge, the key to the strategic alignment of intellectual capital", *Strategy & Leadership*, 24(2): 10-16.

Sawyer, D. (1978), "Social roles and economic firms: the sociology of human capital", *American Journal of Sociology*, 83(5): 1259-1270.
Schultz, W. T. (1960), "Capital formation by education", *The Journal of Political Economy*, 68(6): 571-583.
Schultz, W. T. (1961), "Investment in human capital", *The American Economic Review,* 51(1): 1-17.
Schultz, W. T. (1962), "Reflections on investment in man", *The Journal of Political Economy*, 70(5): 1-8.
Schwalbe, U. (1999), *The Core of Economies with Asymmetric Information,* Berlin: Springer.
Sen, A. (1977), "Rational fools: a critique of the behavioral foundations of economic theory", *Philosophy and Public Affairs*, 6(4): 317-344.
Senge, P. (1990), *The Fifth Discipline*, London: Century Business.
Simon, A. H. (1957), *Models of Man*, London: John Wiley&Sons.
Simon, A. H. (1979), "Rational decision making in business organizations", *The American Economic Review,* 69(4): 493-513.
Solow, M. R. (1956), "A contribution to the theory of the economic growth", *Quarterly Journal of Economics*, 70(1): 65-94.
Stigler, G. (1961), "The economics of information", *Journal of Political Economy,* 69(3): 213-225.
Sveiby, K. E. (1997), *The New Organizational Wealth,* San Francisco: Berret-Koehler Publishers.
Swedberg, R. and J. N. Smelser (1994), *The Handbook of Economic Sociology,* Princeton: Princeton University Press.
Ule, A. (1996), *Znanje, znanost in stvarnost*, Ljubljana: Znanstveno in publicistično središče.
Walsh, J. R. (1935), "Capital concept applied to man", *The Quaterly Journal of Economics,* 49(2): 255-285.
Wiig, M. K. (1997), "Integrating intellectual capital and knowledge management", *Long Range Planning*, 30(3): 399-405.
World Development Report (1999), *Knowledge for Development*, Washington: World Bank.

7. M@nufactnetting antagonism, subversively reengineering cognitive global labor force, and networking class struggles in the age of the cognitive capitalism*

Carlos Prieto del Campo

1. The concept of production in cognitive capitalism: circuits of production and the political imagination

The political autonomy of antisystemic movements requires invention: the inventing of difference, the difference of politics in this moment. To this end, any autonomous political practice must simultaneously construct 1) a theory of capitalism which is theoretically innovative, product of an epistemological rupture with the predominant codification of the concept of capitalism generally accepted in any given moment, which in our case coincides with the crisis of the whole systemic cycle of accumulation and its geostrategic balances; 2) an original theorization of the productive circuit in force in the moment of its historical existance which would permit social subjects to read their immediate productive placement in an innovative way, and to read the balances and structural articulations which bring about the culmination of the processes of exploitation and domination in which they find themselves immersed; and 3) an innovative conceptualization of class composition on the basis of which to comprehend the politics of the *difference* of placement within the structure$_1$ of structures$_2$ of power and thereby to apprehend their antisystemic political practice, which in our case coincides with the first cycle of high-level introjection of living labor's antagonism into the structural metabolism of capitalism at the start of the long 20th century, and the management of that antagonism though the unleashing of recurrent crises restructuring the patterns of social reproduction throughout the century, as well as the emergence of general intellect as the predominant productive paradigm. In the present moment, this means producing a theory of historical capitalism capable of accounting for the variability parameters of the diachronic structures of the system's secular behavior and, at the same time, producing a theory of general intellect as the predominant mode of the labor force's forms of existence as situated within the interior of that structure of reproduction of social power. At the same time we must be very conscious that the present modality of capitalism's behavior cannot be exhausted with the partial description of any of its components or variables (industrial, cognitive or financial capitalism), and that any explicative project must dynamically account for a whole series of variables which allow that the global structure of geoeconomic and geopolitical domination be reproduced and its structural dynamic institutionally

* Translation by Maggie Schmitt.

condensed. Geostrategy and biopolitics thus become horizons of maximum complexity for thinking the politics of autonomy in the present class composition of mass intellectuality.

Following this line of reasoning, the immaterial product *par excellance* which constitutes the process of virtuoso production of our class composition is politics: a political practice which links the complexity and the richness of the current composition of living labor with the really existing forms of structuring power and of stabilizing conflict through the party system and the crystalized forms of the State and of supranational institutions in a revolutionary project of destabilizing the processes of global structuring. If capitalism now exploits the inventive force of the proletarian subject, the fitting antagonistic response would be to make explicit the series of forms and connections which allow the stabilization of exploitation and the accumulation of capital and power in this particular historical moment using all the subversive power of this same inventive force, articulated into a truly revolutionary political project: revolutionary in the sense that it destructures the dynamics of systemic reproduction. For the present class composition which revolves around cognitive work, there is thus no way to think politics except on the basis of a radically original theorization of what capitalism is in the present, and therefore what its patterns of behavior will be in the immediate future, which is not possible to apprehend except through the perfect synchronic and diachronic dissection of its patterns of dynamic behavior throughout its evolution in the last centuries. Thinking through capitalism in the present moment, after the antagonistic cycle of the long 20th century, means to make it revolve around class antagonism as the decisive variable for thinking through the dynamics of the restructuring of capital as a global social relation.

Thus it is only possible to comprehend autonomous class practices if the productive subjects building a new constituitive project are capable of defining a circuit of socio-economic production and reproduction which is radically *different* and which integrates and makes visible the forms of social existence which guarantee the integral reproduction of the model of accumulation and exploitation at a global scale in a given historical moment. The political imagination is irrevocably bound to this new description of the forms of perception of the socio-structural circuit, to the new valences attributed to the networks of connection and the new forms of politization of productive and social subjects within the same. In the current conditions of objective socialization of production and of biopolitical integration, the innovative description of this social circuit requires not only an exhaustive theorization of the forms of exploitation but also, at the same time, a prognosis of those dynamic models of organization of production which might guarantee an ever more equal access to global wealth to the entirety of the planet's population, which, given the present ecological restrictions becomes, by definition, a crucial factor in autonomous practices when it comes to thinking through their adaptations and structural dynamics. And so the primordial manifestation of the political imagination of this new class autonomy based on mass intellectuality is a reivindication of the integral productivity of the economic circuit, which in the present moment requires a theorization of social reproduction as a productive circuit basic to the accumulation of capital. In this sense to theorize production is to reconstruct political representation on a larger scale of complexity and of democratization than in the scenario of the 1970s, and to observe the effects which the processes of economic restructuring deployed globally have had upon each and every one of the fields of social life within each of the discrete societies of global capitalism. These parameters irremediably affect the very concept of production and the concomitant concept of politics (autonomy) to the extent that the autonomy of political and productive behaviors are now stabilized in a differential program of subversive attack upon the present conditions, through which conflict is displaced through selective restructurings inspired by the geostrategy of global capital.

2. Global forces of labor: a nk-class composition cultivated in n-complexity

The present historical moment is the result of the first mature cycle of introjection/exploitation of class antagonism by relation-capital, which has managed to structure its processes of capital accumulation and its models of social structuring through the channelling of antagonism within a social structure which has managed to transform it into the principal set of productive devices for the capitalist world system. This cycle coincides with the systemic cycle of accumulation defined by the long 20th century; that is, it starts with the great depression at the end of the 19th century and extends to the present moment. The management of antagonism which was initiated in this period has not yet been concluded, nor have the possibilities of the diverse strategies of struggle. The end results of these will either shape the future standards of exploitation or lead to the revolutionary transformation of the capitalist system during the next historic cycle. I deliberately use the concept of class both because 1) if we consider the capitalist world economy as a single unit of analysis, the exploitation of the collective labor force continues to be the basic axis which defines social, political, cultural, economic and military antagonism and which marks the dynamics of social constitution, and because 2) the concepts of class and of class struggle have experienced, throughout the cycle of the rise of antagonism (1968) as the crucial category of Marxist thought, an awesome complex of endogenous processes of ontological, theoretical and political wealth, making it possible to initiate a project of deconstruction of the relations of power and the processes by which domination is produced which have transversed its social existence (racism, sexism, Eurocentrism). The presence of these power relations within the social and conceptual existence of class has been historically inevitable given the processes of creation, operation and transformation characteristic of historical capitalism, which joined together to produce the dominated class, ready to circulate like a commodity through the productive and social circuits of capitalist societies. These processes of deconstruction of the power relations which transverse the social existence of the dominated classes and which operate according to complex historical rhythms are experiencing a fundamental qualitative leap that today points towards the implementation of constituent power dynamics, which articulate in political terms the tremendous *potentia* of the criticism of the conditions by which domination is produced, generated in the whole arc of historical capitalism and mapped in the practical-theoretical diagrams conceived since 1968.

Ultimately, it's a question of producing *common epistemologies* which might permit us to think both about the plasticity induced in capitalism by the antagonism of the dominated classes and about the efforts to reconstruct their own production as groups and as dominated subjects inevitably inserted in the collective work force, which was and has been necessarily multinational and global throughout the history of capitalism. It is a question of not losing sight of capitalism as a theoretical object, and of not squandering the processes of self-valorization by the dominated and subaltern classes, which have achieved a high degree of reflection upon the web of processes of definition which have made possible the reproduction of the relations of power and exploitation. We speak of *common epistemologies* because only the original design of such a thing would permit us to think about capitalism as a system, and the "global work force" as a subject endowed with constituent power and force sufficient to generate stable dynamics of reproduction of liberation. It is necessary to think about capitalism in all its historical profundity, spatial and structural, because the processes of restructuration and deconstruction which penetrated societies in the 1970s and 1980s already at that time bore a very high risk of being converted into one more element in processes of restructuration and, as a result, making a mockery of antagonistic criticism while poverty, unemployment and structural adjustment policies turned the subtleties of postmodern theory into bitter sarcasm when that theory fell quiet before the elemental privation of a collective work force which was definitively and irreversibly colored, gendered and geographically situated. The theoretical labor mentioned above was made even more urgent during the 1990s. In the present, the postmodern consensus regarding the uselessness and inanity of criticism in the public perception is gradually being broken, and the profound political crisis which runs through both the forms of national sovereignty and the arena of international relations is being lucidly profiled. The existence of a multinational and global work force occupies anew the epistemic space of a critical theory worthy of its name, and the extraordinary work on capitalism during the last thirty five years emerges as a crucial element in understanding the current political and intellectual stakes faced by the diverse class compositions exploited in the capitalist world-system.

3. General intellect and the possibility of a postnational politics

In order to produce this theory of capitalism and class antagonism to understand the complexity of the social structure in which is exploited the current general intellect's class composition, we have to tackle the process of emergence of real subsumption, which in my opinion can be captured with the concept of the structure$_1$ of structures$_2$ as the process of dynamic stabilization historical capitalism in its process of exploitation of the collective work force. The essential task is to analyze why and how the functioning of the capitalist world economy and the interstate system which corresponds to its arc of development are folded into themselves in order to produce this other productive dimension of social existence which generates mutations of such magnitude in the functioning of contemporary societies. Why should modernity resort to this productive hypertrophy of the whole social structure, which in turn becomes the most sophisticated and complex mechanism of production? Why does the reproduction of the social system become the essential and obligatory condition of existence of all social practice, and how does relation-capital succeed in overcoming a structure so over-codified by the dynamics which historical capitalism tested throughout the last four hundred years of the system's existence? When this process of introjection of class antagonism (antiracist/antipatriarchal) succeeds in establishing itself (Fordism/development) around 1968, the very structure had already succeeded in modifying its material constitution and its profile of strategic functioning according to the precise codification of class struggle. While this process of introjection exploits antagonism 1) it simultaneously accumulates strategic plasticity in order to capture the modifications and mutations which the insertion into its mechanism of exploitation of the tendency to political constitution of the ontology of subversion of productive subjects experiences and 2) it also causes the quality of the basic output which produces such a "system of machines" to mutate: this is one of the key mechanisms which explains the process of "linguistification" of economic activity and the emergence as a new class composition of mass intellectuality, the social and productive figure of which is condensed around the Marxian concept of general intellect. The control of the antagonism of productive subjects within the structure$_1$ of structures$_2$ and its endogenous dynamics of political constitution, which the first wave of antisystemic movements had demonstrated to be of indubitable power, becomes a tremendously complicated process, to the extent that the process of structuration which exploits it becomes for the collective work force an objective possibility for the accumulation of antagonism, for the critical theoretical enunciation and for the political organization of class. This affects the very processes of constitution of society by virtue of the dynamics of self valorization which such dynamics make possible on the capitalist world economy scale. This web of processes should collapse through an abrupt mutation of the dynamics of exploitation and, therefore, of structuration. The system of machines which makes this possible mutates the global dynamic of reproduction.

The concept of $structure_1$ of $structures_2$, by my judgment capable of explaining this productive mechanism of social structuration, has nothing to do with structuralist epistemologies, or worse yet, positivists or functionalists, but neither has it anything to do with rhizomatic or network models. Rather it is a question of a much more complex concept which processes the impact of class antagonism upon the devices of historical capitalism according to a process which denies the latter its dialectic content to the extent that antagonism accumulates from the processes and mechanisms which capitalism employs in order asymptotically to approach its reproduction in ever more solid conditions of political constitution of productive subjects. This is the last element of the set of processes of immanence which define the phenomenology of contemporary class behaviors and at the same time the model of social reality's existence and behavior. Mass intellectuality arises as the result of the variation of the standard commodity (which from now on has the character of flow/output) which should produce the capitalist $structure_1$ of $structures_2$, provoking the confluence of the capital accumulation processes with the process of social reproduction of the conditions of exploitation. The standard flow/output tends to incorporate a progressively greater content of all the flows which shape the social existence of productive subjects. The process of production, as a result, is greatly densified by the incorporation of a number of non-material flows into its material composition, flows which should appear in the average composition of the commodity in as much as the process of production in the strict sense tends to present an ever more notable structural similarity to the power structure which permits the social prerequisites for its productive constitution to exist. The closure of an n_k-process of production demands an n_k-productive treatment to be possible in strictly economic terms, which is effected via its placement in a $structure_1$ of $structures_2$ of power/exploitation of class which is itself a hypercomplex machine of treatment and exploitation of class antagonism operating on the scale of the entire capitalist world economy. Immaterial work is the inverse content of class antagonism productively exploited and utilized by relation-capital after the cycle of the multinational mass worker. Historical capitalism has tried throughout the long 20th century to extract itself as much as possible from this complex productive treatment of the work force in order to convert it into a commodity to be exploited in the economic and political circuit: it has exploited class antagonism just to the point of extracting vectors of structuration/accumulation (Fordism/post Fordism), opting immediately to block the tendency of the latter to situate the process of production in a very high level of potential antagonism and of eventual subversion which at times has bordered on the possibility of the pure and simple destructuration of its social model. Mass intellectuality is the result of historical capitalism's response, specifically from the mechanical order of the process of exploitation after the first phase of the long 20th century (1873-1945) to the asymptotic process of incrementation of political reflexivity of class composition which shapes its cycle of accumulation/structuration. It is also the result of the incorporation of knowledge and productive resources into a work force which should increment and densify the use of cognitive, linguistic and scientific elements in a process of maximal expansion of antagonism. The immaterial content of work is corollary to an ontology of subversion – articulated via a group of highly powerful and historically proven dynamics of proletarian self-valorization– which, nevertheless, have been exploited until now within the productive structure of existent historical capitalism. In this process there is no spurious teleology of scientific progress nor the implicit belief that its concomitant incorporation in the productive process responds to imperatives dictated by a process of neutral rationalization of the economic mechanism: on the contrary, it is about the political necessities dictated by a treatment integral to class antagonism which during the first phase of the long 20th century comes to convert itself into the privileged factor in the process of social structuration and capital accumulation. The crossing of these two asymptotes – political reflexivity of antisystemic movements and productive subjects, and production by means of knowledge, science and language – defines the content of a multinational class composition, whose endogenous dynamics of subversion should be the object of attack and blockage by the $structure_1$ of $structures_2$ of relation-capital. Immaterial work is the incomplete name of a labor process which absolutely transcends the phenomenology of what occurs in the process of individual work, which objectively appears characterized by a greater incorporation of linguistic, cognitive and scientific elements incarnated as much in the productive subject as in the system of machines and instruments used in production. The essential level is constructed, however, by the insertion of that n_k-process of individual work in a much broader process of production through which it incorporates the essential inputs produced in other (n–k)-structural spaces of power which are heteroclite with respect to the n_k-process of production habitually recognized by economic science, but which are essential in agreement with the complex mechanism of treatment of the antagonism which governs the structural devices of capitalism.

The fundamental question, therefore, is how to theorize the productivity of the factory and the society: what exactly, and of what material is this system of machines ($structure_1$ of $structures_2$ of class exploitation and domination) analyzed by Marx in the celebrated fragment about machines in the *Grundrisse* which dazzlingly condenses 1) the historic-structural tendencies of historical capitalism, of antagonism and class struggle, and 2) the emergence of general intellect as an increasingly hegemonic figure of the collective work force and of the real subsumption of society in relation-capital, in an intellectual and political project inseparable from its revolutionary implications? Marx obviously thinks about the enrichment of antagonism, which he foresaw to be exponential, within a complex historical system which should incorporate it according to a model which tends intrinsically towards greater heights of systemic, subjective and political conflict; he understands that for the dominated classes the conflict will bring about an intensification of their productive *potentia* which will be materialized in the very subjective/collective technical and political composition of the proletarian subjects (general intellect), who will experience an irresistible process of endogenization of the intrinsic demands of liberation. This will oblige them to deconstruct the very power relations which synchronically cross through their processes of social existence, and which are produced and recreated diachronically by historical capitalism in a discontinuous process of expulsion from the borders of racism and sexism which are inseparable from it, and to produce an ever more systematic and consistent conceptualization of the global process of socioeconomic and cultural reproduction. With respect to the dominant classes, however, the conflict will tend to turn on the intensification of the process of capitalist production, which Marx considers the privileged site of condensation of historical capitalism according to a schema which always operates on the scale of the world economy, and which will oblige the exponential incrementation of the systems of second generation machines, which are precisely the concatenations of the social machines which define the (re)productive fabric of real subsumption. Thus we can talk about first generation machines and systems of machines, which transform the material through mechanical, chemical, electric, electromagnetic, or informational means, and of second generation machines or systems of machines which transform productive and social processes in accord with a complex logic of social structuration conceived to reproduce the domination of the collective work force as the repressive and systemic ontological closure of an irrepressible antagonism which necessarily tends towards the ontologic, epistemic and political emergence of its historical dynamics of liberation. For Marx, then, the concept of real subsumption simultaneously integrates 1) the tendencies of historical capitalism, 2) the retrospective synthesis and the prospective projection of the collective work force's antagonism and 3) the leap or the successive leaps of social productivity which capitalism should experience in order to contain the web of processes of constitution of revolutionary subjects. The successive scientific-technical revolutions and their involvement in the process of capital accumulation as they are described by conventional economic science only tell the history of the first generation machines (internet included), constituting the necessary infrastructure for applying the second generation machines to social processes triggered by the systemic cycles of accumulation. These second generation machines make possible the structuration of all social n_k-practice, which should experience a much more complex process of production now that they operate with inputs, processes and resources which are only visible from the perspective of class composition, the rhythms of antagonism and the dynamics of subversive semiotization which living work effects on social reality.

Marx said that the principle productive force was the revolutionary class: perhaps this maxim is the final truth of Marxism and of capitalism, but it is obvious that such a complex web of processes of revolutionary constitution constitute the privileged input which should be processed, treated and transformed by the system of machines of real subsumption during the long 20th century. Marx obviously thinks that capitalism exists, and that this process of second generation exploitation of class antagonism, which literally permits relation-capital to map its processes of structuration/accumulation and which doubles the economic exploitation of the proletarian work force, also involves a fierce struggle over the contents and processes of socialization of the class antagonism input and of the concomitant processes of structuration which multiply exploitation to the extent that they socialize the ontological wealth of the collective work force to the benefit of capital. This process of appropriation, necessarily unstable given the existence of an antagonism which despite being exploited continues to carry out a complex of processes of enunciation and semiotization of its conditions of social existence, continually leaves open points of departure for lines of flight which may in turn become partial processes of self-valorization: the *linguistic turn* of the processes of production is the result of this continuous pressure of class antagonism which has historically succeeded in displacing the accumulation of productive social wealth towards the self-valorization of the technical and political composition of living labour, of the collective work force. This partially displaces it from the system of first generation machines which has defined the last two technological revolutions (electro-chemical and informational). The crucial problem, however, is comprehending how class antagonism is exploited through the process of social structuration – thanks to this system of second generation machines which is the $structure_1$ of $structures_2$ –, and simultaneously this antagonism succeeds in generating processes of political constitution which allow it to comprehend and control the reproduction of the social process in as much as its self-valorization is increasingly formed as a network of devices of constituent power which operate or can operate concurrently in the nodes of structural codification of the conditions of possibility of the exploitation which the system produces, and which is capable of blocking its productive coupling and defining possible n-diagrams of new models of concatenation of first and second generation productive processes. These would make possible the accumulation of antagonism in n-structural microdevices which might initiate n-autonomous cycles of social constitution. The Marxian real subsumption, therefore, supposes the crossing of two asymptotic processes which reach their operative maturity in the systemic cycle of accumulation of the long 20th century and which in an increasingly integrated manner structurally adjust 1) the mature process of constitution of the world market with all the phenomenology of behaviors of the capitalist world economy, and 2) the implementation of the first cycle of exploitation of class antagonism by the $structure_1$ of $structures_2$ of relation-capital through its introjection in the rhythm of social structuration, which supposes a whole spectrum of production of structural space essential for orienting the antagonistic strategies of productive subjects.

The essential characteristic of this last point is that it defines an n-dimensional space in which a new concatenation of n-processes of social production is produced. We use the concept of production in the Marxian/Leninian sense, which is to say, the process through which any n-social practice can experience an n_k-productive integration process according to a complex model of integration in its flow/output of social dynamics which are invisible to the economic, not to mention the political, calculation of the dominant epistemes. These are crucial for comprehending the production of surplus value, class power and subjectivity of a given class composition in an n_k-historical moment, and are strictly the result of an n_k-process of production. The concept of $structure_1$ of $structures_2$ defines within itself an n-dimensional space, result of the concatenation of the n-structural spaces of power which define the social existence of class composition and which were shaped during the antagonistic cycle of the worker's masses and the progressive emergence of the social worker, of the intellectuality of the masses which has deployed its antagonism in visible manner since 1968. The productivity of this network of n-structural spaces of power which shapes each one of the $structures_2$ which are ordered by the $structure_1$ takes root in the quality of the flows/outputs which produce and which can incorporate themselves in other flows/outputs of apparently diverse productive processes, but which are inextricable from the point of view of the production of the flows/outputs of power which define and shape the reality of domination and exploitation. Thus an n_k-racist or sexist flow/output is essential in closing a process of economic exploitation in the strict sense, although its production, which has a long genealogy, obviously does not enter into the calculation of expenses of the company which lowers its prices by hyper-exploiting immigrant or female labor; or, more precisely, one can rest easy in the belief that all flows/outputs produced within the capitalist social structure have a sexist/racist component which forms part of their composition as commodities which circulate and are realized in the market. Similarly the flow/output "scientific enunciation" of the independence of the central banks as authorities only accountable to the international financial markets, is crucial in an n_k-historical moment in order to make possible a given strategy of capital accumulation on the world scale through a hypertrophy of the financial markets and the corresponding multistratified strategies of global social explotation; or an aesthetic flow/output becomes part of the production of the worker's subjectivity necessary for the implication of the work force in a process of value-creation within a labour environment increasingly oversaturated by affective behaviors whose absence makes difficult, if not impossible, the closure of the production of surplus value; etc., etc., etc.

The definition of this productive mechanism which exploits the present class composition, increasingly defined by the existence of the mass intellectuality (general intellect), is essential because it demonstrates that the process of exploitation of the latter can play with the phenomenological differential of the diverse forms of social existence and with the apparent incommensurability of the n- existent processes of production in accord with their codification by the dominant epistemes of social analysis or by the machines of ideological enunciation which work to pulverize the productive connection which apparently diverse forms of social existence/economic exploitation experience within a single process of structuration of class power and reproduction of the social structure. The elemental unit of production in this system of complex machines is the *n_k-flow/output of surplus value/class power* whose material content expresses the new social composition of the process of production which takes place in the real subsumption and which historically reaches a state of maturity during the long 20th century and is established around 1968. For the present class composition it is crucial to analyze 1) in capitalism today, what is *the commodity*, how is it produced and of what elements is it composed, as much from the point of view of the inputs which integrate it as of the types and forms of work which make possible its social existence and its validation in the new structural circuits of production of surplus value and class power; and 2) which is its process of production and circulation within the system of second generation machines which shape the $structure_1$ of $structures_2$ which exploits the entirety of the processes of social constitution, economic production, discursive and ideological enunciation and political constitution. In this sense, the elemental productive unit of a second generation machine is, as we mentioned before, the *n_k-structural space of power,* whose insertion in the corresponding $structures_2$ is absolutely compatible with the remaining units which constitute in a given historical moment its architecture and whose flows/outputs can automatically integrate themselves in whatever n_k-process of surplus value/class power production which shapes any n_k-chain of production. The internal architecture of such $structures_2$ and the relation of these with the $structure_1$ defines the substance of the *n-dimensional space* in which productive subjects, and social subjects in general, function, and in whose interior the processes of production and productive concatenation, subjectification, class desegregation and social enunciation are produced, as their material substance is constituted by the circulation of the above mentioned flows/outputs, which simultaneously produce commodities, enunciate reality, and effect processes of constitution of social subjects according to the logic of n-processes of combination of the above, which productive subjects effect according to tremendously varied sequences, but which operate through finite combinations of (n–k)-flows/outputs of surplus value/class power which enunciate the conditions of domination, if they do not succeed in incorporating in this enunciative mechanism (n–k)-antagonistic flows/outputs which distort or make impossible the enunciation of reproduction of an n_k-situation of domination: the process is too complex to expound completely here, but it is obvious that its functioning dissolves all the apparent paradoxes and irresolvable aporias which postmodern theories surprisingly seem merrily to identify in the so-called narratives of modernity. The diatribes about inside and outside, about the no-place of social forms, about the incommensurable, and about the mutations experienced by the processes of subjectification, the new forms of sovereignty and the new models of the statehood should not fail to take into account these new forms of social productivity to which the antagonism of the collective work force has obliged the mechanisms of structuration of relation-capital which have constituted historical capitalism. Diatribes which seem, on the other hand, a bit ingenuous to us antagonistic subjects who had to begin mapping class domination during the 1980s, given that our intellectual and political survival depended crucially upon the overcoming of these false problems which the very reality of domination constantly caused to leap up. The substance and the new productivity which are condensed in this n-dimensional space of the structure_1 of structures_2 may also operate as an n-dimensional space of subversive constitution and constituent power according to a complex of processes of enunciation, class aggregation and generation of organizational practices which make possible other games of destruction/ concatenation of n-structural spaces of power – and in general of the n-subversive flows/outputs, which are generated in the latter by antagonistic proletarian subjects –, and which can become structural spaces of production of subversive practices and, as a result, of flows/outputs which can circulate with that content through the circuits and networks of social production and enunciation.

4. *General intellect*, production, autonomy, hegemony, politics

The intellectual and subjective composition of the general intellect permit us to comprehend in a radically novel way what it means to "produce" now – a new ontology, in fact, an epistemological revolution – and what politics might arise from this transformation of productive, and therefore also constituitive, practices. Present productive subjects are in conditions to 1) integrate an ever higher number, on the one hand, of structural connections which permit the exercise of their productive activity *strictu senso*, and on the other, of inputs which permit the closure of a certain productive process and, as a result, of social reproduction; and 2) to analyze the cumulative impact of the outputs of their immediately economic activities and of the specific organizational and structural forms which these activities assume when placed within the machine of complex production which is the very structure$_1$ of structures$_2$ of power, both from a synchronic and structural perspective and from a diachronic and spacial one, both from the logic of class power which engraves its dynamics upon the whole process from a global perspective as well as from the perspective of ecological and biopolitical impact and with these their ongoing reproduction over time. All this while paying preponderant attention to those options which supress the field of political possibilities in a given conjuncture. In this sense, the functioning of the financial and capital markets presents a fascinating laboratory for studying the chain of restructurings of power relations and the blockage of possible alternative models of productive, economic and commercial organization. In these markets we can trace – from the futures and derivative markets to the *modus operandi* of the hedge funds and of private equity, not to mention the architecture of the international monetary and financial system – a complex spectrum of systemic responses to the processes of class constitution of global productive subjects both from the center of the capitalist world-economy and from the global south. This new paradigm of analysis of class autonomy implies the impossibility and the meaninglessness of isolating one privileged productive subject without reconstructing the very concept of production and without modelling the global productive circuit, that is, the systemic correlations of the capitalist world-economy and the differential placement of productive subjects in its structural functioning. The strategic challenge for autonomy today is not to define a new privileged subject who might realize, in its practices, the politicization of processes of struggle and of political constitution but rather to define the forms of antagonism of the heterogenous subjects present at a global scale, forms which are provoked by the processes of constitution of the diverse social hegemonies active in each region and induced by the very processes of antagonistic constitution and reconstruction of the relation-capital in any given historical moment. Given the mutation of the productive paradigm of historical capitalism, to a great extent fruit of the antisystemic struggles throughout the present US systemic cycle of accumulation, in order to understand autonomy it becomes crucial first to understand the accumulative nature of the diverse processes of the production of the labor force as well as regionally unequal exploitation and the configuration of State forms which have permitted the closure of diverse processes of domination. Heterogenous structural dynamics obviously stabilize themselves through distinct uses of the income and the wealth produced in any given political unit, but they are articulated globally through processes which tend towards the unequal access to resources and above all towards the differentiation of possibilities of politicization and of the antisystemic organization of their heterogeneity.

This subjective and structural heterogeneity finds in the concept of general intellect the material possibility of translation and of autonomous antisystemic accumulation, and ultimately the viability of designing multiform political practices which operate simultaneously in areas and regions which, until recently, were incommensurable due to their socio-economic and political differences, as well as their cultural, national and identitarian diversities. Today the political autonomy of antisystemic movements suposes the possibility of creating transnational planes of consistency which permit that the dynamics of social reproduction be ordered in such a way as to generate descriptions of power relations susceptible to provoking processes of subjectification which in turn might give rise to heretofore unknown models of political relations with the power structures of historical capitalism. A plane of consistency is an attractor which profiles fields of theoretical, epistemological and cultural problematics which might enrich each other exponentially given the level achieved by the struggles and the forms of existence of productive subjects in the capitalist world-economy. These attractors operate transnationally to the extent that the conditions of possibility of their processes of creation and composition reside in a) the very ontological weave of mass intellectuality which tends to operate at a global scale in its productive activity but which until now has expressed its public activity organizing political practices in specific cultural and national idioms, and in b) the growing homogeneization of a productive circuit the entire logic and economy of which is ever more transparent to the general intellect of the productive subjects of the cognitariat. The production of these planes of consistency constitute the elemental condition of political autonomy inasmuch as they function as attractors of theoretical production which radically transform the phenomenological description of really existing power relations, and by modifying this description manage to define irreversible sequences of theorization and politization, incommensurable with the strategies of the modes of exploitation designed by dominant classes and elites. The fundamental characteristic of these modes of exploitation is their accumulative quality and their transversality, which necessarily has to create autonomous discursive political practices, causing important problems in the reproduction of dominant discourses to the extent that they alter and destabilize the predominant diagnoses of how social reality is codified. These specific planes of consistency are placed within axes of antagonistic coordinates, axes which suppose an epistemological and practical space in which the partial descriptions generated in the planes of consistency reach the maximum productivity of their antisystemic and political translation on a scale which finally is global. In order to comprehend autonomy now these micro-planes of consistency should be articulated around the following general problematics:

- *Plane of consistency of the production of the market of general intellect* (The specificity of the instruments of capitalist management of productive processes and the present composition of living labour, as well as their placement relative to the modalities of State and political power in order to isolate the specifically capitalist nucleus of the present social organization which should be the prioritary object of analysis and political attack, beyond the wholesale demonization of the market and the supposed homogenization of the forms of market-oriented management of production and exchange);
- *Monetary, financial and banking plane of consistency of antagonistic mass intellectuality* (The devices of exploitation and hierarchization of material wealth produced on a global scale, and the strategies for the reversion and destruction of their capitalist character, as well as their relationship to strategies of antagonistic social restructuring, not forgetting that historical capitalism has been fundamentally financial and that this modality of its existence has configured a series of functional devices for recreating and strengthening the exploitation and the conservation of class power);
- *Constitutional, material and territorial plane of consistency of common production* (The materiality of the diverse modalities of the national and supranational forms of the State and the public management of common resources according to the reigning geographical patterns of unequal development in a horizon of radical distribution of wealth in a definitively postnational environment for the design of regional macroeconomic options with respect to the super-exploited areas of the surrounding geography, and by extention, the global geography);
- *Ecological plane of consistency of the productive reconstitution of global cognitive subjects* (The strict limits of the reproduction of life in the long term under capitalist conditions of accumulation and exploitation, and the relationship of these current conditions to the apparatus of production, consumption and of distribution of wealth on a global scale within the horizon of ecological crisis and global warming which differentially affect productive activities and social organization);
- *Geostrategic plane of consistency of postcapitalist transition* (The geoeconomy and geopolitics of contemporary capitalism in the context of the crisis of US hegemony and therefore Western hegemony, and the definitive decolonization of the world economic structure in a postcapitalist project which would permit us to read the transition to egalitarian forms of accumulation in an environment presided over by war and systemic chaos in the last decades).

In a most immediate sense, the crucial aspect of autonomy now is that the new productive quality of mass intellectuality of class or of the multitude be translated into descriptions which permit the production of models of knowledge which radically alter the protocols of enunciation of the great machines of social functioning, both on a national scale and on a regional and global one. In this sense, such planes of consistency function as privileged analytical instruments for circulating the knowledges possessed by productive subjects in non-immediate circuits of knowledge and of production in order to alter their present connections and thereby generate new descriptions of the circuits of social reproduction. The concept of general intellect's autonomy today demands this theoretical and epistemological revolution. The politics of the future, indeed the politics of the present, begin with this process of translation through which the creation of these attractors brings about alternative processes of description of the structure and of social processes, which are susceptable to accumulating with other descriptive models in order to provoke a techtonic displacement of the forms of social perception as well as the axes of antagonistic constitution in which the politics of the new class composition of global mass intellectuality is decided.

The paradigm of general intellect requires that we concieve original forms of organizing the processes by which hegemony is produced, which given the current ontological wealth of productive subjects should *per force* operate at a rhythm perceptably faster than the rhythms at which, historically, modalities of political organization have been generated. The productive paradigm of cognitive capitalism has drastically altered the conditions of theoretical production, of intellectual work, of political organization and of cultural practice, such that only a theoretical labour of great intensity, politically concieved with all the resources which the present moment offers and expressed in culturally and asthetically communicative terms as a project of political constitution would be capable of confronting the semiotizing machines of capital. From our perspective, this process by which hegemony might be produced from within global forces of labor's autonomy must start from a complete treatment of the great social macrostructures, using to this end the best theoretical tools which the movement possesses in order to conjugate the best theories of historical capitalism with the best theories of antagonism and antisystemic movements: the instruments of each of these theoretical traditions whould be applied at the planes of consistency indicated above, which in turn must be modulated according to transnational region (not nation) in order to provoke a process of global connection between the ways of comprehending world reality. The productive subject of mass intellectuality (and increasingly all social subjects, given the current average ontological and intellectual wealth) operates and reproduces itself in conditions which are perfect for bringing about such a process of growing politicization and therefore for contributing to the creation of these strategies for the construction of hegemony. The subject's participation in general intellect situates her (or him) in a privileged place (from a subversive perspective) relative to the $structure_1$ of $structures_2$ of power and permits her to contibute to its destructuring, as long as the she has access to powerful political devices through which all of her intelectual, technological and productive force might be expressed. This fluid insertion of productive subjects within the power structure and the structure of production is also the condition of their antagonism and their autonomy. We should not forget that in present day capitalism (real subsumption) all *n_k-social practices*, all *n_k- acts of use of the labour force* and all *n_k-models of public existence*, by virtue of their own conditions of production and their placement within the power structure, as well as by virtue of the modalities of communicative circulation and the ontological consequences of the same, constitute privileged points from which to send out lines of flight susceptable to a posterior process of politically radical subversive treatment and to creatively accrue to an antagonistic project first on the mentioned planes of consistency, then in the construction of hegemony and lastly in the organization of stable political machines. Today the key data for thinking about new processes for creating hegemony and about the political autonomy of the movement is the wealth and the multiple capacities of productive subjects. This is what allows us to imagine the political autonomy of the movement. In this sense, the crucial political task of the moment is to define planes of consistency in such a way that heroclitean productive subjects, trapped in power relations which are functional to the reproduction of the social structure, might incorporate their quota of collective intelligence in order to initiate heretofore unseen processes of description of the functioning of the modalities and strategies of power and exploitation in any given social area. These planes of consistency should create expansive research programs and materially effective communication strategies capable of pushing themselves forward in a virtuoso feedback pattern. These strategies should offer rich ways to articulate the various planes of consistency, thereby producing models for the creation of hegemony at a scale which is clearly postnational and, if regional, then regional with a vigorous tendency towards the global. The productivity of each one of these planes of consistency can be translated into the accumulation of permanent processes of social diagnosis which are intimately interwoven with the productive fabric, with the technological practices of contemporary subjects and with the transversal social perception of those subjects located in other points of the social structure, irrespective of their type of labour or specific productivity. The accumulation of these diagnoses is crucial, because their use in the strategies of creation of hegemony functions to increasingly block and render useless the dominant discourses, and thus the conditions of existence of the current political and constitutional machines and, as a result, the existing balance of power relations.

In the age of real subsumption, of general intellect and of cognitive labor, theory is the nerve of desire. In this senses, the autonomy of antisystemic movements requires the construction of strategies for training, research and empirical analysis which might be harmonously and dynamically integrated in strategies for the creation of social hegemony destined in the short term (or simultaneously) to become political projects vectored in political machines capable of competing at all levels of social existence, and to initiate a direct attack upon all social, economic, constitutional and political balances, as well as their codification and enunciation by administrative institutions, parties and unions. Thus autonomy today means thinking through material constitution with an intensity and a level of confrontation which is exponentially higher than those seen in the political revolutions of modernity. This is so because historical capitalism operates reproducing intense rates of exploitation according to differential development which has been determined historically in the different regions of the capitalist world economy, at the same time as it reproduces modes of regional exploitation in agreement with a complex process of access to global wealth as a function of the systemic modalities of the reproduction of integrated capitalism in the present. Today, this parameter of structural reproduction is elemental in thinking about class autonomy and in constructing its revolutionary organization. The level of displacement should therefore be highly articulated and should be endowed with great depth, which might only be politically organized on the basis of a concept of autonomy capable of apprehending this double structure of exploitative relations and how they have been configured in historical capitalism according to their contemporary articulation in the present systemic cycle of accumulation of capital. Only those processes which comprehend and organize autonomy at this level of complexity will be able to generate irreversable and accumulative processes of politicization, which transcend the functioning of historical capitalism because only they manage to understand in a systematic manner the crucial devices which have permitted the reproduction of the incredible socio-economic inequality which can be observed in specific economic areas as well as throughout the collective of exploited subjects in every phase of their social and life cycles in any given socio-economic area.

Part II: Empirical Analysis – World, South-Eastern Europe

1. The big trade off of "New – Europe": convergence or divergence from USA model of capitalism

Nadica Jovanovska and Natalija Nikolovska

1. The global tendency of capitalism

During last few decades of the twentieth century immense changes have occurred in the global system of capitalism. Two tendencies of changes could be distinguished as essential: Firstly, in the 90's the capitalism became a planetary social – economic system conquering the ideologically expropriated territories (the ex-communist countries). Secondly, in the aggressive competition between different types of capitalism (neoliberal capitalism, state – market economy, welfare state, social market), the neoliberal model of capitalism of USA prevailed and started to "melt" and influence over the other types of capitalism.

There are few contradictory earmarks of the so called neoliberal capitalism. The productivity and competitiveness are generally determined by the generations of knowledge and information processes. The core strategic activities and the economic factors such as, the capital market, science and technology, information, consumer markets, multinational production systems, services, media communications are part of the global network system of inputs and outputs. While the internationalization of the economic system is not a new tendency, what is new is the technological infrastructure which enables dramatic dynamism of the system as well as changes of the value indicators and how they are determined.

In the electronic network systems for fast earnings the profit is not the representative indicator of value but the possible growth of the capital expressed in the price of stocks, a process most clearly visible through the growth of the value of Internet stocks[51]. The global information capitalism, whose fundament is the biggest technological revolution in the history, looks as if it does not have boundaries in their growth and dispersion. However, the other immanent char-

51 The dimensions of growth of the stocks in the field of services can be illustrated through several examples: America On Line employed 10.000 people and was estimated to 66,4 billion US dollars as compared to General Motors that employed around 600.000 workers whereas its market value is 52,4 billion US dollars. The example of Yahoo is also representative because it employed 673 people and its value was 33,9 billion US dollars. Clear speculation!

acteristics of its development contain the contradictions of the new liberal capitalism and in the same time they pose a threat for its survival[52].
Primarily, the main objective here is the most remarkable segment of the new capitalism – the financial markets. The reconstitution of the international economic order in the sense of deregulation and liberalization as universal standards was done in order to bring together the game rules of the single global market. The aim was to support the mobility of the capital worldwide and to abolish the restrictions of possible investments in future. Therefore, the financial magic of the new information technology succeed not just to mobilize the planetary resources of the capital but also to initiate new rules of establishment of the capital value which are not written in the economics books. These rules represent a mix of market rules, political and business strategies, psychologies of masses, rational expectations, irrational expectations, and speculative maneuvers[53]. The complex network of transactions resulted with interactive and contradictory prognosis of the market values in different places and times out of control of the governments, financial institutions and concrete business groups irrespective of the quantity of assets. Consequently, the tendency is based on the dominant prejudice of value regarding the manner in which the process enters into a hazardous network of financial speculations which on the one hand indicate growth and revenue but on the other abandonment of investments and crisis in the moment of facing with the real values[54]. The alchemy of the financial crisis as the Sword of Damocles is above the height of the global capitalism putting the countries in an uncertain process of "bottom bust" cycle and opening possible perspectives for a global crisis.

The significant characteristic of the new global capitalism is presented through the economic policy reduced to a mono-dimensional metaphysical system which focuses on price stability and exchange rate. Therefore, the price stability dogma suppresses the fundamental premises of the economic theory for trade-off be-

---

52 Soros (1998) explains that the contradictions of the new capitalism will bring about its collapse unless the international community does not undertake urgent measures to reform the international institutions.

53 An eminent example of management with mixed strategies and their consequences is the LTCM fund (Long – term capital management) i.e. is the theory of rational expectations headed by two Nobel Prize winners. The fund collapsed and a real shock of the financial markets in the developed countries was at the doorsteps had the FED (system of federal reserves) not intervened. At the moment of collapse, the speculative bubble was blown so that the value of the stocks at the market amounted to 600 million US dollars and the balance leverage was 100 million US dollars (i.e. 167 times more than the capital value).

54 The stochastic process and interdependence of the global financial markets are the fundament of the series of crises in the period from 1997 – 1999 which after the Mexico crisis in 1994 have shaken up the Asian pacific (1997), Russia (1998), Brazil (1999) and sent the shock waves worldwide. However, the global economy absorbed this shock.

tween stability of prices and employment, thus pushing under the "doormat" the more visible unemployment growth, increase of dissimilarities in society, growth of poverty, reduction of social rights,...

Globally, in the new economy the economic reductionism presented through the monetary orthodoxy emphasizes the irrelevancy of the structural economic policies if the price stabilities are not in function of the supreme arbiter of the economic regime – the stable prices. The consequences are evident regarding the possibility of realization of the concept of sustainable development which is multidimensional i.e. contains social, cultural, ecological values. The expansion policy of the business formations (TNC – transnational corporations) through the expansion network of capital (FDI) are in constant search for new investment vs. consumers possibilities. In order to avoid the decline of the average profit rate, societies are being remodelled in terms of "one size fits all" that changes the economic and social system. The requirement for attracting foreign direct investments (FDI) has the advantage over the achievement of the social objectives. This recent capitalism movement tendency is facing at least three threats:

- The risk of expansion of the global financial markets and the consequences as contagion financial crises;
- The risk of economic stagnation produced by the stabilization package of the pro-recessive measures of the economic policy which contrary to the giant growth of the labour productivity, leads to a surplus of capacities that cannot meet the aggregate demand in a time when the fear of inflation through the restrictive policies reduces the purchasing power of the population;
- Degradation of the welfare state, which could lead to social, cultural and political resistance towards the new capitalism that ignores the human dimension of the development.

If USA is the ideological promoter of the neo-liberalism, its future it highly dependent on the EU capabilities to enter in the global regime by keeping the specifics of its own development model (socio–market economy). Therefore, the actual dilemma in EU is how to be strategically positioned in regards to the convergence vs. divergence from the dominant model of capitalism? The dilemma could become more real if EU MP's as well as the general public in the European countries are able to find a way to maintain the specific characteristics of the European development model at a time when the pressure – the global trend of the business elite for changing the economic regime – is extremely powerful.

2. EU in the process of "catching up with" the tendency

The fundamental characteristics of the global capitalism have set to the West – European countries the imperative of creating a highly – integrated economic space, which is going to be able to follow the Information Technology growth, as well as the financial market development. In fact, the pre – structuring of the global economy for the final competition required the starting of mechanisms of European economy, currency and monetary integration, as well as obtaining an eligible position for market – orientated and long – term economic development of the region. That should have been realized through the stronger competitiveness among companies and banks in the region and their enlargement in order to increase the competition in the global flows.

The EU global strategy explicitly emphasized that the integration of the economy space should follow the principles for harmonized, balanced and sustainable development.

The evolution of changes in the EU economy structure, under the market influence, can be followed through the Economic constitution, which represents a framework of core objectives for economy growth stimulation and instruments for realization of those objectives. Since the Rome Treaty, via the European act, and further with Maastricht, Amsterdam, as well as Lisbon treaties, the growth of the competitiveness of the Euro Zone was planned to be realized simultaneously through the process of strengthening the economic and social cohesion among member countries.

In fact, in the initial phase of the EU development, the stimulation of a harmonious development of the union focused on creating a single market, in addition to the strengthening of competition, as well as the strengthening of the economic and social cohesion, in order to reduce the disparities between the different regions. In that manner, the development concept was constituted to mobilize the interest for economic integration of all member countries in a time when the structural funds had to have a corrective function of the market failures on a regional, social and structural level[55].

Actually, the basic characteristics of the Rome Treaty, explicitly reflected in the European act, express such policy (Figure 6).

---

55 The EU Structural Policy comprises of all the measures with which the objectives of regional, sectoral, horizontal or general political character are followed on EU level. There exist 5 financial funds and 4 initiatives of the Union: The European Regional Development Fund (ERDF), European Social Fund (ESF); European Fund for Development and Guarantee of the Agriculture (EFDGA), and initiatives: EQUAL, INTERREG, LEADER and URBAN.

The Maastricht Treaty features a review of the basic economic objectives, constitution of a new institutional system (European Monetary Union), new principles, as well as new activities which had completely different consequences for the future EU development (Figure 7). The Maastricht Treaty calls for three phases in the realization of the European Monetary Union project. The first and the second phase involve economic and institutional preparations for transition into the third phase: Project activation (introduction of the Euro).

The preparations mainly involved the realization of the nominal convergence criteria, which have been measured with performances of the monetary and fiscal policy. The third phase started with the establishment of the monetary Union, i.e. the institutions: The European System of Central Banks and the European Central Bank, which led to centralization of the monetary policy. The transitional project of establishing a synthetic regional currency (Euro) was completed with the Maastricht Act. There is no other example of such a monetary experiment in the most part of the developed countries.

Figure 6: economic structure of the Rome Treaty

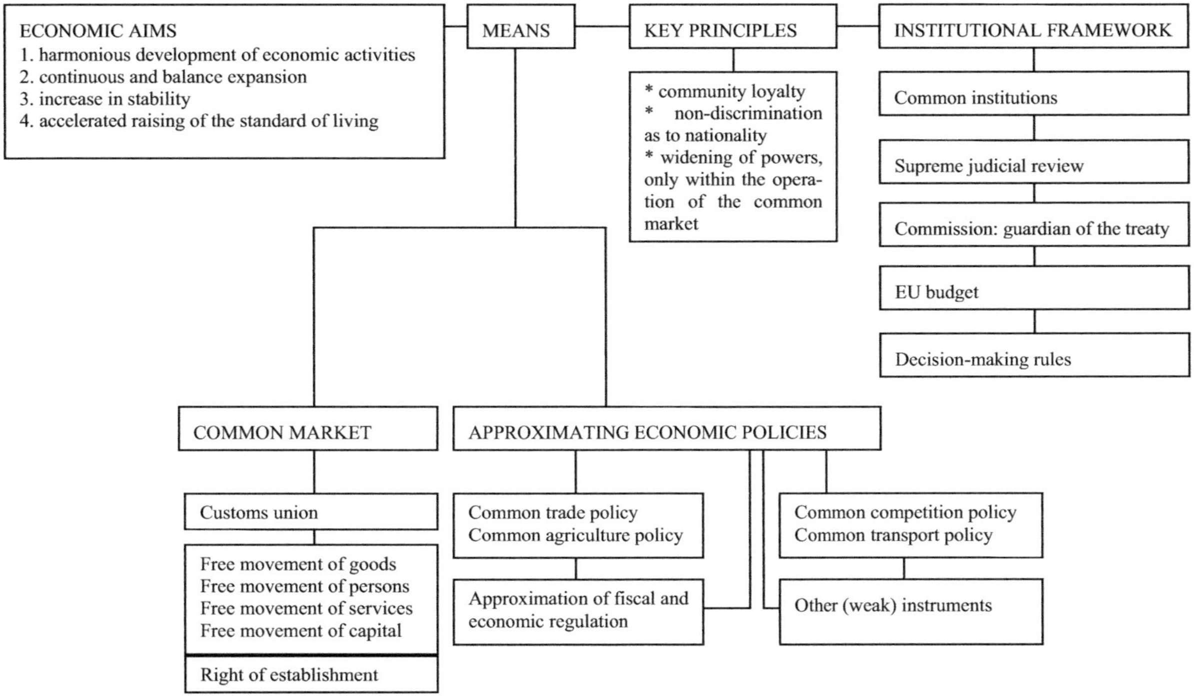

Source: Pelkmans (2006: 2).

Figure 7: economic structure of the Maastricht Treaty

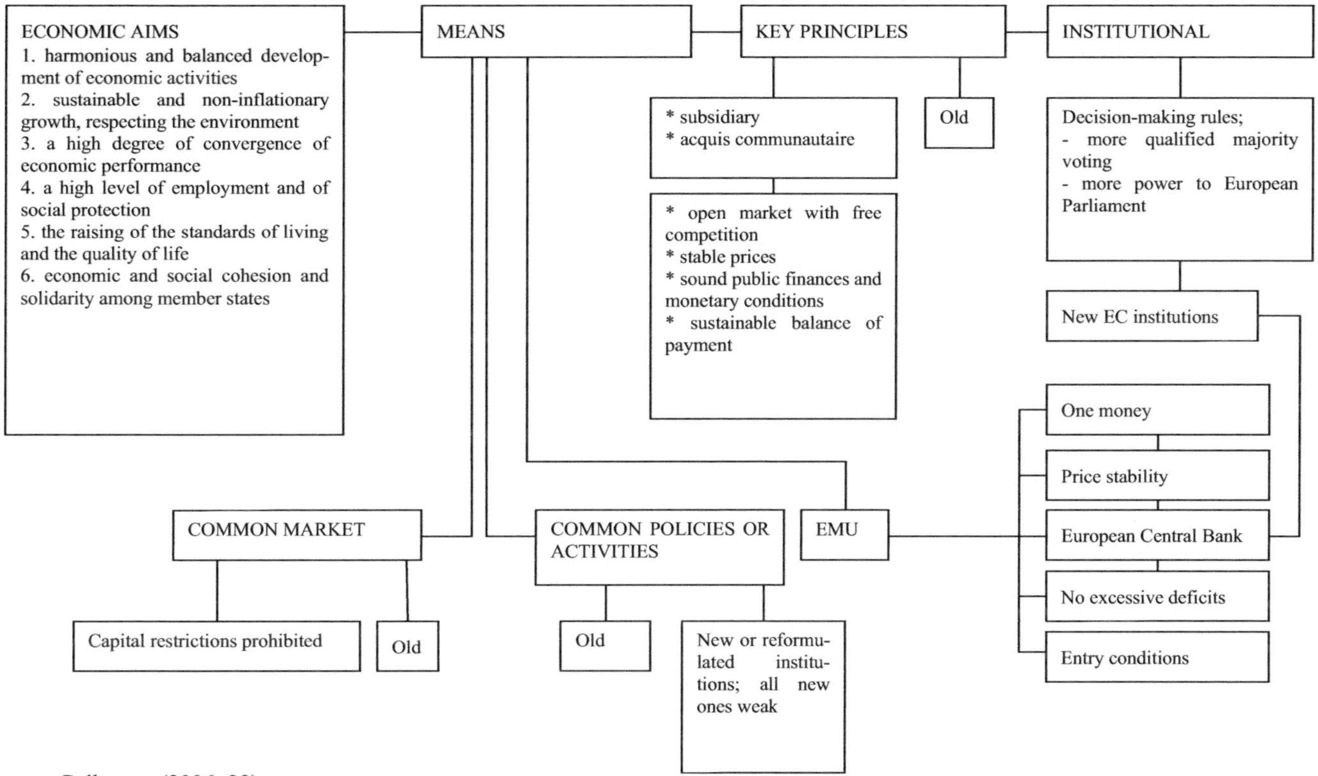

Source: Pelkmans (2006: 29).

The consequences regarding the economic order were determined on the basis of priority, the most important being stability of currency and prices with no trade-off, followed by the employment and regional development and the structural policies.

In fact, despite the previous phase of internal market restructuring, the new phase meant restructuring of the external global market and strengthening the competitive position of the European transnational business (mergers).

Therefore, the main objectives were a result of the priority of the macroeconomic stability policies (on both levels). Furthermore, the principle of subsidizing as part of the cohesion policy is defined today in relation with the competitive power[56]. That is how the conflict among the objectives and the instruments was established[57].

The constitution of the system of goals with the Maastricht Treaty obtained a declarative meaning in the period when instruments acted in opposite direction and depreciated the meaning of the system of goals. On an economic plan, the collision among goals and instruments also became empirically visible in the EU framework through: increase of unemployment, reduction of social rights, regional and social divergences, in spite of the fact that the nominal support of these goals was emphasized.

In the 90s, in addition to the qualitative overturn in the economic policy, quantitative changes also occurred. They were presented in a form of a dilemma for the strategy for eastern enlargement and focused on the question: Will the development be affected by the secondary enlargement trend taking into consideration that its constitutional directions were aimed at the enlargement and broadening of the process of economic and monetary integration? At the beginning the accent was put on the stance that true and credible broadening of the integration required stopping the process of the so called eastern enlargement of

---

56 One of the priority objectives of the cohesion policy stated in the Lisbon Agenda refer to the restructuring of the economic space, supported by the highly technological and competitive production systems that were concentrated in the propulsive centers of power that on the other hand were in conflict with the development support of the less developed regions.

57 An example of that kind of conflict is the employment. Support to the employment policies always occurs in more relaxed monetary – credit policies. In the case of establishment of a stability policy, the trade-off in relation employment – prices was a priori sacrificed and the stable prices became the "holy cow" of the stability policy. However, the growing problem of unemployment was being solving from the budget using different forms of interventions on the labor market.

EU. Similarly, an issue was raised regarding the acceptance of new policies in the mutual corpus of the Union. The dilemmas appeared, on the one hand, as an assessment of the consequences onto the budget as a result of the enlargement, especially from the "net payments" stance for the Common Agriculture Policy (CAP) as well as the support (subsidies) for harmonization with the EU standards for a constitutive regional policy. The other problem referred to the adaptation of the acquis and its implementation as one of the most important measures for business stimulation in the internal market. Can EU successfully manage the process of de facto implementation of the acquis? If not, the European legal system (above all the court) will be blocked and its authority will be discredited thus creating uncertainties among the businesses and the consumers. The risk of all these possibilities was foreseen, however at the end the stance has been made that the strategic course should be "Deepening, widening and enlargement: no trade off's"!

This approach contained the strategic elements of the European global strategy oriented towards consolidation of the economic ambient for the core business and expansionistic policy of accepting new territories for mobilization of new investments and markets. Without doubt, the process of enlargement had to bring benefits at an aggregate level.

In order to lower the risks from the process of enlargement of "premature" member countries, a constitutional platform for their implementation – the Copenhagen Treaty was prepared (Figure 8).

Figure 8: routine elements of enlargement strategy

Origin	Principle conditions
Treaty (Art. 49 EU)	"Every European State" can apply for EU membership
Copenhagen (Dec. 1993)	- Stable institutions, guaranteeing democracy, rules of law, human rights, and respect for and protection of minorities
	- A functioning market economy
	- The capacity (of the economy) to withstand competitive pressures and market forces within the Union
	- The capacity to take on obligations of EU membership, including the objectives of political, economic and monetary union
Madrid (Dec. 1995)	Administrative capacity guaranteeing the effective implementation of the *acquis*

The EU economic constitution obtained amendments in the Copenhagen criteria that were adjusted to the "maturity" of Eastern Europe and pertained to the integration processes. Vividly explained, a second track was established in which the formula 1 race was to take place on cobblestone, whereas the criteria were to absorb the going adrift of the track due to improperly prepared terrain at the start line.

The growth of efficiency and competitiveness as a result of the rapid development and prosperity in the frames of a more equal distribution of the EU growth results were the initial postulates for positive economic integration of the OECD countries. Therefore, the pace of enlargement within a period of three decades (1958 – 1995) arose as gradual process and had a qualitative dimension (the principle of efficiency was balanced with the equivalence). The eastern enlargement emerged on a shock – principle with large deviations from the basic criteria (assumptions for positive integration). Namely, the accent is put on a group of countries that were relatively poor. Never before has the average per-capita salary, been that low as in the period of EU accession. In the period when Ireland and Portugal were accessing in EU, the average salary decreased from the targeted 75% onto 65% compared with EU; with the accession of the EU-10 the average salary per capita decreased to 55,5%. The dispersion among them was also very large. The accession of Bulgaria and Romania additionally decreased the census to 28,7%; 26,7%, respectively.

The political economy of the so called "me-too" association was marked with notable elements of global strategy. In that manner, the eastern countries passed the prime stage of globalization which was presented through the Washington consensus and left marks for most of the countries through emergence of economic depression. The second stage of globalization was presented through the Europeanization. The ideological platform remained the same: The neoliberal concept and the rigid monetarism, in this case the process changed the form suggested from Brussels burdened with bureaucratic procedure. In fact, the regional orientation of the eastern European countries toward EU meant their structural adjustment and functional correlation with the European market. Now it is clear that EU has a double challenge to meet. The first is global competitiveness and the second avoiding the risk and costs of widening disparities of all levels. Are these two goals complementary or in conflict with each other? Is growth and successful restructuring in the East and the South a threat or asset for world competitiveness? Clear answers have not been provided yet. Some facts explain that the differences between the poor and rich EU member states will become deeper in the future[58].

The dramatic changes in the New Europe maintain the budget with decreased financial perspectives. The direct support of the EU funds from the budget for

58 The existence of the difference in the amount of funds that are given by the European funds for surpassing development problems according to the objective 1, shows the fact that the three Baltic countries that are the biggest aid receivers at the moment compared with the new member states which get less than 100 Euro per capita on annual basis the cohesion value for the old member states is 269,9 Euro for Greece, 282,3 Euro for Portugal, 163,7 Euro for Spain.

2006 – 2013 in the process of convergence is implemented through restructuring of the financial instruments and decrease of the financial resources[59].

The other aspect of the disparities was based on the unemployment growth, implicitly the inequalities in society which was directly reflected on derogation of the model of the social market economy. That process is tightly correlated with the monetary stability model in a time when the monetary mechanism of EMU can provide low inflation rates and decreased real interest rates which is important for the process of investment. However, these market process mechanisms are correlated with the national fiscal policies based on the principle of subsidiary. The limit of the fiscal deficits and the total of the public debt in GDP of the member countries are put in function of the purposes of providing stability of the financial markets[60]. Therefore, there is a forthcoming battle for EU for decreasing of the tax rate that is in correlation not just with the traditional government expenditures but with the scope of social transfers that has stable high values.

An impending circumstance is that the mechanisms for shocks absorption due to structural adjusting of the comprehensive offer in the integration process in the European Market do not function in the EU. The limited mobility of the labor increases the unemployment rates (with an average of 9% in EU 27, 2006)[61].

The second mechanism for absorption of the negative shocks is the limited flexibility of the rent – the prices go down. This valve is closed in the European Union because of the high rate of the employees' social care through the social legislation.

---

59 One of the most important structural funds for the future is represented by the cohesion funds that should support the reformed regional policy. The mere future of this fund indicates the extent to which regional policies will be marginalized in a time when the heterogenic economic structure of membership needs a serious approach toward this issue. In that way, up to 2013 the reduction of money in the fund is planned to be decreased up to 0,35% of GDP of EU as it was the case in 1990 when only 15 EU countries were members and their salary per capita was much higher compared with the current 12 new EU member countries.

60 According to the Maastricht criteria the budget deficits are limited to 3% of GDP and the public debt to 60%. These limits are faced with huge reactions in the EU. The euro zone is developing in a problematic fiscal regime in which the economic – political coordination can hardly be realized due to structural reasons.

61 The migration is a very important mechanism in the USA for adjustment of the human resources' supply and demand by profiles in different parts of the country. The migration helps in providing low unemployment rates (3 – 4%). However, similar role of the migration could not be expected in the EU due to lingual, cultural and traditional reasons.

The dynamic changes in the age structure also represent an impending condition. The participation of old people, due to these changes, will increase from 25% to 50% in most European countries. That position is expressed in the planned 4% growth of the allowances and health care expenses until 2050, which is in conflict with the long – term intention of decreasing the budget expenses in the member countries as a part of the stabilization package.

As a matter of fact, the "catching up with" the global tendency by the EU and the rigorousness of the question of companies' profitability, which is strongly monitored by the global capital market, are in direct conflict with the welfare state in the long run. This at the same time opens the question for its reforming (please read: reduction). The creating of a secondary mechanism for social transfers by way of supranational fiscal activism should follow in the future in case of establishing a policy union.

The process becomes more cumbersome as a result of the more heterogeneous structure of members at a time when less effective mechanisms for decreasing the developing disparities exist. In the meantime, the battle for "catching up" with the tendency continues through the comparison of the dollar and the euro currency power on the global market.

3. Comparison of the potentials between the European and the American economies

In order for the model of capitalism to get a comparative advantage in the global economic system it is important that the economic potentials of the regional integrated markets be reviewed, i.e. the comparative advantages and disadvantages of the euro countries vs. USA. Knowing the fact that synthetic representatives of the markets are the international currencies (the Euro and the US dollar) the trends of affirmation of the currencies are clearly connected with the changes in economic power among different regions.

The core factors in the international affirmation of the currency are: 1) the quantity of GDP that presents the standard for measuring the force of the economy; 2) the scope and the quality of the international trade cooperation; 3) the region has to have developed foreign exchange and financial markets that are deep enough to provide financially liquid assets; 4) the currency that aims for status of international assets has to be stabile as compared to the purchasing power parity (low inflation rate) and relatively stable rate of foreign exchange market.

The analysis for accomplishing the above mentioned performances shows that the quantity of the GDP per capita gives a comparative advantage of the American economy (see Table 1). The GDP of USA is 49,5% higher compared to EU-25. In order to obtain a clearer image of the economic potential of the regions, the economic growth factors should be differentiated. The European region has comparative adventives on the goods and services market, i.e. shows better performance in the export sector compared to the USA. Therefore, the deficit in the US trade exchange in 2006 grew up to 857 billion US$ or 6,3% of the GDP vis-à-vis the EU deficit that in normal proportions is 2,2% of GDP (European Economy, 2007). The facts show that the economic growth of EU is based on realistic fundaments (industrial production). Due to the fact that EU has lower labour productivity that is not reflecting on the export flows, the non-price facts of competitiveness of differential products (quality, image, innovation), have immense importance. On the contrary, the basic source of growth in USA is the flow of capital from foreign countries with which the structural imbalance of the American economy is being balanced in the long term. The American economy realizes its supremacy on the basis of the development of the financial foreign exchange markets through which massive flows of capital are taken from countries with surplus and are directed toward the American markets.

Table 1: Europe vs. USA: comparison of the potentials

GDP per capita at current market prices			
	2000	**2005**	**EU-25 = 100 2005**
EU-25	20.100	23.400	100,0
EU=15	22.100	25.400	108,6
Euro Area	21.900	25.00	106,6
United States	30.600	35.000	149,5
Labour productivity			
	2000	**2005**	
EU-25	100,0	100,0	
EU=15	107,5	106,3	
Euro Area	108,5	106,3	
United States	132,1	136,1	
Inflation rate			
	2000	**2005**	
EU=25	2,4	2,2	
EU=15	1,9	2,1	
Euro area	2,1	2,2	
United States	3,4	3,4	
Main players in the world market for goods			

	Exports (2000 - 2005)	Imports (2000 - 2005)	Balance (2000 - 2005)	
EU-25 (1)	858 1.071	996 1.177	-138 -106	
EU=15 (2)	942 1.173	1.033 1.242	-91 - 69	
United States (3)	845 730	1.362 1.226	-517 - 497	
Foreign direct investment (1)				
	Inward	**Outward**	**Outflows**	**Net FDI**
EU-25	69.789	152.541	82.752	-4,5
EU=15	81.115	171.943	90.828	-6,3

Source: Eurostat Yearbook (2007).

In future, the development of the capital market should have a significant role in the restructuring scenario of the financial sector in the euro zone. Currently, the euro zone is a net exporter of capital. The tendency of the flow of the capital in the business will continue to grow strongly. During that process, the restructuring of the financial institutions will be handled through fusions and acquisitions that will help in establishment of a profitable banking sector. The reduction of interest rates should provide a strong incentive for realization of investment projects especially in the high technology sectors.

The Euro zone could be perceived as a banking zone that will, in the forthcoming period be actively involved in redistribution of capital as a result of development performances. That position was, until now characteristic for USA, which throughout the market mechanisms absorbed a substantial foreign capital and then again that same capital was redistributed to other countries. The USA is the biggest importer of capital in the world and part of that capital is used for financing the budget deficit. Cumulatively observed, the USA is the largest world debtor. In addition, its foreign exchange reserves are very modest (73,521 Billion USD in February 2008 (Wikipedia, 2008)) compared to the quantity of foreign exchange trade, the current deficits in balance of payment and the highly cumulative external debt.

The power and the stability of the Euro are significant for its role as a reserve currency. The consolidation of the international position of the Euro depends on the internal stability (the low inflation) and external stability (the currency stability). The performances in the Euro region in the past few years show high stability, and that reflects on the increasing role of the Euro as a reserve currency (Table 2). The role of the Euro grows especially in the insurance of the short – term debts, where its participation is bigger than that of the US Dollar (see Table 3). Such tendencies are connected to the actual USD credibility losing processes, because of its instability. However, USA has acquired the position of the largest world economy due to the quantity of GDP, highly developed capital and money markets and the strong monetary policy. The perspectives of the Euro – zone are based on the larger participation in the world trade, as well as the larger foreign exchange reserves as elements for long – term stability in the region.

Table 2: currency shares in foreign exchange reserves*

	Dec 01	Dec 02	Dec 03	Dec 04	Dec 05	Sep 06
Global (in %)						
USD	71,4	67,0	65,9	65,8	66,6	65,6
EUR	19,2	23,8	25,2	24,9	24,3	25,2

* disclosed currency composition at current exchange rates
Source: ECB based on IMF and ECB calculations.

In the competitive battle for the increase of the regions' attractiveness for foreign capital, the key factor will be the achieving of higher real rates of economy growth. The region which will provide higher long – term rates of economic growth – sustainable GDP growth which is based on profitable export production has better chances of attracting foreign capital. The competitive battle between USA and EU is expected to increase in the future, and new forms of hidden and open political pressures will be used that will also involve the countries which are not directly involved in the two rival regions.

If the strategies, in the process for consolidation of the positions in the USA and EU regions, are orientated towards a global tendency, i.e. financial market strengthening and long – term macroeconomic stability, the development sustainability will largely depend on the fundamental factors where the social and political stability of the region will have a significant role.

Table 3: major currencies' shares in gross issuance of international debt securities

	Average 2004Q3 - 2005Q2	2005 Q3	2005 Q4	2006 Q1	2006 Q2	2006 Q3
Short-term international debt securities						
Euro	37,0	37,9	35,0	33,7	38,0	38,3
US dollar	39,6	36,5	39,2	40,2	36,5	37,9
Long-term international debt securities						
Euro	35,6	30,3	25,1	28,7	26,9	28,5
US dollar	39,5	42,5	48,8	43,8	50,2	49,9

Source: ECB based on BIS and ECB calculations.

4. Model in crisis

The neo-liberal concept requires termination of all limitations for free flow of the capital on an international level. In that way, the countries which accept the capital have not only fully deregulated institutional structures, developed markets of financial derivates and stable macroeconomic policies, but they are ready for unpredictable changes in the flow of the capital. This concept assumes that the unpredictable processes will not be transferred in the most developed regions – USA and EU to a significant extent. The latest developments in the American financial market show a defect in the neoliberal development strategy that even the most powerful economy is not immune to. The answer to the question as to how USA experienced the gigantic house price bubble lays exactly in the fundaments of the neo-liberal model that begin with sustainability in time and quantity of the high trade deficits if they are financed with the business flow of the capital from countries with surplus (see Makin, 1990).

The USA has been running an increasing trade deficit since the early 1980s[62]. The excess of imports over exports is paid for by newly printed dollars or treasury bonds in countries running trade surpluses (like China, Japan) using their increasing stock of dollars to invest in USA assets in order to earn a return. The return flow pushes up assets values in the USA including property and treasury bonds. Higher bond prices go with lower yields and therefore low interest rates. Low interest rates push up US consumption, US domestic debt and cause US deficit to grow. That is the story of the invisible hand of the American empire. The mechanism has generated impressive economic growth in both deficit and surplus countries: but it is inherently unstable. Larger trade imbalance generates large increases in financial transactions and rising financial fragility.

These situations are best reflected through the growth of the stock value. The American stock exchange indexes from the '90s rose extremely compared to the yields of the American companies. The overestimation of the stock exchange indexes indicated a speculative bubble that, through the wealth effect, had an influence on the increase of consumption and recurrently on the growth of pro-

62 The analysts of Bank of International Settlements evaluated that the top external – trade deficits of USA must at some point in time imply weaker dollar as well as appreciation of the yen and the euro. If that happens before the economies of Japan and EU achieve strong growth, the diminished growth of the global economy will become visible. Also, the "overheating" of the American economy through the forthcoming recessions will undermine the stock exchange market that will consequently decrease the financial property and reduce expenditures. If at the same time, the dollar depreciates under the pressure of the flow of the capital and the big trade deficit, the period of stagflation would not be impossible (Bank for International Settlements, 1999: 141-142).

duction of the American economy. The dimensions of the relation between the flows of the stock exchange indexes and the rate of growth is evident from the fact that 30% of the population's assets are kept in securities.

The bursting of the property bubble in the US in 2006 triggered a sequence of events, where slowly, banking and financial operators became aware that the foundation of the debt pyramid was quicksand. The US house buyer (below the top 20% of households) became increasingly insolvent. The large international banks, hoping for the best, waited until the summer of 2007 before they began to acknowledge that many of their complex debt instruments (ABSs) were non-performing: the debts could not be repaid, yet the banks were counting them as revenue-yielding assets. But in August 2007 they jammed on the brakes and cut lending, including to each other and in many other parts of the Atlantic economy (not just the US) as well.

As a result, the year 2008 represented a real purgatory for the global bank industry, and during the first 12 months of the crisis, it was unable to be recognized. The annihilation of billions of dollars of capital was effectuated with disappearance of many banks such as Lehman Brothers and Bear Sterns. The knock-on effect of the fall in house prices and the rise in repossessions in the US means that all other mortgage markets are in trouble. Unemployment is growing, consumption is stagnant. The figure to watch is the ratio of total USA debt to GDP. The ratio of rising debt to GDP has fuelled US growth in the past several decades (it went from 240% in 1990 to 340% in 2006). If total debt to GDP ratio suddenly flattens, the US will experience a recession. However if US debt/GDP falls, the world will experience a recession. The reason is that fall will be accompanied by a decline in US consumption, which, in turn accounts for at least 20% of world consumption. The crisis has already spread to housing markets and mortgage lenders in the US, Germany, France, Spain, and South Korea. It will soon affect China and Japan, which are the two biggest holders by far of US national debt and stand to lose the most from steep dollar devaluation. They, are also large net exporters to the US, and will suffer from a fall in their US exports as the US contracts.

However, it should be noted that the actual recession which resulted from the global financial crisis is not a standard recession, described in the macroeconomic books nor does it look like the World crisis from 1929 – 1933. The current recession appeared from the hyper production of the financial derivatives or from the "crediting of the credit lines" phenomena with suspicious collateral (security). The speculative dimension of the contemporary crisis which started through the financial markets, emphasize the aspect of impossibility of recognition of the depth, width and the time duration of the crisis. In the same time, it highlights the problem of inefficiency of the current instruments for coping with the crisis. In 2008, the USA central bank decreased the discount rate almost to zero and offered a huge amount of liquidity to the banks, but this time without any result. Since the monetary policy became ineffective and the economy fell down, as it is well known from the "the liquidity trap" theory, first the USA and then the other countries started with a substantial application of the fiscal policy in order to rescue the financial systems and the economies from the horrible recession. Fiscal (policies) activism that were not interesting the last few decades are now widely recommended by senior politicians and academic economists, and even by the conservative IMF.

The turmoil might even induce a shift in the neo-liberal consensus about the role of government in governing the market. Even the industrial and financial sectors might become more sympathetic to the idea of more limits on some kinds of markets – limits decided through a political process, in line with a social-democratic vision. However, Larry Elliott (2007) puts a useful caveat: "The sad fact is that only a deep recession is likely to generate enough national self-disgust at the destructive get-rich-quick value system oozing out of the City (of London) to create the political pressure for reform".

The current official consensus (of the IMF, the World Bank and the OECD) is that the world economy faces a serious contraction, and that the developed countries are already in recession. In January 2009, the IMF significantly reduces the corrections of its projections for economic growth in 2009 to 0,5% (as compared to the predictions of 2,2% in November 2008), which would represent the worst result after the Second World War (IMF, 2009). The IMF expect that the real activity of the developed countries will decline for 2%, which means that the drop in the USA will be 1,5%, the Euro zone 2% and in Japan 2,5% (see Table 4)

Table 4: IMF: projections for the global economic development in 2009 – 2010

From year to year				
			Projection	
	2007	2008	2009	2010
World output	**5,2**	**3,4**	**0,5**	**3,0**
Developed economies	2,7	1,0	-2,0	1,1
USA	2,0	1,1	-1,6	1,6
Euro zone	2,6	1,0	-2,0	0,2
Japan	2,4	-0,3	-2,6	0,6

Note: The real effective exchange rates are estimated that they will not be changed on the level that prevailed in the period from December 08 2008 until January 05 2009.
Source: IMF (2009).

Four conclusions can be drawn from the analysis of the long term consequences of the financial crisis both in the developed and developing countries. First, the increase of unemployment and decrease of real estate prices will persist for another 5-6 years. Second, the decline of production will last for only 2 years on average; third, the stock prices will continue their steady decline for approximately 3,5 years. Fourth, almost all crises have had impacts on the increase of the public debt, i.e. this happened in 88% of the crisis episodes that occurred after the Second World War (Reinhart and Rogoff, 2008).

If the consequences from these analyses are taken in consideration, the main risk for the EU economy is the expected increase of the unemployment as well as the growth of the public debt. Within these tendencies, the EU integrative processes become a less sustainable scenario for the neoliberal model. In fact, a new economic curtain is falling down between Western and Eastern Europe, underlining the conflict that the single European Market and EMU opened with a rather heterogeneous economic structure.

Thus, the crisis commenced in USA and spilled over to the EU becoming more complex since it is encumbered with the effort of sustaining the monetary stability in circumstances where the internal tissue is collapsing because of the economic, social, national and political distortions.

The big trade-off of New Europe signifies whether it should wait to be involved in the crisis scenario following the trend of convergence towards fast globalization of the flow of the capital, or by learning from the contemporary experience will draw the red line and be more strictly oriented to establishing protected mechanisms of the financial system as well as reforms and affirmation of the structural policies that will endorse the model of social market economy. Throughout history, Europe has demonstrated a firm ability to make the necessary upturn on time[63].

References

Bank for International Settlements (1999), *69th Annual Report*, Basle: Bank for International Settlements.

Elliott, L. (2007), "When money lenders cry for hand-outs", *Guardian*, 10 September.

63 After the break down of the Bretton Woods system of the fix foreign exchange rates aiming to emancipate from the dominant economic and financial position of the USA in the world economy and the tribulations of the dollar that appeared as world currency in the 60's the developed European economies decided to constitute a European regional monetary system.

European Economy (2007), *Annual Report on the Euro Area*, No. 5, Brussels: European Commission.

Eurostat Yearbook (2007), *Europe in Figures - Eurostat Yearbook 2006-07*, Brussels: Eurostat.

IMF (2008), "Fiscal policy for the crisis", *IMF Staff Position Note*, SPN, 08/01.

IMF (2009), "World economic outlook update", available at http://www.imf.org/external/pubs/ft/weo/2009/update/01/pdf/0109.pdf.

Makin, J. (1990), "International imbalances: The role of exchange rates", in R. O'Brien and I. Iversen (eds), *Finance and the International Economy*, Oxford: Oxford University Press.

Pelkmans, J. (2006), *European Integration Methods and Economic Analysis*, Harlon: Third Ed. Ediugurh Gate.

Reinhart, C. and K. Rogoff (2008), "The aftermath of financial crisis", *Draft Paper*.

Soros, G. (1998), *The Crisis of the Global Capitalism. Open Society Endangered*, New York: Public Affairs.

Wikipedia (2008), "List of countries by foreign exchange reserves", *Wikipedia article*, available at http://en.wikipedia.org/wiki/List_of_countries_by_foreign_exchange_reserves.

2. Old-age pension reforms in the EU: innovation, diffusion and Europeanization

Cristina Matos

1. Introduction

Pension reforms are an important policy concern throughout the EU. Globalisation, population ageing, and irregular working careers are expected to worsen system sustainability.

EU countries have reformed their pension systems for some time now. In most Western European countries, discussions about a pension crisis and reforms started in the 1980s and accelerated in the 1990s (Myles and Pierson, 2001). In Central Europe and Baltics, pension systems were typically reformed twice: in the early 1990s countries established contribution-based systems and in from the mid-1990s reforms usually involved the development of (compulsory or voluntary) private pensions.

In this paper, we investigate how the notions of innovation and dissemination can help us understand the process of pension reforms.

Institutionalism conventionally uses concepts imported from innovation analyses. Institutional evolution approaches have imported considerably from innovation studies, such as the economics of QWERTY (David, 1985; Arthur, 1990). Like technological dynamics, institutional evolution is supposed to be path-dependent. This type of pattern is the result of a branching process, which makes branch switching costly.

Myles and Pierson (2001) applied the notion of path dependence to pension reform. These authors underline increasing returns can account for national pension reform differences. In a pay-as-you-go system those who are working pay the pensions of the retired population and expect that in the future other workers will finance their own pensions. This unfunded system can be contrasted with funded systems where worker's contributions finance their own future pensions. In mature public pay-as-you-go settings, switching to funded settings would be extremely costly. Consequently, mature PAYG systems (as in Canada, France, Germany, Italy and Sweden) introduced only gradual reforms, with a limited shift towards funding, while latecomers (Australia, Denmark, Ireland, the Netherlands, New Zealand, Switzerland and UK) had, by the 1990s, created a virtually universal funded system in addition to the unfunded public program (Myles and Pierson, 2001). As in most institutional analyses, initial conditions, environmental conditions and small events can have a sizeable, lasting impact. PAYG was a good option in the 1950s-1960s: i) it allowed the state to control large capital funds; ii) it was an alternative to distrusted private capitalization; iii) it brought enormous political benefits; iv) it was consistent with modest payroll taxes (actually less important than they would have been in a private system); v) its replacement rates were high; and vi) it was sustainable given high participation combined with high fertility (Myles and Pierson, 2001).

Still, pension reforms have been so important that some authors question the role of path dependence in understanding these processes. Overbye (2008) considers recent pension reforms to be *path breaking*. The divergence between these authors is actually much deeper. What is at stake is to define what a *major* reform actually is. To Myles and Pierson only the transition from a pay-as-you-go to a funded arrangement is a major shift. Others, such as Barr and Rutkowski (2006) distinguish *paradigmatic* changes (introducing private pensions) from parametric reforms (public system reforms). This implicitly downgrades other reforms, some of which have had a major impact. Important shifts of emphasis, other than funding or privatisation, were introduced (e.g. Hinrichs and Kangas, 2004). Some countries changed radically the pension calculation method, reducing considerably pension replacement rates.

In a recent work (Matos, 2009), I have sustained that similar reforms have been hybridised into path dependent pension settings. This approach allows us to consider different types of reform while maintaining the path dependence hypothesis. Path dependence means that, at each moment in time, alternative reform costs depend on the pre-existing system. It does not entail pension evolution is deterministic.

We thus use the term "pension innovation" as a set of pension reforms with a common aim. We will investigate whether EU countries adopted similar "pension innovations" and how important are national differences. Afterwards, we will examine how the notion of "dissemination" can help us understand similarities and differences in "pension innovations". We note, particularly, that the diffusion of ideas on pension reform promotes the adoption of similar principles. Still, this does not mean there will be convergence between the pension systems, since institutional transfer gives rise to hybridisation. At the end we deduce the implications for Europeanization, defined as pension coordination across the EU.

2. Innovation

Table 5 presents selected pension innovations in the EU. These include four sets of pension reforms introduced in most EU counties. It also outlines major inter-country differences. In this section, we will briefly present these reforms as innovations. It should be noted that these were not the only reforms (particularly financing methods have also been reformed and system were increasingly unified). They are a set of intertwined pension innovations, which we have selected because of their direct impact on protection and insurance.

Table 5: selected pension "innovations" in the EU

Similar trends	Variation
Developing complementary pensions	Different national templates; Coverage differences.
Enhancing the benefit-contribution link: -Reference years increase; -NDCs.	Different determination formula; Replacement rates disparities.
Promoting later retirement -retirement age increase; -early retirement limitation.	Different norms; Different retirement ages.
Means-tested protection	There is a major divide between universal and non-universal protection.

2.1. Developing complementary pensions

Complementary pension coverage is generally very weak in Southern Europe and virtually universal in Denmark, the Netherlands and Sweden. In some EU countries complementary systems are obligatory at least to a part of labour market participants; in others, they are voluntary. Complementary pensions arrangements are very different across the EU. Although they have in common that they are not state-run, they can take distinct juridical forms. We can distinguish particularly occupational and individual plans. Individual pensions are run by a private pension fund. While a separate fund can manage occupational pensions, this can also be done by the company, social partners.

Occupational pension arrangements combine elements from pension funds as well as state-pensions (Matos, 2009). Indeed, like public pensions, and contrary to individual funds, occupational pensions are financed through employer contributions. Furthermore, they can be funded or pay-as-you-go. Occupational pensions are dominant in Austria, Belgium, Denmark, France, Ireland, Luxembourg, the Netherlands, Sweden and UK. These often date back longer than a century and pre-existed state-run pensions. They have evolved is specific national contexts and are very differentiated across the EU (Matos, 2009).

Conversely, complementary pensions are dominated by individual accounts in Central European and Baltic new member states, as well as in Finland, Portugal, Greece and Spain. Individual private pensions can be voluntary or compulsory. In the late 1990s-early 2000s, compulsory individual private pensions were introduced throughout CEE (except Czech Republic and Slovenia). Lithuania developed a hybrid system where joining an individual fund is voluntary, yet irreversible.

Throughout the EU, governments have tried to fuel voluntary pension accounts through fiscal incentives. Furthermore, as state-pension replacement rate decreases, people have incentives to supplement their pensions with savings. While national private pension regulations differ, all countries strike to secure private pensions. Private pension regulations include the supervision of fund operations and investments. For example equity allocations have exposed funds to large losses in 2008 (OECD, 2008). These were more limited in countries such as Denmark and the Netherlands where pension funds shifted their portfolio from equities to bonds between 2001 and 2007 (OECD, 2008). This portfolio reallocation appears to be partly driven by the introduction of stricter, risk-based funding requirements.

2.2. Promoting the benefit-contribution link

Consumption smoothing over the life-cycle is a major aim of any pension system (Barr and Diamond, 2008). The benefit-contribution link enhances consumption smoothing. The nature of this link depends on which pension determination model is adopted. These can be defined benefit (DB) or defined contribution (DC). In DC arrangements, future benefits depend strictly on past contributions. As such, in DC settings there is a strict benefit-contribution link. DC templates are based on a considerable benefit individualisation and are based on actuarial fairness. Conversely, in a DB template, benefits are determined by a formula, typically linked to wages earned during a certain time span (e.g. last 15 years, best 20 years). The benefit-contribution link in DB systems depends on the length of wages considered in the formula. The longer the wage record integrated, the stronger that link will be.

While individual plans are often DC, there is a considerable number of DB occupational plans. State pensions in the EU 27 are dominantly DB. These were traditionally final wage systems. Recently, public systems in Latvia, Sweden, and Poland adopted notionally defined contribution (NDCs) systems, where individual contributions, and yielded returns are converted into a stream of pension payments using a formula based on life expectancy. This will also be the case for Italian labour market entrants from 1995. The transition from a DB system to NDC pensions has increased the benefit-contribution link. On the other hand, most countries augmented the wage history considered by the DB pension formula. From 2002, Finland and Portugal consider the entire work history; this is also the case in Austria and Slovakia from 2004. Like in NCD systems, the Finnish and Portuguese new pension systems integrate a lifetime coefficient, adjusting future pensions to increases in life expectancy.

In spite of a similar emphasis on contribution-benefit link, there are important national differences. In Denmark and the Netherlands public pensions are flat-rate and thus independent of contributions. In these two countries, virtually universal complementary systems guarantee the wage-pension nexus. Flat-rate public pensions are more concerned with protection than with consumption smoothing during the life-course.

The aggregate replacement rate is a proxy for the association between average benefit and contribution. It measures the ratio between average pension and average wages before retiring. Figure 9 shows aggregate replacement rates are very different. In general they decreased over the last years; this was not the case in Belgium, Denmark, and Ireland, where they were relatively low. They dropped dramatically in Italy, Latvia, Greece and Portugal.

Figure 9: average replacement rate, 2003-07

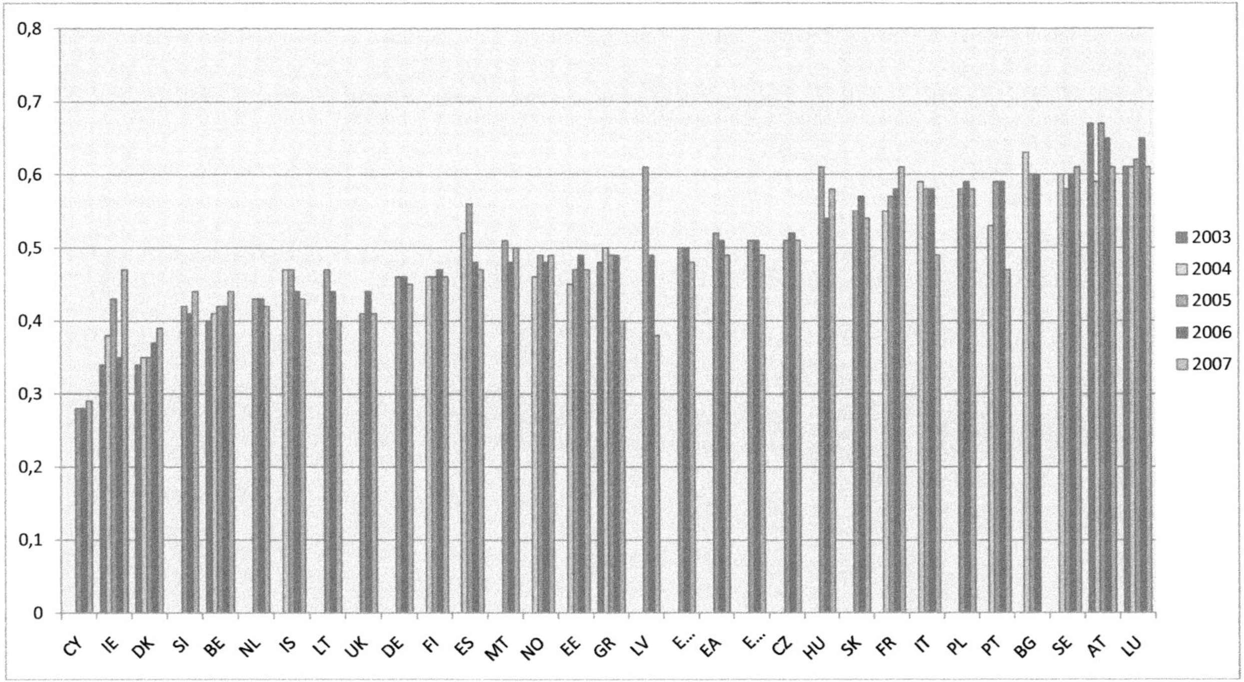

Source: Eurostat.

Since pension calculation changes are phased-out, future replacement rates are expected to decline further. On the other hand, complementary pensions replacement rates are expected to rise. Between 2005 and 2010, total net replacement ratios are expected to decline by 54% in Malta, 33% in Poland, 22% in Slovenia and as much as 17% in France and 15% in Sweden. These projections are based on important increases in voluntary pensions of 21% in Denmark, 16% in Italy and 15% in Germany. The replacement rate for the average worker retiring in 2005 will decline within 10 years by 25 percentage points in Poland, and as much as 16 in Greece, 14 in Hungary and 12 in France.

2.3. Promoting later retirement

Early retirement was used to accommodate unemployment surge in Western Europe in 1970s and 1980s and in Central European and Baltic countries during the 1990s. This strategy was justified by older workers weak re-employment possibilities. Still, it had financial costs because it depressed contributor-to-pensioner ratios. Recent reforms have tried to revert this trend by increasing retirement entitlement age and with incentives to live longer working careers and penalising early retirement.

Statutory ages vary between 60 (in France) and 65 (in most countries) (see Figures 10 and 11). In most countries, men are entitled to retire around 65 (Figure 10). Women entitlement age is sometimes weaker (Figure 11). These do not translate linearly to retirement patterns. The correlation between statutory age and average estimated retirement age is weak: in 2007 it was 0,40 for men and 0,42 for women. Average retirement age is higher in Bulgaria, Ireland, the Netherlands and Sweden. Only Czech men and both men and women in Bulgaria and Romania retire on average after entitlement. Still, the dimension and implications of early retirement are distinct across EU countries. The gap between statutory and effective retirement age was particularly important in Poland, Belgium and Bulgaria until the early 2000s. This gap has been reduced, particularly among men and average retirement age increased in all EU countries except Denmark. Throughout the EU, early retirement reforms integrated a combination of bonus/malus system designed to fuel incentives to labour market participation. While DC arrangements and NDCs automatically establish a set of incentives to retire later, this is not the case in final salary systems. Workers retiring before statutory age are subject to an actuarial reduction. Additionally, most countries also increased the number of contributing years necessary to take-up a full pension.

Figure 10: average exit age for men[64], 2001[65] and 2007[66] and retirement statutory age in 2007

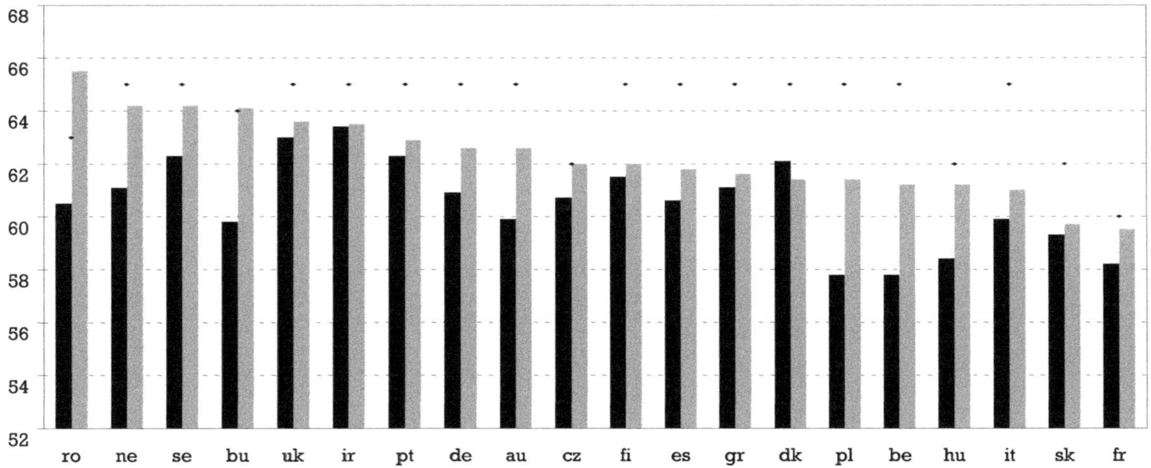

Source: Eurostat (for average retirement ages) and Missoc (for statutory retirement ages).

64 The average exit age gives the average age at which active persons definitely withdraw from the labour market. It is based on a probability model considering the relative changes of activity rates from one year to another at a specific age. The indicator is based on the EU Labour Force Survey.

65 2002 for Bulgaria.

66 2006 for Bulgaria, Ireland and Romania; 2005 for Hungary.

Figure 11: average exit age for women, 2001[67] and 2007[68] and retirement statutory age in 2007

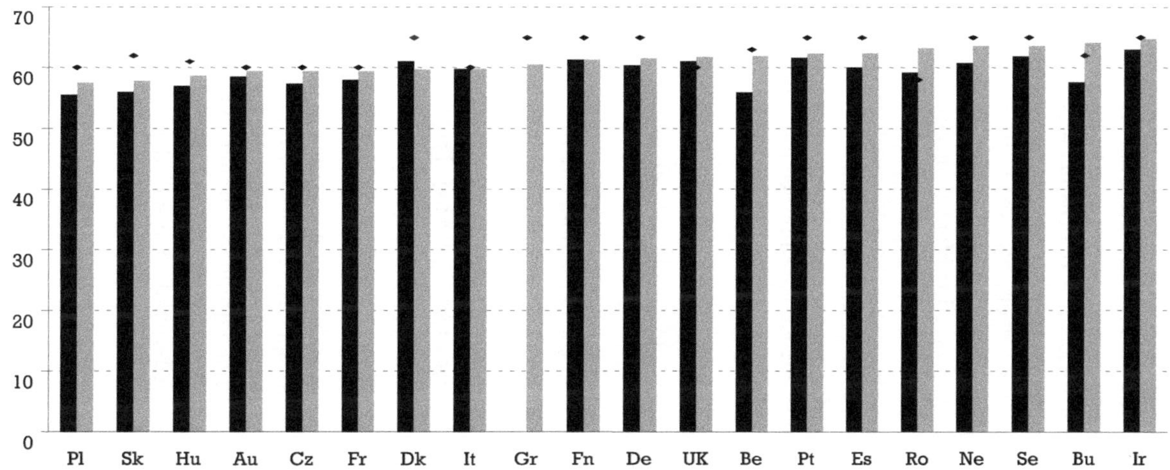

Source: Eurostat (for average retirement ages) and Missoc (for statutory retirement ages).

67 2002 for Bulgaria.

68 2006 for Bulgaria, Ireland and Romania; 2005 for Hungary.

2.4. Means-tested protection

Protection from poverty is one major aim of pension systems. Figure 12 depicts schematically protection arrangements throughout the EU. These are perceived as a set of building blocks. All countries have a means-tested social assistance covering the entire population. In countries like Slovakia and Lithuania this is the only protection available to pensioners. This was also the case in Germany until recently, when a minimum means-tested pension was introduced. Only those who have contributed a minimum number of years are entitled to this type of protection. In addition to these arrangements, some countries also have an universal protection for every person after retirement age whose income is beneath a certain minimum. This third protection block is means-tested.

Denmark, Sweden and the Netherlands have an additional universal protection to every permanent resident; this is not subject to means tests. These arrangements, originally citizenship-based in Sweden and Denmark, evolved, due to EU non-discrimination directives, to residence-based protection. Finland abandoned non-means-tested protection in 1986.

While national trends are different, there is a similar drift. Throughout the EU, means-tested universal pensions are increasingly used and have become the dominant protection arrangement in the EU.

In Sweden and Italy the NDC system carried eliminating the minimum pension, which was formerly paid to everyone after a certain period (as is the case in block two). This would be contrary to NDC functioning.

Sweden increased the universal means-tested pension. Protection was consolidated in Ireland, Portugal and Spain where basic pension growth exceeded inflation.

In conclusion, while EU countries introduced similar pension innovations, there are important national differences; specific reforms were different and the emerging pension systems are differentiated. We will use the process of dissemination to explain i) why countries introduced similar reforms; and ii) why existing systems remain different. We will address the first question using the notion of epistemic communities. Afterwards, we will develop an institutional account for diversity, based on how ideas are integrated into path-dependent settings.

Figure 12: protection arrangements and reforms 1980s and 1990s

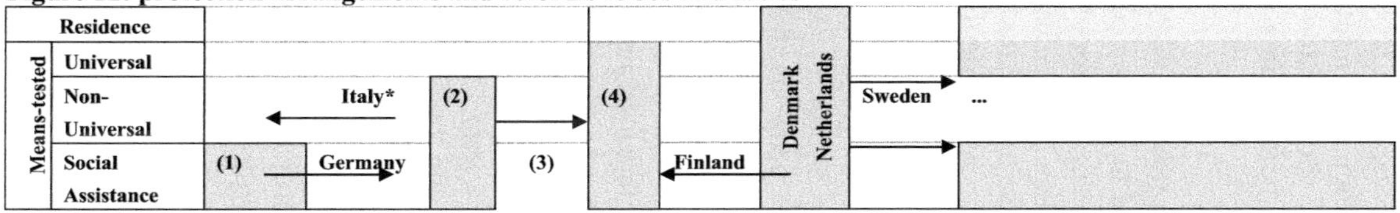

Notes:

1) Lithuania and Slovakia.

2) Austria, Belgium, Bulgaria, Italy (for those on the labour market before 1995), Greece, Latvia, Luxembourg and Poland.

3) France, Estonia, Hungary, Romania and the Czech Republic.

4) Ireland, Portugal, Spain and the UK.

3. Understanding dissemination: epistemic communities

Across the EU, pension reforms were diffused through a pension epistemic community. Epistemic communities are a "network of professionals with recognized expertise and competence in a particular domain and an authoritative claim to policy-relevant knowledge within that domain or issue-area" (Haas, 1992). While professionals may be from different disciplines, they share a set of normative beliefs providing a "value-based rationale for the social action of community members" (Haas, 1992). Additionally, these experts maintain a set of causal beliefs, on which they base their advice.

While most reforms were oriented toward pension cuts, means-tested protection was often consolidated. This reveals reform cannot be reduced to pension cuts. Interdependent upgradings and downgradings suggest a system recalibration (Ferrera and Hemrijck, 2003). We will analyse in this section how such pension recalibration reveals a set of normative and causal beliefs. These are repeated in documents presenting pension reforms. Still, as our discussion will underline, taken for granted normative and causal beliefs, neglect some complexities. This allows the epistemic community on pensions to present its pension innovation project as self-evident.

Orenstein (2003) analysed the diffusion of public and private pensions in the World. He underlines the World Bank was a vehicle of private pension dissemination. Müller (2003) and Stubbs (2003) also emphasized the role of the World Bank in promoting the introduction of compulsory private pensions in Central European countries. The World Bank advised, promoted conferences and debates, and also financed pension reforms. Therefore, its influence was limited in Western Europe. Whereas most Central European and Baltic countries introduced compulsory private pensions, these remain voluntary in some Western countries arrangements. Nevertheless, private plans represent a very important part of pensions in Denmark, the Netherlands, Ireland, Sweden and the UK.

In any case, throughout the EU, experts promoted complementary pensions on two main grounds. On the one hand, these would decrease the pressure on public systems. On the other, this would promote savings. Theoretical controversies have been left out of pension reform debates. We will briefly discuss here the major controversies.

While the desirability of voluntary private pensions is not considered to be an issue by most specialists, there are certain controversies over compulsory private plans (Barr and Diamond, 2008). There are specific causal beliefs and values behind the case for private pension development. The first is the idea that a private scheme will always outperform any public scheme. Rate of return comparison often relies on gross rate of return, which includes administrative costs and does not take into account stock returns variation (Orszag and Stiglitz, 2001). Furthermore, real fund returns dropped considerably in recent times, particularly were fund portfolios are dominated by equities (OECD, 2008). Second, compulsory private pensions have been sustained because of their effect on growth. This relies on a neo-classical, Solow-type, growth model where savings promote growth. This hypothesis is not accepted by Keynesians; furthermore even in endogenous-growth models the relation between savings and growth is more nuanced. In any case, it assumes private plans foster savings, assuming implicitly that other forms of savings will not decrease (Orszag and Stiglitz, 2001).

While pension privatisation implies risks to future pensioners, experts underline the need for a strict regulation. Still, there are two main questions. First, do states have the capacity to regulate financial markets? Second, regulation on voluntary pensions is less stringent and thus these are more volatile. Promoting private pensions was also a means to increase actuarial elements in pension determination. Public pensions reforms also enhanced actuarial fairness, through a stronger benefit-contribution link and through early retirement restricting.

Both benefit–contribution link and early retirement actuarial penalisation aim at promoting a longer working life. The longer the wage record integrated in the pension formula, the greater the incentives to retire later. Barr and Diamond (2008: 57) clearly state "*analysts agree that a well designed plan should base benefits on a fairly long period of contributions*".

Final wage plans favours workers whose wages steep at the end on the career and weakens incentives for increased effort in the early and middle years (Barr and Diamond, 2008). This can also produce incentives to under-declare wages, thus depressing social security contributions.

Increasing the benefit-contribution link is based the normative value of actuarial fairness, where what each person gets is related to what he or she contributed with. It should be noted that, the resulting pension inequalities will only be fair if the underlying wage distribution was just. The argument for increasing the link between benefits and contributions relies on four hypotheses: i) workers are motivated by monetary considerations alone; ii) leisure is a superior good; iii) retirement decisions are made by the employee; and that iv) there is job creation. These hypotheses actually rely on some taken for granted causal relations and should be nuanced. The first two hypotheses are derived from the simple homo oecunomicus representation. Indeed, although the idea that people prefer leisure to work may seem quite reasonable, retired persons are not always happier after retirement than when working. The social evaluation of ageing and retiring is important to understand how individuals evaluate incentives. Furthermore, work can also have a positive value; it is not simply forgone leisure. Work is a source of social status; its evaluation is culturally embedded. This does not mean monetary incentives are unimportant. It means motivations are complex. These complexities are neglected by official documents on pension reform.

Mainstream economics assumes the labour market, as any other market, suppliers respond to price signals and control the quantity they supply. This implies that activity rates depend on worker decisions. Still, unlike other commodities, work relationships are intrinsically hierarchical relations and involve asymmetrical authority. If activity rates decreased it is because firms used early retirement schemes as a way to downsize and let off older workers.

Job creation is also another important issue. Even if retirement decisions are partly decided by employees and partly based on monetary incentives, later retirement will not boost contributor to beneficiary ratios unless there is job creation. Otherwise, there will only be a substitution between younger workers and older workers. If people stay on the job longer and there is no job creation, younger workers will find it harder to come across a job.

Furthermore, working longer can be linked to the values of *activation*. Social benefits are increasingly dependent on labour market participation. More generally, there has been a shift toward expanding labour supply (Taylor Goody, 2005). While in the early 1990s, the discourse on the unintended consequences of social assistance dominated only Anglo-Saxon countries, dominant discourse shifted in this direction across the EU; "*intellectuals close to social democracy increasingly argue that traditional redistributive social democratic policies are no longer possible*" (Aust and Arriba, 2005: 118).

Actuarial elements foster individual fairness. This should not endanger other aims of the pension system, such as poverty relief and social insurance (Barr and Diamond, 2008). Protection reforms increasingly used means-tests. These were for decades dominant in the liberal welfare state alone (Esping Andersen, 1990). Means tests separate those in need from the rest of the elderly, who are concerned by actuarial justice. Still, controversies over means-testing are very old. Particularly, Beveridge considered means-tests create injustice and harm incentives to work (Harris, 1997). Consistently, flat rate benefits were at the heart of the Beveridge report. Means-tests developed in England in spite of the Beveridge report and only more recently diffused throughout the EU.

Means-tested assistance is part the World Bank pension reform proposal. World Bank (2005) considers the first pillar of any pension system should be made of a universal means-tested pension. This pillar is actually part of the general social safety-net. This framework was introduced in most Central European and Baltic countries (see Figure 12).

There are two major problems affecting means-test effectiveness. First, in order to limit the incentives effects, means tested benefits have to be extremely low. This limits protection effectiveness. Second, means testing effectiveness depends on how good are its instruments. If informal economy is endemic, income measures are inaccurate, thus multiplying the demands of minimum pension.

To conclude, this section has focused on identifying the common ideas behind the selected old-age pension innovations, presented previously. We have shown these articulate around certain values and causal beliefs. These associate with changes in other social protection fields.

These ideas diffuse through an epistemic community on pensions. Consequently, the some causal relations are taken for granted and controversies obscured. Still, controversies open the space of pension reform to some diversity. This is particularly the case in the field of private pensions, where the promotion of supplementary systems was interpreted differently across the EU. Moreover, our pension innovation overview showed important national differences. In the next section, we will analyse how an institutional approach can help explain national differences.

4. Understanding dissemination: hybridization

In this section we analyse how disseminated ideas are imported into national pension innovations. Institutionalism refuses a *tabula rasa* perspective of reforms, where new systems simply replace existing ones. Both institutional complementarities and switching costs entail path dependence. The process of adaptation can be perceived as institutional *bricolage* (Campbell, 2004).

Institutional analyses have increasingly integrated the role of ideas. Ideas can promote or limit reforms. Campbell (2004) distinguishes between programs, paradigms, frames and public sentiments. Causal relations sustained by the epistemic community on pensions provide a paradigm on which to base reforms; they give a set of cognitive taken for granted assumptions. These identify valid reform alternatives. Namely, the epistemic community on pensions considers reforms should promote supplementary private pensions; it also sustains pension reforms should enhance actuarial fairness and use means-tests.

These general common principles are afterwards translated into explicitly articulated national programs. In turn, programs will be translated into specific reforms. Cultural embeddedness influences these successive translations.
Culture limits the range of programs both constituents and decision-making elites consider acceptable or legitimate (Campbell, 2004). It also affects the way people evaluate their interests. Furthermore, reformers manipulate shared values and select some ideas from paradigms in order to frame their programs. Framing influences how individuals evaluate incentives. Namely, pension reform framing has involved some compensation mechanisms, which created a certain complexity. This effect is increased by lack of information.

Increases in retirement age give us an interesting example. Indeed, in the past, there was a trend to consider *social progress* should reduce statutory ages. This idea and this trend have been abandoned in the last two decades. Nevertheless this involved strategies of *blame avoidance*, through a *crisis narrative* (Kuipers, 2006). This discourse shifted responsibilities away from reformers and pointed the finger at "globalisation" or "ageing". These were presented as self-evident processes. Apart from this framing, statutory age increases were phased-out (Bonoli and Palier, 2007).

Apart from *blame avoidance* framing can also enhance *credit claiming* (Natali and Rhodes, 2008). Indeed, promoting supplementary pensions, actuarial fairness and working longer are part of a *positive* discourse; this contrasts with the *negative* discourse on "cutting pensions" or "later retirement".

Institutional analyses underline the role of institutional complementarities and coherence. Complementarities between institutions boost increasing returns as a result of *supplementarity* or of synergies arising through selection (Deeg, 2005). This explains why real-world diversity is actually less important than it could theoretically be (Boyer, 2005). Still, institutional complementarities will eventually be disrupted by the emergence of tensions; the "*fit among institutions is always partial and transitory*" (Boyer, 2005). These frictions may emerge from environmental dynamics and from the reform process itself. For example, while attitudes towards retiring are changing (slowly), employer attitudes towards older workers may not be evolving at a corresponding pace. This can create a friction, which disturbs previous institutional complementarities. Cultural embeddedness and institutional complementarities entail path dependence. We have seen that in spite of similar innovations, national differences did not disappear. Pension innovations were hybridised into national pension settings. "Hybridization *describes the process through which tentatively imported institutions are transformed via their interaction with domestic institutional forms*" (Boyer, 2005).

Hybridisation appears distinctively in the case of private pensions. While all EU countries sought to promote supplementary, non-state pension systems, emerging templates are diverse. We should distinguish particularly occupational pensions and individual pension plans. Occupational arrangements are collective and quite different from individual account pension funds (Matos, 2009). They often date back longer than state pensions and co-evolved with them.

Occupational pensions emerged from the organisation of internal markets. These included job ladders and work organisation routines, which were different across EU countries. Consequently, in some countries, occupational pensions are traditionally managed by collective agreements. On the other hand, some employers used final salary schemes to reduce labour turnover. This was the case in British big firms. Elsewhere, governments promoted branch – or national-level schemes in order to facilitate labour turnover (Denmark, France, the Netherlands, Sweden).

While employer pension plans are moving from DB to DC, final wage schemes remain frequent. Furthermore, contrary to pension funds, occupational pensions are often unfunded. While new schemes are overwhelmingly funded, pre-existing unfunded schemes will not probably be transformed into funded schemes because the *implicit debt* represents a sizeable switching cost[69]. To be sure, occupational plans are increasingly DC, funded and managed by professional funds. Still, reforms did not purge final wage arrangements, unfunded arrangements or union involvement. This can be explained by switching costs (e.g. the implicit debt) and cultural embeddedness (e.g. collective bargain legitimacy). These complementarities enlighten national differences. Neither Southern European, nor Central European and Baltic countries had such an occupational pension tradition. Here private pensions were introduced only recently and designed top-down.

The World Bank promoted private account introduction in Central Europe and Baltics (Müller, 2003; Stubbs, 2003). Some Bank experts were also involved in designing and framing national reforms. Only two countries in the region did not adopt compulsory private pensions. In Czech Republic social democratic values dating back to the beginning of the XIXth (Vecernik, 1996). On the other hand, Slovenian finance minister opposed these because of the switching cost involved. These reasons show the importance of path dependence. Even in other countries, the introduction of compulsory individual plans was phased-out, as a way to control switching costs.

---

69 We adapt here the Myles and Pierson (2001) argument on pay-as-you-go arrangement path dependence.

The introduction of compulsory private pensions in Central Europe and Baltic countries was complementary with a more general ideology of privatisation and state disengagement. Voluntary private accounts developed throughout the region and were backed by fiscal incentives. On the other hand, occupational funds and legislation have been imported from neighbouring EU countries. Still, their development has been limited. This can be explained by the weaknesses of institutional complementarities, such as a consistent primary market or collective agreement traditions.

Southern European experiences also stress institutional complementarities. Primary labour markets (i.e. good jobs) have traditionally been extremely limited in these countries (Ferrera, 1996). This has limited the expansion of occupational pensions. Recently, governments have thought to promote both occupational settings and private plans. While these institutions are imported from other EU, their transfer involved adaptation. For example, professional financial organisations often manage both forms of supplementary pensions. Private pension coverage remains relatively weak. The lack of synergies can explain this situation. Labour markets are extremely fragmented. The limited primary markets, on the one side, and endemic informal economy, on the other, restrict professional as well as individual funds.

Overall, the development of private pensions has been linked to the role state pensions play in specific national pension arrangements. These elements interplay with state pension innovations. Actuarial fairness innovations dissemination also involved hybridisation. Countries introduced different measures aimed at benefit-contribution link and longer working life. While BD formula has been reformed, we have seen that there are still important replacement ratio differences. Indeed, although these are decreasing and expected to decrease even further in the next decades, there is some replacement ratio evolution has been incremental in most countries. Changes were more important in Latvia, Poland or Sweden, where NDC introduction changed radically the calculation method. Portugal and Finland also introduced radical changes and started using life expectancy. In these countries, the complexity of the calculation and the different transition systems reduced popular dissatisfaction. They should reduce significantly future pension replacement rates. Conversely, in most countries, progressive benefit calculation changes and phasing-out were used to frame reforms. In an extreme case, Italian reforms will only apply to those who entered the labour market in 1993.

Cultural embeddedness can partially help understand reforms. The public pension systems are more central in corporatist countries, such as Austria, Belgium, France or Germany. These contrast with the UK, where employees can opt-out of the public system. Pension reforms have also been less radical and involved phasing-out (Bonoli and Palier, 2007). Institutional complementarities are also important, since private pension arrangements have an almost universal coverage in Denmark, the Netherlands or Sweden.

We have seen that most EU countries use means-tested assistance. Still, Figure 12 also shows intra-EU diversity. Furthermore, countries use different means tests. Some control only for the pension earned. Others control for all other household income.

There are different welfare state traditions in the EU (Esping Andersen, 1990). Of these, means-tested assistance is typical of the residual-liberal welfare state. Conversely, in the social-democratic world protection was typically universal, while in the corporatist countries it was employment-related. If we observe Figure 12, we can see that, relative to those ideal-types, means-tests have progressed in the other two worlds. Still, as this component has been added to existing arrangements, emerging arrangements remain diverse. These differences can be explained by cultural embeddedness, because pre-existing forms of protection are valued by the population as well as reformers. It can also be explained by complementarities vis-à-vis other protection arrangements.

Still, it has been noted that while the residual approach has become dominant in reform discourse, national social inclusion and activation policies remain distinct (Taylor Goody, 2005). This does not mean change was only incremental. For example, Finland abandoned residence-based protection for pensioners. This has divorced this country from the social democratic welfare world in neighbouring countries. On the other hand, France has become dissimilar from corporatist countries because it introduced an universal (therefore non-employment-related) basic pension. These changes reflect shifts in the organisation of social assistance. Social assistance is very modest in Southern Europe. Actually protection lagged behind in the construction of the welfare state. This dimension has been developed hesitantly in most countries (Ferrera, 2005).

World Bank sponsored the introduction of means-tested universal basic pensions in Central European countries. This was a part of the three-pillar model advocated by this organisation. In countries with no Bank assistance, there are different evolutions. Czech Republic uses means-tested universal protection, while Slovenia does not. These options have an affinity with general universalistic approaches in social assistance.

5. Concluding remarks: pension Europeanization

The EU created an open-method of coordination (OMC) on pensions in 2000. This was united with social inclusion and health, giving rise to the social protection and social inclusion OMC in 2006. In this section we will deduce the implications of dissemination analysis to this process. The open-method of co-ordination methodology developed from the European Employment Strategy, through which EU countries have been discussing and benchmarking their employment policies from 1997. The Pensions OMC establishes guidelines, which are approved by the EU Council, and against which National Strategy Reports are evaluated by peer review.

Guidelines are qualitative and organized around three topics:

i) Pension adequacy matters include preventing social exclusion, maintaining living standards and promoting inter- and intra-generational solidarity;
ii) Financial sustainability themes comprise extending working lives, increasing employment rates and providing sustainable pensions in the context of sound public finances;
iii) Societal dynamics (adapting to more flexible employment and careers, promoting gender equality and promoting consensus); and
iv) A governance topic was added in 2006 to promote secure private pensions and to support pension systems governance.

The OMC process was conceived to promote policy diffusion and good practice dissemination (*learning from the partners*). Yet, there is considerable discussion over the actual impact of OMC on national pension reforms. Contrary to the European Employment Strategy (EES) which is Treaty-based, the Pensions OMC has an ambiguous status (Citi and Rhodes, 2007).

Still institutional transfer can also have mimetic and normative sources (Radaelli, 2000, cited by Borrás and Jacobsson, 2004). These correspond to persuasion through peer review, as well as naming and shaming. Additionally, framing and norm internalization can emerge from the participation in discussions, from the use of a common language (e.g. active ageing), from building Euro-indicators and from establishing common (quantitative or qualitative) objectives (Borrás and Jacobsson, 2004; Jacobsson, 2004).

Our analysis has sustained ideas are important and that they are diffused through epistemic communities. There are three main implications to analysing the OMC. First, guidelines are defined by political agreement. They emerge from a process of political bargaining. As such, they represent the common principles upon which EU government agrees. How the issues are expressed is interesting and enlightening. Second, the choice of guidelines is relevant and a bad review can be used to trigger reform domestically. As such, the OMC reports can be used to frame specific reforms. Third, the pensions OMC is integrated on the epistemic community and its documents echo the pension innovations we have analysed. Indeed, the pension innovations we analyse in this paper are at the heart of OMC documents. Private pensions are thought to "*strengthen the sustainability of the statutory pay-as-you-go old-age pension scheme in the long run while allowing individuals to accrue additional pension rights through privately-managed funds*" (EC, 2006). OMC guidelines also include securing private pensions.

Pension adequacy relates both to pension calculation and to protection. These are established very generally. While a list of indicators is produces, there is no benchmarking against which to confront replacement rates or poverty rates.

Financial sustainability topic is oriented toward increasing the contributing careers. The only quantitative targets influencing pension reforms result from the European Employment strategy. They orient countries towards increasing the working life. The Barcelona target aims at "*a progressive increase of about 5 years in the effective average age at which people stop working in the European Union should be sought by 2010*". The Stockholm European Council agreed "*to set an EU target for increasing the average EU employment rate among older women and men (55-64) to 50% by 2010*". The Commission monitors progress in the older worker employment rate and the "average exit age from the labour force". This shows how the European Employment strategy is central and how it structures social protection issues. It is revealing of the place activation occupies in the pension coordination process.

Therefore, the OMC can be perceived as part of the epistemic community on pensions. It intensifies the diffusion of certain ideas. Although it is not enforced, it limits the cognitive and normative definition of legitimate pension innovations. Innovations will be hybridised into specific pension systems. We have stated in this paper that hybridisation is influenced by cultural embeddedness and institutional complementarities. These limit the range of valid innovations. They can also enhance certain features, while refraining others.

References

Arthur, B. (1990), "Positive feedbacks in the economy", *Scientific American*. 262(2): 92-99.

Aust, A. and A. Arriba (2005), "Towards activation? Social assistance reforms and discourses", in P. Taylor-Gooby (ed), *Ideas and Welfare State Reform in Western Europe*, Basingstoke: Palgrave Macmillan, pp. 100-123.

Barr, N. and M. Rutkowski (2005), "Pensions", in N. Barr (ed), *Labour Markets and Social Policy in Central and Eastern Europe. The Accession and Beyond*, Washington: The World Bank, pp. 135-170.

Barr, N. and P. Diamond (2008), *Reforming Pensions: Principles and Policy Choices*, Oxford: Oxford University Press.

Bonoli, G. and B. Palier (2007), "When past reforms open new opportunities: comparing old age insurance reforms in Bismarkian welfare systems?", *Social Policy and Administration*, 41(6): 555-573.

Borrás, S. and K. Jacobsson (2004), "The open method of co-ordination and new governance patterns in the EU", *Journal of European Public Policy*, 11(2): 185-208.

Boyer, R. (2005), "Coherence, diversity, and the evolution of capitalisms – the institutional complementarity hypothesis", *Evolutionary and Institutional Economics Review*, 2(1): 43-80.

Campbell, J. (2004), *Institutional Change and Globalization*, Princeton: Princeton University Press.

Citi, M. and M. Rhodes (2007), "New modes of governance in the EU: common objectives versus national preferences", *European Governance Papers (EUROGOV)*, 07/01, available at *www.connex-network.org/eurogov/pdf/ egp-newgov-N-07-01.pdf.*

David, P. A. (1985), "Clio and the economics of QWERTY", *American Economic Review Papers and Proceedings*, 75(2): 332-337.

Deeg, R. (2007), "Complementarity and institutional change in capitalist systems", *Journal of European Public Policy*, 14(4): 611-630.

EC (2006), *Synthesis Report on Adequate and Sustainable Pensions*, Brussels: European Commission.

EC (2007), *Joint Report on Social Protection and Social Inclusion*, Brussels: European Commission.

Esping Andersen, G. (1990), *The Three Worlds of Welfare Capitalism*, Princeton: Princeton University Press.

Ferrera, M. (1996), "The 'Southern model' of welfare in social Europe", *Journal of European Social Policy*, 6(1): 17-37.

Ferrera, M. (2005), "Welfare states and social safety nets in Southern Europe: an introduction", in M. Ferrera (ed), *Welfare State Reform in Southern Europe: Fighting Poverty and Social Exclusion in Italy, Spain, Portugal and Greece*, London and New York: Routledge, pp. 1-32.

Ferrera, M. and A. Hemerijck (2003), "Recalibrating Europe's welfare states", in J. Zeitlin and D. Trubek (eds), *Governing Work and Welfare in a New Economy: European and American Experiments*, Oxford and New York: Oxford University Press, pp. 88-128.

Haas, P. M. (1992), "Introduction: epistemic communities and international policy coordination", in P. Haas (ed), *Knowledge, Power and International Policy Cooperation*, Columbia: University of South Carolina Press, pp. 1-35.

Harris, J. (1997), *William Beveridge: A Biography*, Oxford: Clarendon Press.

Hinrichs, K. and O. Kangas (2004), "When is a change big enough to be a system shift? Small system shifting in German and Finnish pension policies", in P. Taylor-Gooby (ed), *Making a European Welfare State? Convergences and Conflicts Over European Social Policy*, Malden, MA: Blackwell Publishing, pp. 34-52.

Jacobsson, K. (2004), "Soft regulation and the subtle transformation of states: the case of EU employment policy", *Journal of European Social Policy*, 14(4): 355-370.

Kuipers, S. (2006), *The Crisis Imperative: Crisis Rhetoric and Welfare State Reform in Belgium and the Netherlands in the Early 1990s*, Amsterdam: Amsterdam University Press.
Matos, C. (2009), "Unreformed or hybrid? Accounting for pension arrangements diversity in the EU.", *Forum for Social Economics*, forthcoming.
Müller, K. (2003), "The making of pension privatization in Latin America and Eastern Europe", in R. Holzmann, M. Orenstein, and M. Rutkowski (eds), *Pension Reform in Europe: Process and Progress*, Washington: The World Bank, pp. 47-78.
Myles, J. and P. Pierson (2001), "The comparative political economy of pension reform", in P. Pierson (ed), *The New Politics of the Welfare State*, Oxford and New York: Oxford University Press, pp. 305-333.
Natali, D. and M. Rhodes (2008), "The 'new politics' of pension reforms in continental Europe", in C. Arza and M. Kohli (eds), *Pension Reform in Europe. Politics, Policies and Outcomes*, Oxon and New York: Routledge, pp. 25-46.
OECD (2007), *Pensions at a Glance*, Paris: OECD.
OECD (2008), "Private pensions and the 2008 turmoil in financial markets", *Pension Markets in Focus*, 5.
Orenstein, M. (2003), "Mapping the diffusion of pension innovation", in R. Holzmann, M. Orenstein, and M. Rutkowski (eds), *Pension Reform in Europe: Process and Progress*, Washington: The World Bank, pp. 171-194.
Orszag, P. and J. Stiglitz (2003), "Rethinking pension reform: ten myths about social security systems", in P. Orszag and J. Stiglitz (eds), *New Ideas about Old Age Security*, Washington: The World Bank, pp. 17-56.
Overbye, E. (2008), "How do politicians get away with path-breaking pension reforms? The political psychology of pension reforms in democracies.", in C. Azra and M. Kohli (eds), *Pension Reform in Europe, Politics, Policies and Outcomes*, Oxon and New York: Routledge, pp. 70-86.
Solow, R. (1991), *The Labour Market as a Social Institution*, London: Blackwell.
Stubbs, P. (2003), "International non-state actors and social development policy", *Global Social Policy*, 3(3): 319-348.
Taylor-Gooby, P. (2005), "Paradigm shifts, power ressources and labour market reform", in P. Taylor-Gooby (ed), *Ideas and Welfare State Reform in Western Europe*, Basingstoke: Palgrave Macmillan, pp. 12-29.
Vecernik, J. (1996), *Markets and People. The Czech Reform Experience in a Comparative Perspective*, Avebury: Aldershot.
World Bank (2005), *Old-Age Income Support in the 21st Century*, Washington: The World Bank.

3. Growth, inequality and poverty in emerging and transition economies*

Pasquale Tridico

1. Introduction

World economic growth was well sustained in the last decade, although many industrialised countries, western European in particular, did not experience fast growth. Emerging economies (EEs), such as low-to-middle per capita income economies, and transition economies (TEs), such as former communist countries, are experiencing a process of fast growth and institutional change in most cases. This paper aims first of all to explore the social sustainability and the quality of such growth in those countries. The economic growth that occurred in Emerging and Transition Economies (ETEs) during the period 1995-2006 was, on average, 4,7%, and above the average world growth. The paper examines, in particular, whether, this growth resulted in income distribution, measured as a reduction of the Gini coefficient, and in a reduction of poverty, measured by a cut-off line of $4 a day. Secondly, the paper addresses important issues of the economic development process, such as the dynamics of life expectancy and education, and of human development variables more generally. In particular the paper tries to understand whether or not economic growth increased human development in ETEs.

Such an issue is crucial to the identification of a process of economic growth with a process of economic development. In their widely quoted *economic development* book, Perkins et al. (2007) stress the difference between economic growth (understood as the rate of growth in goods and services produced) and economic development (which involves economic growth together with change in some human development variables, such as life expectancy, infant mortality, education, and other goals such as environment sustainability, political democracy, income distribution, participation, access to resources, etc). Cypher and Dietz (2004) also make such a differentiation between economic growth and (economic) development. The latter "...encompasses a wide range of social and human goals that, while including the level of income and economic growth, goes well beyond this as well" (Cypher and Dietz, 2004: 29). This differentiation must not be confused with that discussed among institutional economists

* The paper was written during a visiting research fellowship at the Global and Urban Research Centre (GURU) of Newcastle University, in November-December 2007. The author is very grateful to Prof. Frank Moulaert for his help and support at Newcastle University and to Prof. Fadda for his comments. The usual disclaimer applies. An ealier version of this paper was published in Review of Transition Studies, 2010, 16(4).

(cf. Brinkman (1995) for a review on this perspective) who perceive economic growth as a static phenomenon and economic development as a wider perspective of development that includes structural and institutional change, social dynamics and cultural change (Myrdal, 1974). However, it has to be said that these two perspectives of economic development (the one put forward by Perkins et al. (2007) and Cypher and Dietz (2004), and the other put forward by Myrdal (1974)) would easily converge in the end because, as Myrdal (1974: 729) himself states, economic development would bring about improvements in health, education and other collective goods.

Through a series of cross-country regressions, using OLS models, the paper assesses the type of development in a sample of 50 Emerging and Transition economies. Economic growth during 1995-2006 is regressed against poverty, inequality and human development variables. The main findings are that growth did not reduce poverty and that inequality increased, on average, among Emerging and Transition economies during this period. Moreover, economic growth occurred at the expense of an important human development variable i.e., life expectancy and an important indicator of political democracy, i.e., Voice and Accountability.

The rest of the paper is organised as follows: section 2 presents an essential review on poverty, inequality and growth; section 3 analyses more deeply the institutional change occurring in ETEs, putting forward a model of development path (Figure 13); section 4 describes the sample of ETEs; section 5 shows the results of the OLS regression models on poverty and inequality in ETEs; section 6 concludes the paper.

2. Growth, inequality and poverty: a brief review

In the terminology of the International Monetary Fund (IMF) and of the World Bank (WB), economic development is not just about economic growth in general but a particular kind of economic growth, identified by the words "high-quality growth" (HQG), which both the IMF and the WB claim to promote (IMF, 1995). In particular, IMF defines HQG as "...growth that is sustainable, brings lasting gains in employment and living standards and reduce poverty. HQG should promote greater equity and equality of opportunity. It should respect human freedom and protect the environment"; and it should "...bear the primary responsibility for the care, nutrition, and education. Achieving HQG depends, therefore, not only on pursuing sound economic policies, but also on implementing a broad range of social policies" (IMF, 1995: 286). Hence, great emphasis is put on reduction in levels of poverty and inequality, together with

the pursuit of social goals, such as improved health and education, which should increase accordingly during the process of economic growth.
Poverty and inequality are key concerns nowadays among economists of development. However, social attitudes towards poverty and inequality can change through time, basically because tolerance of high levels of poverty and inequality varies across countries, cultures, and times. Western societies have become less tolerant against poverty over time; East Asia, mainly following Confucianism, does not, in general, tolerate high economic inequality. Unfortunately this promising field of research has not produced many cross-cultural studies. Alexander and Kumaran (1992) studied culture and development in India. They discovered that the lowest tolerance of inequality is not in the richest States of India, but in those with the highest education levels. *If* it were possible to make some generalization on the basis of this, one could say that variation in values that concern inequality is influenced by education. Indeed within both developed and less developed countries, those which have achieved higher levels of education seem to show less tolerance towards inequality and poverty (Cypher and Dietz, 2004).

Gary Fields (1989) reviewed all the major empirical studies on growth, inequality and poverty and found out that there is no general predictable relationship between inequality and GDP growth; the relationship can work in both ways round. Nevertheless, there seems to be some evidence of poverty reduction associated with economic growth. However, he did not conclude that economic growth reduces poverty. It is possible that during GDP expansion the poor become less poor, and during GDP contraction the poor become even poorer (Dollar and Kraay, 2002). However, eradicating poverty can take generations and it is not only a matter of economic growth. Moreover, social policies and income distribution are, as will be shown below, strictly linked to poverty reduction. Hence, as Myrdal (1974) and many others, such as Pronk (1993) and Street (1987) argue, a *holistic approach* is required to defeat poverty. Poverty has a social and political dimension; both should be addressed in order to arrive at a deeper understanding of the meaning of poverty, its causes and its consequences. Poverty alleviation comes as a result of a complex analysis and of the implementation of strategies that bring together both different disciplines and the poor themselves in the process of policy-making.

2.1. Poverty

The World Bank claims the defeat of poverty as its main target, and policies which "make poverty a dream" are now at the core of its agenda. Over time, however, WB policies on poverty have changed consistently. During the 1960s, the WB believed that the best way to reduce poverty in Less Developed Countries (LDCs) was a rapid industrialisation. During the 1970s the WB understood the need to develop the rural sector in LDCs as a vehicle for both economic growth and poverty reduction. In the 1980s, the WB was more committed to structural adjustment, as the International Monetary Fund was implementing structural adjustment programmes in Developed Countries (DC). In the 1990s the WB embraced a more general approach to combat poverty involving investments in human capital, macroeconomic adjustment, fostering economic growth, environment attention, etc. Finally, in the 2000s, the WB and the IMF together developed a new approach to poverty reduction, the so called Poverty Reduction Strategy Papers (PRSPs). PRSPs set policies and agendas to reduce poverty and integrate economic, social and environmental issues into a general framework. They are developed in a participatory way, with the involvement of individuals, NGOs, international organisations, local and national authorities (Marcus and Wilkinson, 2002). So far the aim of defeating world poverty has not been achieved; from the analysis in this paper it has emerged that growth did not contribute to poverty reduction between 1995-2006. Most of the criticism directed at the WB and the IMF lies in the fact that the approach they adopted towards LDCs during the 1980s and the 1990s relied exclusively on structural adjustment and economic growth, transplanting policies and institutions from developed countries. The World Bank (2000) estimates that poverty, measured with a cut-off line of poverty of $1 a day, increased from 1.116 million to 1.200 million people from 1985 to 1998. With a cut-off line of $2 a day, people falling within the poverty trap form nearly half of the global population (2,8 billion) (cf. World Bank, 2000: 3, 13). In terms of percentages, while poverty is stable in Sub-Saharan Africa (46,3% of population) and in Latin America and the Caribbean (15,6% of population), it fell in the Middle East and North Africa (from 4,3% to 1,9%), in Southern Asia (from 44,4% to 40%) and in particular in Eastern Asia (from 26,6% to 15,3%).

In Sub-Saharan Africa and in many other LDCs the main problem causing poverty seems to be deprivation of basic human necessities such as food, basic medicines, water, illiteracy etc (Cypher and Dietz, 2004). In richer countries, such as Emerging and Transition Economies with low-to-middle per capita income, the main problem causing poverty seems to be also deprivation (Sen, 1999); however, different forms of deprivation are prevalent here, such as education, nourishment, health, employment etc. Such deprivations, in both groups of countries, do not allow people to develop their capabilities and to achieve liberation from poverty[70]. In many cases, these deprivations do not depend on

---

70 On this concept is drawn the Human Poverty Index (HPI), a composite index which measures deprivations in the three basic dimensions captured in the human development index: a long and healthy life (health), knowledge (education) and a decent standard of living (income) (UNDP, 2006).

money, but a cut-off line of poverty of $1 or $4 a day can be considered just as a proxy for such a problem.
In addition, when poverty is measured through the concept of "poverty gap"[71], the strong link between poverty and distribution immediately becomes clear. In fact, the poverty gap appears to be relatively modest in size when compared to current income in LDCs. Theoretically, the poverty gap can be interpreted as the amount of income that must be created and received by the poor in order to bring income above the poverty line (Cypher and Dietz, 2004: 7). For instance the poverty gap, in the 1990s, was around 10-12% in Sub-Saharan Africa and Southern Asia and around 2% in the rest of LDCs (World Bank, 1990). These figures underline that in the final analysis eradicating poverty is a political economy matter and not a technical one. However, it has to be added that distribution alone would not be enough for a permanent poverty reduction; a process of development would have to reproduce basic need satisfactions, goods and jobs.

2.2. Inequality

The very foundation of the problem of inequality is the concept of social welfare. According to the utilitarian approach, social welfare is the sum of individual welfare. Social welfare improvements are not possible (or would not be "Pareto efficient") by re-distributing resources from one individual to another, because a "Pareto" improvement is only a situation in which it is possible to make someone better off, without making someone else worse off. On the other hand, an egalitarian approach would consider re-distribution of resources to avoid the situation where an individual could become richer by taking advantage of the fact that the other is in poor health or in poor education, or is handicapped (Sen, 1973). In this latter approach, the application of the Rawls' criterion would be the best policy; the aim is not individual welfare but the level of welfare in the society. If one individual (A) has a lower level of welfare that another (B), and if B can be made better off by re-distributing resources from A, then the Rawls criterion of justice requires that B should have sufficiently more income to make B's utility equal to A's. In Rawlsian thinking, inequalities have to be adjusted following two principles: 1) offices and positions must be open to everyone under conditions of *fair equality of opportunity*; 2) they have to be of greatest benefits for the least-advantaged members of the society (Rawls, 1971:

71 The poverty gap is the percentage by which the income of the poor falls short the poverty line measured usually as a percentage of total consumption of the country. In other terms, it is the amount of additional income needed to raise all the poor above the poverty line. This measure would help towards a better understanding of the severity of the poverty. For instance, if a country has half of its population in poverty but each person is only $2 away, per year, from the poverty level, it is in a better position than a country with half of its population in poverty but each person is $50 away, per year, from the poverty level.

303). To be applied, these criteria require more than meritocracy. “Fair equality of opportunity” requires not only that positions are distributed on the basis of merit, but also that all have equal opportunity, in terms of education, health etc., to acquire those skills on the basis of which merit is assessed. The application of these principles would, in the end, produce much greater advantages for the society as a whole.

Another way to look at the problem of inequality is through social peace and cohesion. Sen (1973) saw inequality as strictly linked to the concept of rebellion and indeed the two phenomena are linked in both ways. Inequality causes rebellion, but it may happen that income inequality may increase after a rebellion where it brings power to a specific apparatus or a nomenclature or a social class; this has happened many times in history when, for instance, rebellions were led by army generals or by elites of nobles. In several transition economies, inequality increased after a “rebellion” which brought to power oligarchs. In particular, in the former Soviet Union inequality increased dramatically after the 1991 August Coup which deposed Soviet president Mikhail Gorbachev and dissolved the USSR. In some African countries, such as Congo, Sudan etc. the same happened: rebellions, carried out by generals and warlords, deposed previous authoritarian or less authoritarian regimes, but such a change brought about an increase in inequality. Nowadays, economists try to capture a causality nexus (inequality → rebellion → inequality) through the use of some modern governance indicators such as political stability. The link between political stability and inequality is demonstrated in numerous empirical works such as Alesina and Perrotti (1996) and Easterly (2001), where it emerges that income inequality increases during political instability.

An interesting explanation of inequality in the Americas is put forward by Sokoloff and Engerman (2000), who, in order to explain inequality in wealth, human capital and political power, suggest an institutional explanation, historically founded, which lies in the initial roots of the factors of endowment of the respective colonies. In general, political institutions set up by the Spaniards and Portuguese in Latin America were different from the ones set up by the British in North America. Moreover, the latter sent educated people and skilled work forces, along with the lords, to the New World, and these started to build their own future; while the Spaniards and the Portuguese did not encourage massive migration from the motherland but sent landlords who basically exploited slaves from Africa.

One of the first cross-country works on inequality was made by Kuznets (1955). He showed that in the early stage of economic growth income tends to be unequally distributed among individuals. In the early stage of a growth process, over time, the distribution of income worsens. In the later stages, national income starts to be more equally distributed. Hence, inequality declines in the end, after the country has accomplished the "U"-shaped trajectory. Several later empirical studies confirmed this relationship (Chenery and Syrquin, 1975; Ahluwalia, 1976). The reason for such a relationship was attributed to structural changes, which at the beginning of the "transition" bring about job losses and inequalities.

Nevertheless, the implicit trade-off behind the Kuznets curve (economic growth/ inequality) and the idea that an increase in inequality is sometimes necessary for a rapid growth has been often criticized (Atkinson, 1999). An alterative hypothesis to explain why income inequality differs among countries is put forward by Milanovic (1994), who shows that inequality decreases in richer societies because social attitudes towards inequality change as those societies get richer, and inequality is less tolerated. Birdsall and Sabot (1994) showed, contrary to the Kuznets hypothesis, that inequality may be a constraint for growth and, if inequality is lowered, then a country could have a GDP per capita 8,2% higher than a country with income inequality 1 standard deviation higher.

A similar hypothesis is suggested by Voitchovsky (2005: 273) who, however, stresses *the shape* of the distribution and suggests that inequality at the top end of the distribution is positively associated with growth, while inequality lower down the distribution is negatively related to subsequent growth. Moreover, empirical evidence in cross-countries analysis, from Latin American to East Asian Countries, would pose the question why Latin America has high inequality and low growth and, on the contrary, why East Asia has high growth and low inequality. Birdsall and Sabot (1994) suggest that it is a matter of policies and social attitude towards inequality. In Latin America, dictators, generals and the ruling classes acted, for long time after WWII, with little respect for the poorest part of their society, implementing fiscal and trade policies that provided little benefits to the poor. On the contrary, in East Asia the ruling classes were more aware of social needs, and implemented policies such as land reforms, public housing, public investments in rural infrastructures and public education which had a positive effect on both growth and income distribution; better educated people can get a better job and earn more; public investment in the rural sector can bring farmer productivity and income higher; public housing and other social services can increase the purchasing power of people, and so forth.

3. Institutional change and economic growth in emerging and transition economies

Emerging and transition economies are countries which are experiencing a huge process of institutional change, involving both a social and cultural transformation and a political and economic reform (Kornai, 2006; Mauro, 2000)[72]. However, in order to be socially sustainable and macro-economically stable, the incumbent process of institutional change in ETEs has to be consistent: the change occurring in the formal sphere of the institutional framework (which involves laws, organization and state institutions) should move coherently with that in informal institutions i.e., with social rules and uncodified laws and values, which prescribe certain behaviours and affect in several ways the economic behaviour of agents and their choices (Hodgson, 2006; Nugent and Lin, 1996). Moreover, and most importantly, the change has to guarantee equal gains to people who otherwise would resist to the transformation. Inertia towards a new institutional framework occurs when the social benefits of transformation are not universal and where many people, during the transformation, become losers in terms of unemployment, purchasing power, education, etc (Tridico, 2006). Therefore the change should be radical and should involve as well as relationships between the various powers, and lobbies (Mabogunje, 1989) which are able to change *political institutions*.

My assumption, concerning political institutions, is that a country which is governed more democratically and where political institutions are oriented towards freedom guarantees, people participation and political rights, is a country where citizens can have some power and can make some lobbying on the governors. Consequently public decisions, in this country, would be more oriented towards collective benefits than a country where the level of democracy and freedom is less marked. The country which enjoys better democracy, freedom and political rights would extend people opportunities easier than a country where these rights are restricted. Such a restriction would cause lower level of human development and lower economic growth.

Following this approach, development might be defined as a process that involves economic growth and institutional change (Toye, 1995). As Kuznets put it in referring to developing countries (1965: 30): "the transformation of an underdeveloped into a developed country is not merely the mechanical addition of a stock of physical capital: it is a thoroughgoing revolution in the patterns of life and a cardinal change in the relative powers and positions of various groups in the population". The process of institutional change has to guarantee two im-

72 The term "emerging economy" was coined in 1981 by Antoine Van Agtmael of the World Bank, and refers to countries that are "emerging" from under-development, and are restructuring their economies along market-oriented lines (cf. Agtmael, 2007). Transition economies refer strictly to former communist countries which are transforming their economies from a planned system to market economies.

portant factors: first, a breaking with previous institutions, routines and norms and overcoming "...the resistance of a whole complex of established interests and values" that previously impeded economic growth (Kuznets, 1965: 30). Secondly, it has to guarantee the distribution of growth and of the social benefits of development. It is crucial therefore to know how to change institutions and how to enforce a new institutional deal which will bring about economic development i.e. improving both living condition, in terms of income and distribution, and quality of life, in terms of health and education. Hence, institutional policies and an active role of the State are needed during such a transformation in order to guarantee a stable and sustainable economic development.

Such a definition of change, strictly connected with the process of economic development, can be summarised by a graph where, on the vertical axis there is the level of institutional change, which involves social, cultural and political change; on the horizontal axis there is the speed of economic growth. These two variables, institutional change and economic growth, identify the path of the development process which, if the speed of change of the two variables is appropriate and consistent, will be positively inclined, as shown approximately in the graph below:

Figure 13

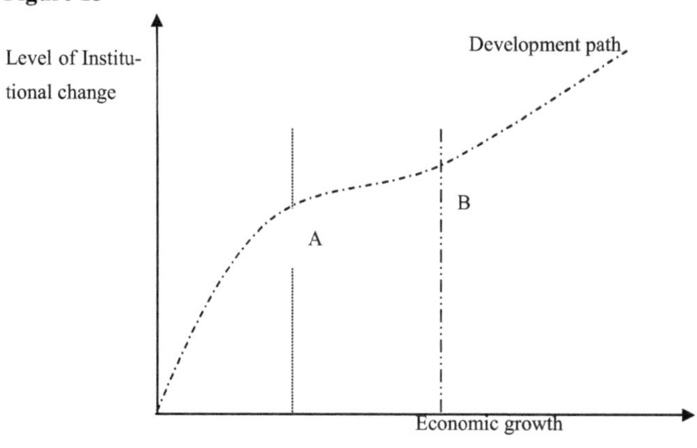

Note: during the first period, from the origin to the point A, the speed of institutional change is faster than the speed of economic growth. In the second period, from point A to B, the economic growth is faster than the speed of the institutional change. In other words, economic growth follows the institutional change.

This path of development is the one that many current industrialised countries experienced after WWII. In these countries, economic growth, together with a process of institutional change in the system of values, the culture and the society, brought about economic development also, in the sense that poverty was defeated or substantially reduced, inequality was reduced, political democracy was achieved and human development improved, because social policies were implemented and simultaneously an important Welfare State was created. Will ETEs replicate such a development path? I maintain that the type of development will not necessarily be the same, in the sense that institutions and strategies for development can be different. Informal institutions are also different. However, insofar as the specific country strategy includes an appropriate institutional change with consistent social institutions, accompanied by economic growth, the trend of the path could be replicated – although with different policy prescriptions.

Given the concept of institutions as including both formal and informal institutions, changing formal institutions alone in order to achieve another system is no longer sufficient. More important is to "change the mentality" of economic agents. Both prevalent rules and the mentality of agents can be considered in Veblen's sense of shared "habits of thought" (Veblen, 1919: 273). If the formal economic institutions are neglected, informal institutions and processes of spontaneous forces prevail. These forces fill the *power vacuum* of the system. Consequently, the transformation would favour better organised groups, elites, the better educated and the groups in a dominant position. Simultaneously, it would cause disadvantages to less organised groups, unskilled workers, the poor and the less well educated.

As a consequence, economic growth, if it occurs, will not be distributed, inequality will rise and poverty will not be defeated. Development would therefore be uneven, opportunities and *capabilities* for many people would decrease, and there would be many more losers than winners. Moreover, this informal institutionalisation may also be parastatal or illegal. Hence, such uncontrolled transformation strongly favours the emergence of organised crime, corrupt bureaucracy, informal economies, negative informal economic networks, rent-seeking, illegal lobbies and so forth.

4. Emerging and transition economies: a description of the sample

Most of the reputable studies on the dynamics of poverty, inequality and growth, focus more on LDCs and less on ETEs. This is mainly because emerging and transition economics is a relatively new field of research, and a good assessment on the relationship between poverty, inequality and growth would need quite a long time span, ten/fifteen years at the minimum. Secondly, all transition economies experienced a huge recession at the beginning of the 1990s, hence economic growth started in many countries in the second half of the 1990s.

Therefore, most of the studies on poverty and inequality in transition economies, focus on the worsening of these two variables during the recession period (Atkinson and Miklewright, 1992; Milanovic, 1995, 1998; Gradstein and Milanovic, 2004), and not really on their evolution during a process of growth acceleration.

This paper tries to fill this hole and examines, empirically, poverty, inequality and growth in a wide sample of Emerging and Transition Economies. This group consists of two elements: Emerging Economies (EEs) as defined by the World Bank and the International Monetary Fund i.e., countries with low-to-middle per capita income in a process of institutional reforms and integration in the world economy (IMF, 2001; World Bank, 1998); and transition economies, i.e., former communist countries such as current members of the Confederation of Independent States (CIS) and Central and Eastern European Countries (CEECs). Of course Emerging Economies and Transition Economies are very different from each other, from many different points of view, historically, socially and economically. However, they are often considered, by international financial organisations such as Morgan Stanley, Grant Thornton, Goldman Sachs and The Economist group, as part of the group of Emerging Economies, broadly speaking, in the sense that they are experiencing a process of reform and of institutional change. Nevertheless, I would say that although Transition Economies can be considered, in some ways, as Emerging Economies, the opposite is not true. Transition economics is a very specific concept that was applied to former communist countries which, after the fall of the Berlin wall (1989) and the dissolution of former Soviet Union, began a transition from a planned to a market economy. In general, most of these countries were already industrialised and middle per capita income economies. Taking the beginning of the 1990s as a starting point, most of them had better initial conditions than the Emerging economies, in terms of both infrastructure and quality of life (captured by life expectancy, poverty levels, infant mortality, education, etc.).

Emerging economies can be small, medium and large, and, in general, they appear on the global scene because they are becoming more open, in terms of trade and flows of foreign investments. Brazil, China and Tunisia, for instance, are part of the category of emerging economies because they have been experiencing a process of reform over the past decade, with openness, economic growth, institutional and structural change. By this definition, some European countries, such as Spain and Ireland, could have been considered as emerging economies in the 1980s and 1990s when they experienced fast growth and structural change. For this reason I include them in this analysis as reference countries for current emerging economies. However, since the aim of this paper is to look at the effects of economic growth on income distribution and poverty I selected, from among ETEs, a group of 48 countries that experienced a *growth acceleration* process in the last 11 years (1995-2006). A growth acceleration is defined by Hausmann, Pritchett and Rodrik (2005: 305) as an increase in per-capita growth of 2 percentage points or more for at least eight years (Rodrik et al., 2005: 305). In this way I included only the ETEs that grew at an average rate of more than 2% in the period 1995-2006[73]. Moreover, I started the cross-section analysis from 1995 because many transition economies experienced a huge recession at the beginning of the 1990s.

Average growth in these countries during 1995-2006 was 4,71%; this was above the world average growth of 4,33% (IMF, 2007). At the same time, the average income inequality, as measured by the Gini coefficient, grew in the same period (1993-2004), reaching an average level of 39%; the average of Gini variation was +7%; poverty, on average, decreased from 52% to 42%, as measured by a cut-off line of $4. However, the average of poverty variation was +20%, showing that many countries experienced a huge increase in the poverty level between 1993-2004[74]. Hence, when assessing the quality of economic development also inequality and poverty dynamics need to be addressed, as it will be done below.

5. Poverty and inequality in transition and emerging economies

This section deals with the specific path of development in ETEs. Firstly, I analyse whether ETEs experienced, together with a growth acceleration process, a reduction of poverty, an increase of political democracy, and an improvement of the human development variables. The second part of this section will focus on income distribution. In other words I will explore whether those countries experienced development or just economic growth.

5.1. Poverty

73 The complete list of countries considered in our sample include the following: Albania, Algeria, Argentina, Armenia, Azerbaijan, Belarus, Bolivia, Botswana, Brazil, Bulgaria, Chile, China, Croatia, Czech Republic, Ecuador, Egypt, Estonia, Georgia, Hong Kong, Hungary, India, Ireland, Israel, Kazakhstan, Republic of Korea, Kyrgyzstan, Latvia, Lithuania, Macedonia TFYR, Malaysia, Mexico, Pakistan, Peru, Philippines, Poland, Russian Federation, Saudi Arabia, Singapore, Slovakia, Slovenia, South Africa, Spain, Tajikistan, Tunisia, Turkey, Turkmenistan, Ukraine, Uzbekistan, Venezuela, Viet Nam. These are 23 transition economies (former communist countries), 25 non former communist emerging economies and 2 old European Union member States (Spain and Ireland), included in the sample as reference countries for current emerging economies.

74 Table 7 explains this apparent contradiction.

In order to answer this question I used the sample of 50 ETEs described above. In the first regression below I found that economic growth in 1995-2006 was associated with more poverty, less democracy, as underlined by the coefficient voice and accountability, more authoritarianism, as underlined by the coefficient government effectiveness, and with negative variation of Life Expectancy during the period 1995-2004.

Table 6: economic growth in ETEs

OLS model - Obs 50 **Dependent Variable: Economic growth 1995-2006**	
Variables	**Coefficient**
Poverty (1993)	0,060977* (0,012766)
Poverty Variation (1993-2004)	0,008892* (0,002588)
Voice & Accountability (1998-2005)	-0,830378** (0,394578)
Government Effectiveness (1998-2005)	1,499615** (0,467849)
Life Expectancy Growth (1995-2004)	-0,165477** (0,051299)
Life Expectancy (1995)	0,236490* (0,069520)
Constant	-14,60425** (5,180183)
R-squared 0,547555	
Adjusted R-squared 0,469993	
Log likelihood -69,94339	
Durbin-Watson stat 1,524590	
Mean dependent var 4,752131	
Prob(F-statistic) 0,000055	

Significance level at * = 1%, ** = 5%. Standard Errors (in parenthesis) are heteroscedasticity–robust after White test. Multicollinearity not relevant.
Source: own elaboration on data in Appendix

In the regression table 6, it is surprising to see how well the observed variables fit with economic growth. In particular, an initial high level of poverty in 1993, an increasing level of poverty (1993-2004), a negative value of the indicator Voice and Accountability between 1998-2005 (a proxy for democracy and pluralism), a positive value of the indicator Government Effectiveness[75] and a nega-

75 Both Voice and Accountability and Government Effectiveness are World Bank indicators of Governance. World Bank indicators, elaborated by Kaufmann et. al. (2008) reflect the statistical compilation of responses on the quality of governance given by a large number of enterprise, citizen and expert survey respondents in developed, transition and developing countries, as reported by a number of survey institutes, think tanks, non-governmental organisations, and international organisations. Indexes are estimated between -2,5 and +2,5. They concern five fundamental governance dimensions: Voice and Accountability, Political Stability, Government Effectiveness, Regulatory Quality, Rule of Law and Con-

tive variation of Life Expectancy from 1995 to 2004, despite an initial higher level of the latter, are all functions of the economic growth that occurred during 1995-2006. The values of these variables do not identify a process of development of quality. Growth occurred at the expense of fundamental development variables such as life expectancy, poverty, and voice and accountability. The fact that an initial higher level of life expectancy, in 1995, is also functional to economic growth does not contradict the results; it just underlines that life expectancy, initially higher, declined during the process of economic growth.

Table 7: averages of relevant variables of the regression Table 6, for group of countries

	Eco. growth 1995-06	Poverty 1993 (% of pop)	Poverty 2004 (% of pop)	Poverty[76] variat. 1993-04 (in %)	Life Exp in years (1995)	Life Exp in years (2004)	life Exp growth 95-04 (in %)
All countries	4,71	52,11	42,39	20,1	69,7	70,16	1,5
CIS (12 countries)	6,1	54,1	53,3	74,8	68,5	67,2	-1,9
CEECs (11 countries)	4,1	31,3	21,2	9,9	71,8	72,3	0,7
Latin American (8 countries)	3,5	50,2	50,0	1,3	69,8	68,3	-1,3
Asia (9 countries)	5,5	80,7	62,7	5,5	67,3	68,7	2,2
Africa, Middle East and Turkey (8 countries)	4,2	60,5	49,8	-10,1	65,6	71,0	11,3
EU – 2 old MS	5,6	Na	15,0	Na	77,0	77,0	0,0

Source: own elaboration on data in Appendix. Table 9 reports also averages for Voice and Accountability and Government Effectiveness.

By contrast, a process of development of quality, (High Quality Growth), is brought about when there is an improvement in human development variables, causing an increasing of the Human Development Index (HDI); this is an alternative means of measuring well being to GDP per capita (UNDP, 1990). The UNDP Human Development Index is a composite index, ranking between 0-1. It is the combination of two non-income dimensions of people's lives and one income dimension. The first one is life expectancy at birth which also reflects infant mortality; the second is educational attainment which is a combination of

---

trol of Corruption. Slovenia, Hungary, Estonia, the Czech Republic and Poland have the highest indicators.

76 Data on this column reflects the average values of variation of the poverty levels for each group of country from 1993 to 2004. Although the aggregate poverty level, on average, fell from 52% to 42%, average variations for all countries is +20%. An example would explain better this case which seems a truism. In Slovakia poverty, between 1993-2004, increased from 2% to 6%, that is more than 200%. Hence, average of poverty variation can be very high although average poverty level is falling. For more details and examples on this see Table 16 in appendix.

primary, secondary and tertiary educational levels and adult literacy rate. The third element is an adjusted GDP index which reflects income per capita measured in Purchasing Power Parity (PPP) at US$ (UNDP, 1990). In fact, the idea that the GDP is an absolute and reliable measure of development has been widely criticized by development economists (Morris, 1979; Sen, 1985; Noorbakhsh, 1996). A great deal of empirical evidence shows that, both in developing and in developed economies, some countries have relatively high GDP per capita but very low indicators of development such as literacy, access to drinking water, rate of infant mortality, life expectancy, education, etc. This is partly due to the fact that wealth is unequally distributed. Conversely, there are cases of relatively low GDP per capita and high indicators of development in countries where income is more equally distributed (Ray, 1998)[77]. The HDI is determined, in the following regression, by voice and accountability and low poverty. In the sample, countries having a lower poverty level (2004) and higher Voice and Accountability 1998-2004 also have a higher HDI 2004 – which is indeed different from having a higher GDP per capita.

Table 8: HDI in ETEs

OLS model - Obs 50 Dependent Variable: Human Development Index 2004	
Variables	**Coefficients**
Voice & Accountability 1998-2005	0,026915* (0,009763)
Poverty (Variation 1993-2004)	-0,002351* (0,000316)
Constant	0,886631* (0,015218)
R-squared 0,696647	
Adjusted R-squared 0,683165	
Log likelihood 75,52770	

77 For instance, Guatemala has a GDP per capita that is higher than Sri Lanka but inequality is much higher in Guatemala. Development indicators are much better in Sri Lanka than in Guatemala. Life expectancy (years): 72 compared with 65; infant mortality rate (per 1000): 18 compared with 48; access to safe water (% of pop.): 60 compared with 62; adult literacy rate (%): 89 compared with 54 (UNDP, 1995). Examples like this are numerous and non-perfect correspondence between GDP and development indicators can be observed even in industrialized countries where there are more resources to distribute. For instance, Ireland has the highest GDP per capita after Luxemburg yet its non-income dimension indicators i.e., education and life expectancy are lower than Italy or Portugal (UNDP, 2006). Saudi Arabia has a GDP per capita which is higher than many transition economies such as Poland, Czech Republic, Hungary etc, but its non-income dimension indicators are lower. USA has an income per capita which is much higher than most of the countries in the world, yet life expectancy of black American citizens is lower than in China or in the Indian State of Kerala. As a result of all these contradictions and exceptions, the UNDP taxation of Human Development Indexes and GDP rank is not at all coincident (UNDP, 1999).

Durbin-Watson stat 2,111577
Mean dependent var 0,786104
Prob(F-statistic) 0,000000

Significance level at * = 1%. Standard Errors (in parenthesis) are eteroschedasticity–robust after White test. Multicollinearity not relevant., Source: own elaboration on data in Appendix

The results of the regression in Table 8, which is in a sense the reverse of the regression in table 6, confirm my hypothesis. Among ETEs, countries with a higher level of development – represented here by the index HDI, would have lower poverty and higher political democracy, represented by the index Voice and Accountability.

Table 9: averages of relevant variables of the regression Table 8, for group of countries

	HDI 04 (between min 0 – max)	**Voice & Accountability Average 1998-2004** (min - 2.5 max +2.5)	**Government Effectiveness Average 1998-04** (min - 2.5 max +2.5)
All countries	0,788	-0,06	0,02
CIS (12 countries)	0,746	-0,9	-0,7
CEECs (11 countries)	0,848	0,7	0,5
Latin American (8 countries)	0,792	0,2	-0,2
Asia (9 countries)	0,699	-0,7	-0,1
Africa, Middle East and Turkey (8 countries)	0,733	-0,3	0,0
EU – 2 old MS	0,947	1,2	1,5

Source: own elaboration on data in Appendix

Interestingly enough, poverty appears to be reduced by three variables: public expenditure in education, public expenditure in health, and political stability (see Table 10). Political stability is an important indicator, which in general is a consequence of cohesion and social peace; in this circumstance, it is most likely that appropriate poverty reduction policies have been implemented. Conversely, economic growth (1995-2006) did not contribute to poverty reduction as the coefficient for the variable economic growth (1995-2006) is not significant (see II regression). A predictable model which would represent poverty reduction and which is in fact confirmed by the result below is the following:

$$Poverty = \alpha - \beta_1 \cdot Edu - \beta_2 \cdot Health - \beta_3 Pol.Stab + \varepsilon$$

In other words poverty increases when public expenditure in education and in health decreases and when political troubles and political instability increases.

Table 10: poverty in ETEs (1)

OLS model - Obs 50 Dependent Variable: Poverty 2004			
I Regression		II Regression	
Variables	Coeff.	Variables	Coeff.
Public Education Expenditure Av. 2000-04	-5,128180* (1,833510)	Education Expenditure 2000-05	-5,133575* (1,857425)
Public Heath Expenditure Av.2000-04	-8,742550* (1,853532)	Heath Expenditure 2000-05	-8,832262* (1,897523)
Political Stability 2000-04	-9,256239** (3,685674)	Political Stability 2000-05	-9,296939** (3,735670)
		Economic Growth 1995-2006	-0,551997 (1,685981)
Constant	95,83431* (9,177251)	Constant	98,75598 (12,88641)
R-squared 0,6512		R-squared 0,6514	
Adjusted R-squared 0,6274		Adjusted R-squared 0,6189	
Log likelihood -163,7369		Log likelihood -163,6755	
Durbin-Watson stat 1,985574		Durbin-Watson stat 1,966940	
Mean dependent var 42,51769		Mean dependent var 42,51769	
Prob(F-statistic) 0,000000		Prob(F-statistic) 0,000001	

Significance level at * = 1%, ** = 5%. Standard Errors (in parenthesis) are eteroschedasticity–robust after White test. Multicollinearity not relevant.
Source: own elaboration on data in Appendix

A theoretical explanation of this evidence can be traced back to Amartya Sen's thought. Since public expenditure in education and health would improve education level and life expectancy, crucial indicators of development, poverty will be reduced because individual capabilities of doing and being will increase (Sen, 1999).

Table 11: averages of relevant variables of the regression Table 10, for group of countries

	Political Stabil. Av. 1998-04 (min – 2,5 max +2,5)	**Health Expenditure average 2000-04** (% of GDP)	**Education Expenditure average 2000-04** (% of GDP)
All countries	-0,04	3,3	4,5
CIS (12 countries)	-0,7	2,3	5,8
CEECs (11 countries)	0,4	5,1	5,3
Latin American (8 countries)	0,1	3,0	3,2
Asia (9 countries)	-0,1	1,5	3,1
Africa, Middle East and Turkey (8 countries)	-0,5	3,6	5,2
EU – 2 old MS	0,8	5,7	4,7

Source: own elaboration on data in Appendix

Another way of seeing the relation represented in table 11 is to regress Poverty (2004) with infant mortality reduction (1975-1995) (a good proxy also for health public expenditure), and adult literacy variation (1990/95) (a good proxy also for education expenditure). Similarly, economic growth (1995-2006) does not appear to be significant in this regression. Basically, the evidence which emerges from this exercise is that poverty is lowered by infant mortality reduction (1970-1995) that occurred previously to the current economic growth. The variable Adult literacy in 1990/95 is also significant, in the sense that an initial higher level of education would cause a lower level of poverty.

Table 12: poverty in ETEs (2)

OLS model - Obs 50 **Dependent Variable: Poverty 2004**			
Regression I		Regression II	
Variables	Coeff.	Variables	Coeff.
Infant Mortality reduction 1970-1995	-0,6186608* (0,125173)	Infant Mortality reduction 1970-1995	-0,5632049* (0,1330992)
Adult Literacy 1990/95	-1,054593* (0,202224)	Adult Literacy 1990/95	-1,066044* (0,2015496)
		Economic Growth 1995-2006	1,1281490 (1,711285)
Constant	170,3155* (20,2291)	Constant	159,3541* (22,15867)
R-squared 0,5078		R-squared 0,5231	
Adjusted R-squared 0,4860		Adjusted R-squared 0,4906	
Log likelihood -211,2259		Log likelihood -210,92220	
Durbin-Watson stat 2,149447		Durbin-Watson stat 2,181335	
Mean dependent var 42,38229		Mean dependent var 42,38229	
Prob(F-statistic) 0,000001		Prob(F-statistic) 0,000005	

Significance level at * = 1%. Standard Errors (in parenthesis) are eteroschedasticity–robust after White test. Multicollinearity not relevant.
Source: own elaboration on data in Appendix.

Hence, it can be concluded from these regression results in table 10 and 11 that economic growth occurred during the last decade did not contribute to a reduction in poverty or to an increase in human development variables. On the contrary poverty appears to be much lower in countries enjoying higher levels of political stability, and which improved human development variables such as infant mortality and adult literacy during the period before the current economic growth, and thanks to public investments done in the health system and in education.

Table 13: averages of relevant variables of the regression Table 12, for group of countries

	Adult literacy 1990/95 (% of pop)	Reduction of infant mortality 1970-95 (in %)
All countries	90	55,4
CIS (12 countries)	99	30,7
CEECs (11 countries)	97	56,7
Latin American (8 countries)	90	62,3
Asia (9 countries)	75	52,5
Africa, Middle East and Turkey (8 countries)	74	70,2
EU – 2 old MS	98	73,9

Source: own elaboration on data in Appendix.

5.2. Inequality

During the last 10-15 years Emerging and Transition Economies experienced an increasing trend in the Gini coefficient. In the sample of ETEs, the average of Gini, in 1993, was 37%, while in 2004 it was above 39%. The average of Gini variation for the same period was +7%. The lowest values of Gini are in Slovakia and the Czech Republic (25,8%), Hungary (27%) and Slovenia (28%), among former communist countries, and in South Korea (31%) for non communist countries. The highest values are in Botswana (61%), Bolivia (60%), South Africa, Chile and Brasil (57%) and, for former communist countries, in Russia (42%).

Table 14: growth and inequality for group of countries

	Economic growth 1995-06	Gini coeff. 1993 (in %)	Gini coeff. 2004 (in %)	Gini variation 1993-04 (in %)	Public Exp. Av 00-05 (% of GDP)	Life exp. Growth 1970-95 (in %)	Adult Literacy Variat. 1995-04 (%)	Adult Literacy 2004 (% of pop)
All countries	4,71	37,1	39,2	7,7	23	10,1	6,5	92,2
CIS (12 countries)	6,1	34,9	35,5	4,4	32	1,6	-0,2	99
CEECs (11 countries)	4,1	28,3	31,6	13,2	27	3,2	1,7	98,9
Latin American (8 countries)	3,5	49,1	53,4	10,3	18	17,6	4,7	91,4
Asia (9 countries)	5,5	36,2	38,5	6,8	22	21,3	15,1	78,9
Africa, Middle East and Turkey (8 countries)	4,2	43,3	44,5	3,8	21	15,8	21,1	80,4
EU – 2 old MS	5,6	30,0	34,0	13,8	15	7,4	1,9	99

Source: own elaboration on data in Appendix

Hence, although economic growth occurred for a quite long period (1995-2006), inequality did not decrease as predicted by a hypothetical inverted "U"-shaped Kuznets curve. The following figure invalidates such a hypothesis, scattering ETEs in two periods, in the 1990s and in the 2000s, with GDP per capita on the horizontal axis and Gini on the vertical axis.

Figure 14 – Gini 1993 vs GDP per capita 1995 Figure 15: Gini 2004 vs GDP per capita 2006

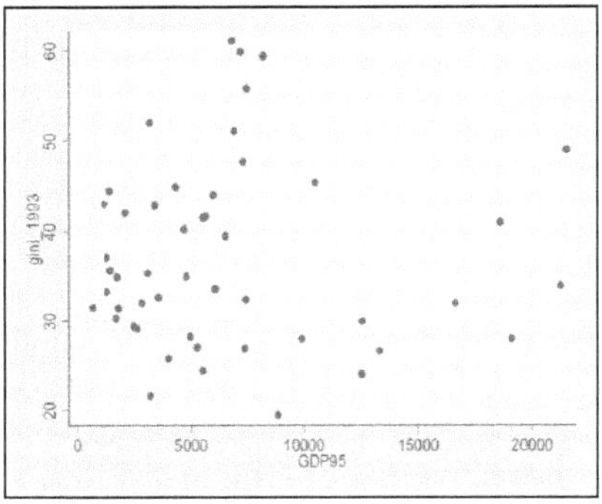

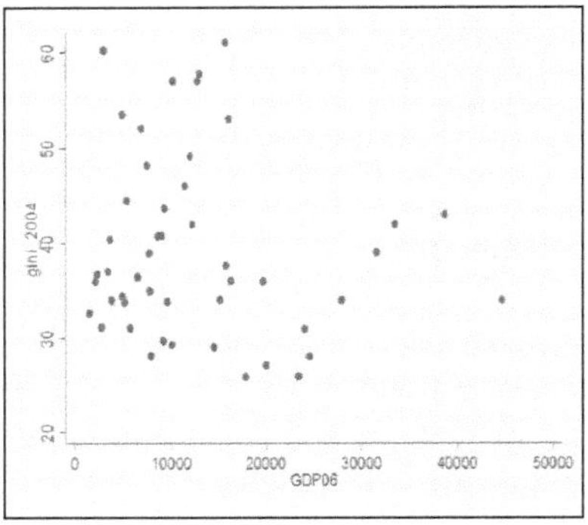

Source: own elaboration on data in Appendix.

Why did income inequality increase? I assume because education and other human development variables (such as life expectancy) worsened. Consecutively, income distribution worsened. A theoretical model which would represent such a prediction would be the following:

$$Gini = \alpha - \beta_1 \cdot literacy - \beta_2 \cdot lifeExpe - \beta_3 \cdot PubExpe + \varepsilon$$

In order to test such a hypothesis I used an OLS regression model in the usual sample of 50 ETEs. The results are very interesting, although are a bit more complex than the model above, as shown in table 15. The Gini coefficient in 2004 is negatively correlated with Adult literacy in 2004, Adult literacy growth (1995-2004), Public expenditure (2000-05) and life expectancy growth eventually occurring before the current economic growth (1970-1995). Economic growth (1995-2006), which would increase income inequality in this model by a coefficient of β=0,2410, is not statistical significant (cf. Regression II).

Table 15: income inequality

OLS model - Obs 50 Dependent Variable: GINI 2004			
Regression I		Regression II	
Variables	Coeff	Variables	Coeff
Adult literacy 2004	-1,05157* (0,151033)	Adult literacy 2004	-1,065728* (0,155722)
Adult literacy growth (1995-2004)	-0,5566862 * (0,1139592)	Adult literacy growth (1990-2004)	-0,5663246* (0,1170401)
Life expectancy growth (1970-1995)	-0,3470506 (0,1298205)**	Life expectancy growth (1970-1995)	-0,3456583** (0,1310583)
Public expenditure (2000-05)	-0,3385873 (0,1291205)**	Public expenditure (2000-05)	-0,3460278** (0,1313586)
		Growth (1995-2006)	0,241014 (0,5423469)
Constant	76,94141* (5,969043)	Constant	76,32705* (6,180829)
R-squared 0,5599		R-squared 0,5619	
Adj R-squared 0,5199		Adj R-squared 0,5110	
Log likelihood -174,6677		Log likelihood -174,5815	
Durbin-Watson stat 1,940153		Durbin-Watson stat 1,952846	
Mean dependent var 39,24		Mean dependent var 39,24	
Prob(F-statistic) 0,0000		Prob(F-statistic) 0,0000	

Significance level at *=1%; **=2%. Standard Errors (in parenthesis) are heteroschedasticity–robust after White test. Multicollinearity not relevant.
Source: own elaboration on data in Appendix.

Education and public expenditure are crucial variables in this model for a reduction of income inequality. Public expenditure finances, among other, a national health system with positive advantages for life expectancy, which should growth too in order to reduce income inequality. Life expectancy grew consistently before the current economic growth in most of the ETEs as shown in table 14. However, during 1995-2004 life expectancy worsened in many countries (cf. table 7). This is the reason why the variables life expectancy variation between 1995-2004 and life expectancy in 2004 would not be significant in reducing inequality, and are therefore excluded from the regression in table 15. In fact, following a capability approach, basic dimensions such as health and education should be guaranteed by public policies in order for people to live a long and healthy life, become knowledgeable and acquire a decent standard of living. If these basic capabilities are not achieved, many choices are simply not available and many opportunities remain inaccessible (UNDP, 1999). Lack of opportunities will lead to income inequality and poverty. Very simply, if education is subject only to market rules, then higher education will be available only to children whose parents can pay market prices. Poorer parents, who in most of cases are unskilled workers, could not afford such a cost; consequently unskilled parents will tend to have unskilled children. In this way, inequality will be "crystallized" within the initial conditions and will not be reduced during economic growth.

Moreover, if growth requires more and more skilled workers, inequality will increase accordingly.

It seems that economic growth in ETEs requires higher education and ignores basic education. This is confirmed by the increase, in all the emerging economies, of exports in the ICT sector (UNCTAD, 2006), which of course has a high employment ratio of skilled workers. This is likely to be one of the elements of the growing inequality in ETEs. Unskilled workers, i.e., people with basic education, remain outside of the socio-economic model of growth in ETEs, which includes skilled people with high education. Such a model produces education inequality and consecutively income inequality, with an increasing level of people at risk of poverty.

6. Conclusion

Using Emerging and Transition Economies during the period 1995-2006, this paper analyses the *process of development* perceived as a wider process of economic growth and of institutional change bringing about poverty reduction and income distribution alongside an improvement in human development variables. During this period, ETEs experienced an acceleration growth in the sense of Hausmann, Pritchett and Rodrik (2005), with average growth equal to 4,7%, and above the world average growth. However, such a growth did not bring about a *process of development* as above defined. The results suggest that the economic growth occurring during the last decade contributed neither to a decrease in poverty between 1993-2004, measured through a cut-off line of $4 a day, nor to an increase in human development variables, particularly in life expectancy. On the contrary, these variables worsened, as did Voice and Accountability, the proxy for political democracy and pluralism.

Income inequality, measured as a reduction of Gini coefficient between the years 1993-2004, worsened too. One can say that growth in ETEs occurred despite the worsening of income inequality. Nevertheless, this does not identify a "U-shaped" Kuznets curve because a subsequent inequality reduction, after a long period of growth (11 years) was not observed. On the contrary, inequality increased constantly. The results suggest also that countries with a lower level of adult literacy and public expenditure, suffer higher income inequality. Hence, inequality is not inevitable during economic growth but higher education and State intervention in strategic dimensions of human development may reduce inequalities; a more educated population and an active role of the state in creating equal opportunities increase individual capabilities with consequent positive effects on individuals' income.

In the same way poverty appears to be much lower when countries improved, during the period before the current economic growth, and thanks to public investments, human development variables such as infant mortality and adult literacy. Hence, the holistic role of the State, in the sense of Myrdal (1974) is crucial in reducing poverty. In fact, as the regression results suggest, the public expenditure in education and health increases skills and life expectancy, and provides great opportunities, essential for escaping the poverty trap, and for people to build creative and long lives. On the contrary, lack of opportunities will lead to both income inequality and poverty.

References

Agtmael, A. (2007), *The Emerging Markets Century: How A New Breed of World-Class Companies is Overtaking the World,* New York: Free Press.

Alesina, A. and R. Perotti (1996), "Income distribution, political instability and investment", *European Economic Review* 40(6): 1203–1228.

Alexander, K. C. and K. P. Kumaran (1992), *Culture and Development, Cultural Patterns in Areas of Uneven Development*, New Delhi, Newbury Park and London: Sage Publications.

Atkinson, A. (1999), *Is Rising Inequality Inevitable? A Critique of the Transatlantique Consensus*, WIDER Annual Lectures 3, Helsinki: UNU World Institute for Development Economics Research.

Atkinson, A. and J. Miklewright (1992), *Economic Transformation in Eastern Europe and the Distribution of Income*, Cambridge: Cambridge University Press.

Birdsall, N. and R. Sabot (1994), "Inequality as a constraint on growth in Latin America", *Development Policy,* Newsletter on Policy Research, Inter-American Development Bank: 1-5.

Brinkman, R. (1995), "Economic growth versus economic development: toward a conceptual clarification", *Journal of Economic Issues*, 29(4): 1171-1188.

Chenery, H. B. and M. Syrquin (1975), *Patterns of Development, 1950-1960*, Oxford: Oxford University Press.

Cypher, J. and J. Dietz (2004), *The Process of Economic Development*, 2nd edition, London and New York: Routledge.

Dollar, D. and A. Kraay (2001), "Growth is good for the poor?", *The World Bank Policy Research Working Paper Series*, 2587.

Easterly, W. (2001), "The middle class consensus and economic development", *Journal of Economic Growth*, 6(4): 317–335.

Field, G. (1989), "Changes in poverty and inequality in developing countries", *World Bank Research Observer*, 4(2): 167-185.

Gradstein, M. and B. Milanovic (2004), "Does libertè = egalitè? A survey of the empirical links between democracy and inequality with some evidence on the transition economies", *Journal of Economic Surveys*, 18(4): 515-537.

Hausmann, R., L. Pritchett, and D. Rodrik (2005), "Growth accelerations", *Journal of Economic Growth*, 10(4): 303-329.

Heston, A., R. Summers, and B. Aten (2006), "Penn World Table Version 6.1", Center for International Comparisons of Production, Income and Prices at the University of Pennsylvania.
Hodgson, G. (2006), "What are institutions?", *Journal of Economic Issues*, 40(1): 1-25.
IMF (1995), "Gender issues in economic adjustment", *IMF Survey*: 286-288.
IMF (2001), *World Economic Outlook*, Washington, D.C.: International Monetary Fund.
IMF (2007), "World economic outlook", *online database*.
Kaufmann, D., A. Kraay, and M. Mastruzzi (2008), *Governance Matters IV: Governance Indicators*, Washington DC: World Bank.
Kornai, J. (2006), "The great transformation of Central Eastern Europe. Success and disappointment", *Economics of Transition*, 14(2): 207-244.
Kuznets, S. (1955), "Economic growth and income inequality", *American Economic Review*, 45(1): 1-28.
Kuznets, S. (1965), *Economic Growth and Structure: Selected Essays*, New York: Norton.
Mabogunje, A. L. (1989), *The Development Process. A Spatial Perspective*, 2nd edition, London: Unwin Hyman.
Marcus, R. and J. Wilkinson (2002), "Whose poverty matters? Vulnerability, social protection and PRSPs", *Childhood Poverty Research and Policy Centre Working Paper* No.1.
Mauro, P. (2000), "Stock returns and output growth in emerging and advanced economies", *IMF Working Paper*, 89.
Milanovic, B. (1994), "Determinants of cross-country income inequality: an augmented Kuznets hypothesis", *The World Bank Policy Research Working Paper Series*, 1246.
Milanovic, B. (1995), "Poverty, inequality, and social policy in transition economies", *The World Bank Policy Research Working Paper Series* 1530.
Milanovic, B. (1998), "Explaining the increase in inequality during the transition", *The World Bank Policy Research Working Paper Series* 1935.
Morris, D. M. (1979), *Measuring the Condition of the World's Poor: The Physical Quality of Life Index*, New York: Pergamon Press.
Myrdal, G. (1974), "What is development?", *Journal of Economic Issues*, 8(4): 729-736.
Noorbakhsh, F. (1996), "Some reflections on UNDP's human development index", *University of Glasgow Cds Occasional Paper*, 17.
Nugent, J. B. and J. Y. Lin (1995), "Institutions and economic development", in H. Chenery, T. N. Srinivasan, and J. Behrman (eds), *Handbook of Development Economics*, Amsterdam: North-Holland.
Perkins, D., H. Dwight, S. Radelet, and D. Lindauer (2007), *Economics of Development,* 6th Edition, ISI.
Pronk, J. (1993), *The World Bank and Poverty Reduction*, The Hague: Ministry of Foreign Affairs.
Rawls, J. (1971), *A Theory of Justice*, Cambridge, Mass.: Harvard University Press.
Ray, D. (1998), *Development Economics*, Princeton: Princeton University Press.
Sen, A. (1973), *On Economic Inequality*, Oxford: Clarendon Press.
Sen, A. (1985), "A sociological approach to the measurement of poverty: a reply to professor Peter Townsend", *Oxford Economic Papers*, 37(4): 669-676.
Sen, A. (1999), *Development as Freedom*, New York: Oxford University Press.
Sokoloff, K. L. and S. L. Engerman (2000), "History lessons. Institutions, factor endowments, and paths of development in the new world", *Journal of Economic Perspectives*, 14(3): 217-232.

Street, J. H. (1987), "The institutionalist theory of economic development", *Journal of Economic Issues*, 21(4): 1861-1887.
Toye, J. (1995), "The new institutional economics and its implications for development theory", in J. Harris, J. Hunter, and C. Lewis (eds), *The New Institutional Economics and Third World Development*, London: Routledge.
Tridico, P. (2006), "Institutional change and governance indexes in transition economies: the case of Poland", *The European Journal of Comparative Economics*, 3(2): 197-238.
UNCTAD (2006), *Statistical Yearbook*, online database.
UNDP (various years: 1990; 1995; 1999; 2000; 2004; 2006), *Human Development Report*, Oxford University Press.
Veblen, T. (1919), *The Place of Science in Modern Civilization,* New York: The Viking Press.
Voitchovsky, S. (2005), "Does the profile of income inequality matter for economic growth? Distinguishing between the effects of inequality in different parts of the income distribution", *Journal of Economic Growth*, 10(3): 273-296.
World Bank (1990), *World Development Report*, Oxford University Press.
World Bank (1998), *East Asia: The Road to Recovery*, Washington, D.C.
World Bank (2000), *World Development Report*, Oxford University Press.
World Bank (2007), *Millennium Development Goals*, online database.

APPENDIX

Table 16

	growth 1995-06	1993 -pov-erty	2004-poverty	poverty var 93-04	life exp. 1995	life exp. 2004	life exp. growth 95-04		growth 1995-06	1993 – poverty	2004-poverty	poverty var 93-04	life exp. 1995	life exp. 2004	life exp growth 95-04
Albania	5,2	66,9	47,9	-28,3	73	73	0,0	Kyrgyzstan	4,5	34.79	72.48	108.3	68	66.8	-1.8
Algeria	3,6	48,85	42,3	-13,3	69	72	4,3	Latvia	6,7	48.25	26.3	-45.5	68	72	5.9
Argentina	5,5	25,4	36,6	44,0	73	71	-2,7	Lithuania	5,3	87.63	36.04	-58.9	70	77	10.0
Armenia	10,1	75,6	80,5	6,4	71	71,4	1,3	Macedonia	2,2	27.17	21.95	-19.2	73	73.7	1.0
Azerbaijan	7,3	86,9	57,6	-33,7	70	66,9	-4,4	Malaysia	4,1	40.07	25.45	-36.5	72	63	-12.5
Belarus	6,7	1,1	8,3	609,4	68	68,1	0,1	Mexico	3,9	50.43	35.14	-30.3	72	72	0.0
Bolivia	2,9	61,7	67,8	9,9	61	75	23,0	Pakistan	3,8	93.74	92.75	-1.1	64	63	-1.6
Botswana	5,7	80,3	73,1	-8,9	47	75	59,6	Peru	3,2	65.26	60.03	-8.0	68	78	14.7
Brazil	2,0	46	41,9	-8,9	67	65	-3,0	Philippines	3,9	82.88	75.66	-8.7	68	70	2.9
Bulgaria	2,0	19,5	39,8	104,2	71	64	-9,9	Poland	4,1	38.21	17.45	-54.3	73	71	-2.7
Chile	3,9	*36,1*	23,5	-35,0	75	35	-53,3	Russia	3,7	53.39	35.36	-33.8	67	65	-3.0
China	8,7	82	56,9	6,7	70	73	4,3	Saudi Arabia	2,9	Na	Na	Na	71	47	-33.8
Croatia	3,4	5,4	5,5	3,1	73	70	-4,1	Singapore	5,9			Na	77	67	-13.0
Czech Republic	2,2	0,51	0,5	-2,0	74	71	-4,1	Slovakia	3,9	2.01	6.69	232.8	73	70	-4.1
Ecuador	2,4	66,9	63,7	-4,8	70	76	8,6	Slovenia	3,7	Na	8	Na	74	78	5.4
Egypt	4,3	*85,5*	84,8	-0,8	66	73	10,6	South Africa	2,9	58.01	55.92	-3.6	55	72	30.9
Estonia	6,3	36,8	33,1	-9,9	69	75	8,7	Spain	3,5	Na	14	Na	78	80	2.6
Georgia	6,7	22,7	61,8	172,5	73	70,5	-3,4	Tajikistan	5,0	79.36	84.71	6.7	67	63.5	-5.2
Hong Kong	3,8	Na	4	Na	78	81	3,8	Tunisia	4,8	*38.04*	24.93	-34.5	70	80	14.3
Hungary	4,1	12,1	10,6	-12,8	71	73	2,8	Turkey	4,9	52.37	52.54	0.3	69	79	14.5
India	6,0	96	94,1	-2,1	63	72	14,3	Turkmenistan	9,3	89.99	66.88	-25.7	65	62.4	-4.0
Ireland	7,6	Na	16	Na	76	74	-2,6	Ukraine	2,6	23.49	44.68	90.2	69	75	8.7
Israel	4,3	Na	15	Na	78	70	-10,3	Uzbekistan	4,9	69.4	16.92	-75.6	68	66.5	-2.2

Kazakhstan	6,2	58	56,7	-2,3	68	63,2	-7,1	Venezuela	4,0	49.76	71.48	43.6	72	74	2.8
Korea	4,0	Na	4	Na	72	73	1,4	Viet Nam	6,6	89.4	62.65	-29.9	67	71	6.0

Source: Heston et al., (2006) and IMF (2007) for growth data; World Bank (2007) for poverty data; UNDP, (various years) for Life expectancy. data;

Table 17

	HDI 2004	P.Edu Exp. 00-05	P.Health Exp. 00-05	Voice & Accountab 98-05	Pol Stability 98-05	Gov effect. 2000-05		HDI 2004	P.Edu Exp. 00-0	P.Health Exp. 00-05	Voice & Accountab 98-05	Pol Stability 98-05	Gov effect. 2000-05
Albania	0,78	na	2,7	-0,69	-0,69	-0,04	Kyrgyzstan	0,70	6	2,2	-0,98	-1,04	-0,78
Algeria	0,72	5,1	3,3	-1,61	-1,61	-1,05	Latvia	0,84	4,1	3,3	0,9	0,81	0,81
Argentina	0,86	3,3	4,3	-0,3	-0,07	0,35	Lithuania	0,86	5,5	5	0,94	0,8	0,8
Armenia	0,76	na	1,2	-0,57	-0,38	-0,53	Macedonia	0,79	na	6	-0,09	-1,07	-0,33
Azerbaijan	0,75	7,7	0,9	-1,24	-0,85	-0,96	Malaysia	0,81	5,1	2,2	-0,36	0,29	0,73
Belarus	0,79	5,7	4,9	0	-1,08	-1,48	Mexico	0,82	3,8	2,9	0,26	0,13	0,03
Bolivia	0,69	2,4	4,3	-0,6	-0,35	0,05	Pakistan	0,54	2,6	0,7	-1,28	-1,46	-0,68
Botswana	0,57	6,2	3,3	0,78	0,78	0,73	Peru	0,77	2,8	2,1	0,03	0,86	-0,46
Brazil	0,79	na	3,4	-0,04	-0,13	0,37	Philippines	0,76	3	1,4	0,12	0,98	-0,08
Bulgaria	0,82	5,4	4,1	0,22	0,03	0,54	Poland	0,86	5,2	4,5	1,09	0,45	0,6
Chile	0,86	2,5	3	0,82	1,09	0,94	Russia	0,80	3,6	3,3	-0,65	0,81	-0,51
China	0,77	2,2	2	0,14	0,08	-1,55	Saudi Arabia	0,78	5,8	2,5	-1,52	-0,38	-0,12
Croatia	0,84	5,5	6,5	0,3	0,3	0,44	Singapore	0,92	3,1	1,6	-0,05	1,12	1,12
Czech Republic	0,89	na	6,8	0,77	0,75	0,96	Slovakia	0,86	5,6	5,2	0,97	0,72	0,72
Ecuador	0,76	3,4	2	0,95	-0,95	-0,13	Slovenia	0,91	4,8	6,7	1,06	1,01	0,92
Egypt	0,70	3,9	2,2	-0,66	-0,18	-1,01	South Africa	0,65	5,9	3,2	0,83	-0,25	-0,25
Estonia	0,86	na	4,1	0,83	0,83	1	Spain	0,94	4,3	5,5	1,11	0,44	1,37
Georgia	0,74	na	1	-1,34	-0,7	-0,33	Tajikistan	0,68	na	0,9	-1,13	-1,41	-1,13
Hong Kong	0,93	2,8	na	1,05	1,22	0,1	Tunisia	0,76	6	2,8	-0,97	0,23	0,61
Hungary	0,87	6,1	6,1	0,82	0,82	1,11	Turkey	0,76	2,4	5,4	-0,32	-0,85	-0,19

India	0,61	3,7	1,2	-0,96	-0,19	0,33	Turkmenistan	0,75	3,9	2,6	-0,32	-0,85	0,1
Ireland	0,96	5	5,8	1,15	1,61	1,36	Ukraine	0,77	6,2	3,8	-0,51	-0,32	-0,63
Israel	0,93	6,5	6,1	-1,25	0,7	0,63	Uzbekistan	0,71	9,4	2,4	-1,66	-1,41	-1,08
Kazakhstan	0,76	3,9	2	0,12	-0,75	-1,14	Venezuela	0,78	4,5	2	-0,43	-1,13	-0,88
Korea	0,91	3,8	2,8	0,32	0,32	0,7	Viet Nam	0,71	1,8	1,5	-1,54	0,29	-0,21

Source: UNDP (2006) for HDI, Public education and Heath Expenditure data; Kaufman et al. (2006) for institutional variables.

Table 18

	Adult Literacy 1990/95	**Adult Literacy 2004**	**Var. Adult Literacy 1995-04**	**Reduction Infant Mortality 1970-95**		**Adult Literacy 1990/95**	**Adult Literacy 2004**	**Var. Adult Literacy 1995-04**	**Reduction Infant Mortality 1970-95**
Albania	77	98,7	28	61,5	Kyrgyzstan	98,7	98,7	-1	44,0
Algeria	52,9	69,9	32	79,0	Latvia	99,8	99,7	-1	14,3
Argentina	95,7	97,2	2	47,2	Lithuania	99,3	99,6	-1	17,4
Armenia	97,5	99,4	2	42,0	Macedonia	95	96,1	-2	85,0
Azerbaijan	98	98,8	1	17,0	Malaysia	80,7	88,7	10	80,4
Belarus	99,5	99,6	0	59,0	Mexico	87,3	91	4	64,6
Bolivia	78,1	86,7	11	55,1	Pakistan	35,4	49,9	41	20,8
Botswana	68,1	81,2	19	61,6	Peru	85,5	87,7	3	62,6
Brazil	82	88,6	8	62,1	Philippines	91,7	92,6	1	42,9
Bulgaria	97,2	98,2	1	50,0	Poland	99,7	99,7	-1	68,8
Chile	94	95,7	2	85,9	Russia	99,2	99,4	-1	27,6
China	78,3	90,9	16	55,3	Saudi Arabia	66,2	79,4	20	81,4
Croatia	96,9	98,1	1	76,5	Singapore	88,8	92,5	4	81,8
Czech Republic	98,7	98,7	-1	76,2	Slovakia	99,6	99,6	-1	64,0
Ecuador	87,6	91	4	65,5	Slovenia	99,6	99,6	-1	80,0
Egypt	47,1	71,4	52	67,5	South Africa	81,2	82,4	1	40,0
Estonia	99,8	99,8	-1	14,3	Spain	96,3	99	3	77,8

Georgia	98	98	-1	32,0	Tajikistan	98,2	99,5	1	13,0
Hong Kong	98	99	1	62,5	Tunisia	59,1	74,3	26	81,5
Hungary	99,1	99	-1	72,2	Turkey	77,9	87,4	12	75,3
India	49,3	61	24	45,7	Turkmenistan	98,8	98,8	-2	24,0
Ireland	98	99	1	70,0	Ukraine	99,4	99,4	-1	18,2
Israel	91,4	97,1	6	75,0	Uzbekistan	98,7	98,7	-1	31,0
Kazakhstan	98,8	99,5	1	30,0	Venezuela	88,9	93	5	55,3
Korea	98	99	1	88,4	Viet Nam	90,4	90,3	-1	70,2

Source: UNDP (various years).

Table 19

	Life expectancy growth 70 -95	**Public Exp. 00-05**	**Gini 1993**	**Gini 2004**	**Gini variation 1993-04**	**GDP 1995 $PPP**	**GDP 2006 $PPP**		**Life expec-tancy growth 70-95**	**Public Exp. 00-05**	**Gini 1993**	**Gini 2004**	**Gini varia-tion 93-04**	**GDP 1995 $PPP**	**GDP 2006 $PPP**
Alba nia	7,2	19	29,12	31,09	6,8	2.636	5.727	Kyrgyzstan	9,0	41	43	36	-16,3	1.171	2.121
Al-geria	28,1	21	35	35	0,0	4.776	7.747	Latvia	-1,9	31	26,99	37,66	39,5	5.244	15.806
Ar-gen-tina	9,1	17	45,35	53	16,9	10.474	16.080	Lithuania	-1,1	28	33,64	36,01	7,0	6.026	16.373
Ar-me-nia	1,0	23	44,42	33,8	-23,9	1.418	5.177	Macedonia	9,0	29	28,21	38,95	38,1	4.939	7.680
Azer bai-jan	2,0	36	34,96	36,5	4,4	1.764	6.476	Malaysia	14,6	18	47,65	49,15	3,1	7.232	11.957
Bel-arus	-5,0	26	21,6	29,73	37,6	3.213	9.143	Mexico	16,6	13	51,06	46,05	-9,8	6.861	11.369
Bo-livia	31,5	19	42,04	60,24	43,3	2.100	2.931	Pakistan	23,8	18	30,31	31,18	2,9	1.711	2.744
Bot-swan a	-17,5	29	61	61	0,0	6.739	15.692	Peru	22,5	17	44,87	52,03	16,0	4.293	6.856
Bra-zil	11,7	22	59,82	56,99	-4,7	7.134	10.073	Philippines	18,3	15	42,89	44,48	3,7	3.390	5.365
Bul-garia	0,4	30	24,32	29,24	20,2	5.494	10.022	Poland	2,4	17	32,39	34,05	5,1	7.358	15.149
Chil e	19,2	18	55,75	57	2,2	7.395	12.811	Russia	-4,7	26	44	42	-4,5	5.947	12.178
Chin a	11,3	29	29,4	35	19,0	2.495	7.722	Saudi Arabia	32,8	28	na	na	na	11.89 4	16.505
Croa tia	4,0	28	26,82	29	8,1	7.313	14.523	Singapore	12,0	9	41	42	2,4	18.58 9	33.471
Czec	5,9	31	26,6	25,82	-2,9	13.302	23.399	Slovakia	4,4	26	19,49	25,81	32,4	8.834	17.913

h Re-public															
Ecuador	20,2	21	52	53,53	2,9	3.183	4.835	Slovenia	6,6	22	24	28	16,7	12.519	24.571
Egypt	28,3	10	*32*	34,45	7,7	2.835	4.895	South Africa	0,4	24	59,33	57,77	-2,6	8.171	13.018
Es-tonia	-1,4	31	39,5	36	-8,9	6.489	19.692	Spain	7,0	17	32	34	6,3	16.628	27.914
Georgia	3,0	41	37,13	40,37	8,7	1.286	3.642	Tajikistan	4,0	32	31,52	32,63	3,5	668	1.494
Hong Kong	9,2	6	49	43	-12,2	21.530	38.714	Tunisia	24,6	14	*40,24*	40,81	1,4	4.678	8.975
Hungary	3,0	28	27,94	27	-3,4	9.883	20.047	Turkey	21,6	16	41,53	43,66	5,1	5.494	9.240
India	25,8	36	31,465	34,025	8,1	1.823	3.802	Turkmenistan	5,0	34	35,38	40,77	15,2	3.096	8.539
Ire-land	7,9	13	28	34	21,4	19.104	44.676	Ukraine	-1,4	34	25,71	28,05	9,1	3.999	7.832
Is-rael	8,2	25	34	39	14,7	21.259	31.561	Uzbekistan	5,0	35	33,27	36,72	10,4	1.293	2.304
Ka-zakhstan	0,0	20	32,65	33,85	3,7	3.556	9.568	Venezuela	10,0	17	41,68	48,2	15,6	5.613	7.480
Ko-rea	17,1	11	30	31	3,3	12.540	24.084	Viet Nam	34,0	15	35,68	37,05	3,8	1.446	3.393

Source: Heston et al., (2006) and IMF (2007) for GDP and Public Expenditure data; World Bank (2007) for Gini data; UNDP (various years) for Life expectancy data.

4. South-Eastern Europe between socialism, transition and capitalism*

Siniša Kušić

"The worst thing in communism is what comes afterwards" (Adam Michnik)

1. Introduction

After the collapse of socialism and the fall of the "Iron Curtain", a new social order had to be built in East, Central and South-Eastern Europe for the second time in half a century. Formerly socialist countries accordingly began transition towards a market economy and democracy at the end of 1980s. Although there were no role models for this historically unique process, there was no lack of concepts for such thorough transformation. Reform suggestions grounded in economic theory were partially pragmatic but to a large extent also ideologically coloured. A number of reformers were convinced – at least at the beginning of the transition – that it was sufficient to apply mainstream neoliberal economic policy concepts to post-socialist countries, even regardless of their initial positions. The search for alternative routes to the market economy was clearly rejected and slogans like "no experiments" or "market economy without attributes" dominated the political debate on transition. By now we know that the success of the transition countries on their way to the market economy differed, and that economies in South-East Europe lagged far behind the successful countries of Central and Eastern Europe (CEE). These countries were supposed to become more "modern" during the course of transition so that they could catch up with "Europe" and be able to "get back to Europe". Therefore, almost twenty years since the beginning of the transition, we may ask ourselves what went wrong, especially because in the social and economic fields – particularly in the South-East European countries – frequently apparent is a "chaotic" or even "wild" capitalism with its unwanted consequences. What were the reasons for the different approaches taken to transition and for the different characteristics of capitalism in South-Eastern Europe?

2. Socialism, reforms and transition

As well known, economic systems exist in a certain environment. Hence they must adapt to the conditions of this environment, and to changes in it. Some economic systems develop constantly; others remain almost unchanged until they suddenly collapse and transform into another economic system. The latter variant describes processes in East, Central and South-Eastern Europe at the end

---

* Translated by Vladimir Cvijanović.

of the 1980s, when it finally became clear that the socialist experiment had failed.
Whilst there existed an illusion in the Eastern bloc of countries even in the 1950s that they could match the economic performance of the Western industrial nations, this catching-up process failed in the 1970s (Bergson, 1987). A merely extensive economic growth of the socialist countries in the sense of "conservative modernization" ended with depletion of resources and workforce. A low efficiency of investments, together with deficient innovative ability, led to a growing technological gap between East and West (Brus and Kowalik, 1983). The East European countries did not lack attempts to reform the existing socialism with all its facets and nuances. However, the reforms that were introduced regularly failed because of the restorative tendencies of the political leaders and bureaucracy[78]. Only Hungary and the former Yugoslavia managed to push through far-reaching reforms in the direction of market socialism and to draw the line between their systems and the classic centrally-administered system.

Declining living standards and the backsliding of the Comecon countries behind the Western industrial nations led to an increasing loss of legitimacy by socialist governments and the system as a whole (Vodička, 1996). The better ability of broad strata of the populace to gain information about consumption patterns in the Western industrial societies contributed to the decreasing ability of socialist parties to persuade the population about the superiority of the socialist economic systems. At the end of the 1980s, the competition between the systems was finally decided. Institutional changes much more radical than previous ones initiated the transition of economic and social systems in individual socialist countries (Kornai, 1992). To be observed with hindsight is that in almost all cases the growing dissatisfaction of the populace – or the "newly emerging citizens" – was crucial for radical societal change (Dvornik and Solioz, 2007). The dissatisfaction sprang from deficient economic provision, the pronounced economic crisis, the desire for larger democratic participation, and rejection of political claims by the communist parties for sole representation.

At the beginning of the 1990s the responsible actors – the new (old) elites – in the former socialist countries of East, Central and South-Eastern Europe were faced with the major challenge of initiating and designing thorough transforma-

78 Some economists, Janos Kornai for instance, maintain that two forms of change came about in the classic socialist systems: *reform* and *refinement*. Refinement made planning easier and bureaucratic control better. The institutional frame of the societal order remained intact during the process, and the power of the communist party and its elites was preserved. On the other hand, reforms were more far-reaching and changed individual characteristics of the system without questioning the power of the party with its ideological basis.

tion of the existing economic and societal order in the direction of a market economy and democracy. But economics had no self-contained transition theory to offer[79]. Like economists, scientists in associated disciplines were caught completely unawares by events. Just as manifold as the terms used for the change ("transformation", "systemic change", "transition") were the theoretical approaches and the proposals on how best to handle the process – because transition theory was lacking and there were no historic role models (Kušić, 2006). Reform suggestions well founded in economic theory ranged from demands for radical intervention in the economic and societal structure to gentler reforms. In expert circles, different positions were taken up in the debate on shock therapy versus gradualism. However, consensus was reached on the lifting of state controls on prices, on liberalisation of the markets, and on the need to privatise state-owned enterprises. These reforms were to be undertaken within a policy framework that ensured macroeconomic stability[80].

It was at first assumed that it sufficed to apply the neoliberal concepts of economic policy dominant at that time to the whole of Eastern Europe, regardless of a country's initial situation. The negative results of the first phase, as well as the enormous slump in economic activities connected with a rapid rise in unemployment and inflation rates came as a surprise to some economists, reformers and consultants; and so did increasing rejection of the new economic system by the population[81]. Only later was it realized that some reform measures could not be transferred to all transition economies in equal measure, and that there were completely different routes to capitalism (Biggart and Guillen, 1999), which were also visible in the case of the Central and Eastern European countries

---

79 The prevalent opinion was that the market economy, i.e. capitalism, could only coexist in combination with a democratically structured social order. Therefore the recommendations in the transition debate predominantly envisaged a simultaneous shift towards a market economy and democracy.

80 At that time, the neoliberal course prevailed at international level, fuelled by "successes" in Chile, Argentina and Bolivia, as well as later on in Great Britain. The neoliberal school was especially boosted by the radical actions of M. Thatcher after she had drastically reduced the government's role and initiated one of the largest waves of privatization among the Western industrial nations.

81 The economic and social consequences of introducing a market economy are a matter of controversy in the literature. Economists like Tamás Bauer argue that the negative consequences were not solely caused by the transition process but were determined by the socialist system itself. Some of the negative consequences of the transition process could be described as legacies from the past system, since certain phenomena in the old systems were concealed and hidden. Other economists believe that the economic and social consequences were caused by the transition process itself. They argue that material and non-material burdens on economic actors – which can be described as transition costs – were caused by transition alone (Boxberger, 1997: 53).

(Stark, 1996). This is unsurprising given there are different variants or characteristics of modern capitalism worldwide[82]. From the second half of the 1990s onwards, the concepts and reform measures selected led to divergent transition pathways with different implications for the productive capacity of the economies (Streit, 1996). In regard to evaluation (in terms of growth rates, price stability, balanced budgets, rate of unemployment and the development of the private sector) of progress by individual transition economies towards a market economy, the Central and Eastern European countries were especially successful among the transition countries according to international studies and diverse rankings (Kušić, 2002).

3. "Competitive advantages" on the way to the market economy

The aforementioned countries adopted a transition policy which was predominantly pragmatically oriented and consisted in a combination of different reform measures. It is consequently difficult to relate it to concepts like shock therapy or gradualism. Contrary to the approach of the rest of the transition countries, which were less successful, the Central and Eastern European ones implemented the necessary reform measures early, and they coherently sequenced the individual steps in reform. A further feature shared by the more successful countries was their consistent application of the transition policy of their choice, in which process a very important role was played by the new elites. The question of how rapidly the old system should be abandoned and the new one established – and the form that the new one should take – depended largely on the rapidity with which individual countries experienced a comprehensive change of elites. Transition processes – regarding the degree of democratisation reached and establishment of market structures – have to date varied from country to country. This can be largely explained by the degree of replacement of elites, the change of elites, and the continuity of elites[83].

Extensive room for manoeuvre was opened for the new and old elites especially in regard to change of property rights, i.e. privatisation of the sector of former state-owned enterprises[84]. The same applies to the basic decision concerning the

82 Examples are the "Anglo-American" and "Japanese-Rhenish" variants of capitalism. See Albert (1993), Berger and Dore (1996), and Berger (2000).

83 Adequate and illustrative material is offered by the literature on transition with the focus on "deficient democracies" i.e. "market economies with functional deficits".

84 It was essentially possible to choose among pure methods of selling, privatisation by free transfer of company shares to the population, or privatisation by management- or employee-buyout. Depending on goals like speed, allocative efficiency or acceptance in society, these methods exhibited advantages and disadvantages. From the theoretical point of view, and particularly from the perspective of property-rights theory, the most efficient

process of modernisation and restructuring – whether to organise it predominantly by using own resources, i.e. with domestic capital, or with help of foreign capital (FDI). Besides the method of privatisation chosen, a range of other factors have influenced the success of transition policy. The later phase of transition, especially, was characterised by intensified reforms at institutional level and adaptation to market structures of West European type. That meant turning away from the model of the market economy "without attributes" and towards the building of a social market economy. Moreover, the role of prospective accession to the EU, which came early for several Central and Eastern European Countries (CEEC) (approximately in the mid-1990s), should not be underestimated. Owing to various development programmes like PHARE and the strategy of adopting acquis communautaire, questions on particular legal provisions, institutional framework conditions and infrastructure were the predominant ones raised. Coupled with their respective transition policies, this made it possible for the aforementioned countries (CEEC) to largely accomplish the transition process (König and Kušić, 2004). Apart from these aspects, a few so-called "competitive advantages" in the transition process can be identified in connection with the establishment and design of the capitalist system. The relevant factors in this regard have been, besides historical experience of market/democratic systems, the degree of industrialisation of the transition countries as well as geographic proximity to the Western industrial countries (Balcerowicz, 1995). It is consequently possible to argue that there is a path dependency in the transition process that has co-determined some activities.

4. Capitalism in South-Eastern Europe

Before going into details on transition and the design of capitalism in South-Eastern Europe, first to be dealt with is the question as to where the spatial borders of South-Eastern Europe actually lie. Experts in different disciplines have often disagreed as to which countries should be counted as constituting South-Eastern Europe, especially when historical, cultural, religious or geopolitical aspects are considered. The main problem is exact definition of the north-western border, i.e. the questions of whether Slovenia, Hungary or Slovakia belong to South-Eastern Europe or to Central Europe, and where the actual border runs between different regions. It should also be borne in mind that the notion "South-Eastern Europe" only became current during the twentieth century. The debate on what is to be included in the notion of "Balkans" has been equally controversial. This space comprises numerous valleys and mountains that have

privatisation method – as to the subsequent restructuring and establishment of efficient corporate governance – was sale to strategic investors with participation of foreign capital. For further discussion see Kušić (2001).

no shared centre and have been largely separated from both the coast and the Danube area. However, this controversial debate will not be addressed here; nor the fact that the aforementioned countries anyway identify themselves with the notion of Central and Eastern Europe[85]. Employed here is the common delimitation of this space used by the international institutions and which regards it as comprising the following countries: Bulgaria, Romania, the countries that succeeded the former Yugoslavia (Croatia, Bosnia and Herzegovina, Serbia, Montenegro, Kosovo, Macedonia), as well as Albania[86].

Inspection of the map of Europe shows that the region of South-Eastern Europe comprises small regions of different sizes and with limited connections with the neighbouring spaces. On the other hand, the fact that all of the aforementioned countries are located in the periphery of the old continent not only explains their historical development but is also indicative of the region's current and future potential[87]. According to the above-mentioned competitive advantages of the transition, one may also draw conclusions about the framework conditions for the transition and about establishment of the capitalist system. The entire region has to date had only little experience with market/democratic systems, and its degree of industrialisation has been less than that of both Western Europe and the CEEC. In addition to factors like geographic position and distance to the dynamic regions of Western Europe (centre vs. periphery), there are several others that have stopped the far-reaching engagement of foreign capital: increasing political instability since the 1990s, ethnic animosities, fragmentation of the common internal market, war conflicts, often unclear property rights, and last but not least strong corruption. This has been reflected in a relatively low inflow of FDI in South-Eastern Europe, with the exception of Croatia. In light of these considerations, it is not surprising that the South-East European countries – as the usual indicators show – have lagged far behind the successful CEEC in economic transition (Altmann, 2005).

---

85 It is most prominently Slovenia which refuses to be mentioned in connection with South-Eastern Europe, attaching great importance to delimitation from its south-easterly neighbours.

86 The term "Western Balkans" used by the EU for South-Eastern Europe serves to delimit it from two other EU member countries, Romania and Bulgaria. Hence it is used for the other South-East European countries which are not yet in the EU.

87 The historical processes in South-Eastern Europe lack a functional core; there has been no indigenous shaping power that would have influenced the environment in the long run. Instead, developments in the region were interrupted by a long period of foreign dominance. After the period of Turkish-Ottoman dominance, numerous young and relatively small national states sprang up, without any of them being able to establish primacy over the others (Heppner, 2006).

Closer inspection reveals different characteristics of the new capitalist economic system. In fact, systemic transition was initiated everywhere, occasionally it was also implemented, but it is still far from being accomplished. Overall, the societies of South-Eastern Europe have been highly influenced by legacies from the socialist era. In spite of the substitution of elites – a process which has undergone different dynamics – the old system of values shows inertia in many areas and the consequent polarisation has on occasion increased. Furthermore, the new economic system in South-Eastern Europe – in spite of regional differences – has been far from characterized as an efficient market economy accepted by the majority of the population and connected with improvement in the material standards of the preponderant number of citizens[88]. Instead, this form of economy is often described with the help of attributes like "chaotic" and "wild" capitalism, or "crony" capitalism with close connections between the political and economic levels. There is often talk of overweening clientelism, attempts to restrict power to a few influential families, and the exclusion of foreign actors. However, it should not be forgotten that these latecomers are not homogenous – neither in levels of development and economic competitiveness nor in the state of reforms. If nothing else, this is clear with regard to various statuses of individual countries in the process of accession to the EU[89].

The heterogeneity among the countries of South-Eastern Europe has been reinforced from time to time by the actions of international institutions like the IMF and the World Bank, as well as by the policy of Brussels towards the region within the framework of the Stability Pact for South-Eastern Europe. Besides the structural level, i.e. cooperation mechanisms with the EU, this has also been reflected at the psychological level. As a study by ESI reported as early as 2000 (with regard to building functioning institutions) both candidate countries, Bulgaria and Romania, could draw on much better expert advice than their South-East European neighbours concerning the TAIEX programme and the twinning process (East West Institute and European Stability Initiative, 2000: 3). Moreover, the candidate countries of the first round had far easier access to various EU support programmes and did not have to expose themselves to the protracted

88 At the beginning of transition, falls in GDP were followed by drastic decreases in standards of living because savings were eaten up. Only lately have the successor countries of the former Yugoslavia returned to the levels recorded at the beginning of the 1990s under the old regime.

89 Whereas all the CEEC became members of the EU in 2004, the situation in South-Eastern Europe is mixed. Bulgaria and Romania have been EU member states since 2007, Croatia has been in accession negotiations with Brussels since 2005, Macedonia is a EU candidate country. The other countries, Serbia or Bosnia and Herzegovina, have been waiting to complete the Stabilisation and Association Agreement (SAA), i.e. for concrete steps in accession to the EU.

and conditional project mechanisms of the Stability Pact in order to access funds.

4. What is different in South-Eastern Europe? – Diverse starting conditions

As opposed to the CEEC, capitalism came to South-Eastern Europe more slowly, and as a rule not as planned. When Prague, Warsaw and Budapest knew relatively soon after revolutionary upheavals what they longer wanted, and sometimes even precisely what the new economic model should be, Sofia, Bucharest, Belgrade or Zagreb were busy with other problems at the beginning of the 1990s. Instead of “capitalism without attributes”, as some slogans in the capitals of the CEEC put it, the South-East European countries were focused on overcoming the old system, and only thereafter considered what should take its place. In contrast to the CEEC, the transition was much less radical and the substitution of elites was less dynamic, even when events in Bucharest gave another impression. At times of upheavals, old and new elites have acted with each other, side by side or in conflict, commensurately with various forms of revolution and various interaction patterns between old and new elites during regime change. Hence, following Sterbling, we may speak of both the replacement or change of elites and the continuity of elites (Sterbling, 2001). Some of the negative societal concomitants in South-Eastern Europe of the change from a socialist planned economy to a market economy were hence also direct consequences of the policy of ex-communist politicians. The latter strove to transform their earlier political privileges into new economic resources, often opting for nationalism.

But what were the reasons for the different approaches to transition and for the different characteristics of capitalism in South-Eastern Europe? In addition to different historical and cultural characteristics, disparate starting economic and political conditions eventually led to an enormous gap with the CEEC, but also among individual countries of South-Eastern Europe. In comparison to some CEEC like the Czech Republic, the South-East European countries were generally much less industrialised, and the share of agriculture in GDP was consequently more pronounced. But also within the region there was a clear north/south divide in the level of development, that is, between the relatively highly developed Yugoslav Republic of Croatia and Kosovo, Macedonia or Albania, in which developmental deficits inherited from the socialist era, and partially also from the pre-socialist period, are still evident today. Hence, Albania – which opened up only in 1991 after decades of isolation – belongs among the poorest European countries in spite of high growth rates in recent years[90]. In ad-

90 GDP per capita in Albania in 2005 was about 2100 EUR, and GDP growth is today around 6 or 7 per cent – although the starting point was very low. With 150 internet users and 61

dition, country-specific characteristics of the old system in the individual South-East European countries were also responsible. Open borders in the former Yugoslavia, combined with extensive decentralisation, worker self-management and societal ownership of the production factors since the 1960s, represented the polar opposite to Bulgaria's planned economy, which was isolated from the West. This country was not exposed to reforms until just before collapse, and it adhered strongly to the central administrative system of the Soviet Union. All these factors naturally influenced economic development in individual countries. A traveller at the end of the 1980s between Bucharest, Sofia, Zagreb or Tirana could not fail to notice these enormous differences.

5. The new system and economic development in South-Eastern Europe

With the decline of the socialist systems, the fall of the Soviet Union and of the "Iron Curtain", the South-East European countries were faced with the task of introducing an all-encompassing transition to a market economy. Whereas some strategic decisions were to be made by each country in transition, so that the necessary reform measures in the individual countries showed some similarities, matters were different in the region of the former Yugoslavia. The countries of that region were soon afflicted by further problems triggered by the fall of Yugoslavia, collapse of the common market and eventually by the war in the entire region. The consequence was *inter alia* that the new elites in the individual successor countries of the former Yugoslavia did not prioritise the establishment of market framework conditions. In the end, this was not demanded by sufficient forcefulness by a wide section of the population. The elites were instead preoccupied with setting up governance structures or raising funds for the war, but often also with themselves.

This was especially apparent in the ownership transformation of societal enterprises, which proceeded relatively slowly in all the successor countries of former Yugoslavia, and in many cases left inefficient ownership structures behind. Under the strong influence of the management and workers consequent on inherited structures inherent to the system (workers' self-management), the privatisation strategy was not conceived to comprise pure selling methods but rather a mix of management-buyout (MBO) and worker-buyout (WBO) (Kušić, 2001). Moreover, the necessary privatisation of large enterprises was either postponed, as in Bosnia and Herzegovina and Serbia, or undertaken in the shadow of a defensive war with an opaque privatisation strategy in the 1990s, as in Croatia (Kušić, 2005). As a consequence, the governance and control structures of the privatised

cars per 1000 population, Albania is way below the European average (Statistisches Bundesamt der Bundesrepublik Deutschland, 2008).

enterprises were largely concentrated in the hands of insiders. The new "owners" were little interested in sharing control over the enterprises with external (foreign) investors. At the same time, the insider-dominated enterprises had little appeal for potential investors, who refrained from participating in them. This impacted negatively on the modernisation and restructuring of enterprises and did not generate the expected drive to growth. Insiders, moreover, were given a chance to acquire majority shareholdings in "their" enterprises with little commitment of their own funds – in Croatia through so-called "manager credits". Hence the temptation for them to asset strip was great. Because they could not (or did not want to) invest in these enterprises after privatisation, the option was often divestiture, with far-reaching consequences on the performance of the domestic economy.

For the countries of South-Eastern Europe, and especially for the region of the Western Balkans, this means that quite favourable conditions at the beginning of transition were not utilised to sell enterprises to strategic investors – and hence to exploit the advantages of the transition from social ownership to private ownership of the production factors. In the early phase (end of the 1980s) there were indeed domestic and foreign actors willing to invest their money. In the meantime, numerous internationally operating enterprises made their investment decisions, with the consequence that they engaged and located in the region of the Western Balkans only to a minor extent – as opposed to Hungary, the Czech Republic and Poland. They were thus unable to contribute positively to the transition and EU-integration of the countries in the region as they did in the rest of CEEC[91]. This may be the reason why, overall, privatisation gave only minor impetus to growth. These were especially absent in the sector of export-oriented industry, with negative consequences for the current competitiveness of individual successor countries of the former Yugoslavia, as confirmed by growing trade deficits and small adjustment to intra-EU trade (Kušić, 2003). Therefore, not surprisingly, neither the way in which capitalism entered South-Eastern Europe nor the current characteristics of the individual South-East European countries have been the same as in the CEEC (all of which have become members of the European Union in the meantime). Moreover, South-Eastern Europe has had no "Indiana Jones of economics", as the American Solidarnosc-consultant Jeffrey Sachs was dubbed by the US newspapers[92]. Nor can one suppose that his advice would have found as widespread support as it did in Poland at the end of the 1980s. This was to become clear later in light of attempts by the IMF to shift the countries of South-Eastern Europe onto this road. However, the reformers often

91 To be noted is that various studies have found no unambiguous connection between FDI and economic development in the transition countries (on this see Bandelj, 2002).

92 "Cowboy of Poland's Economy", Los Angeles Times, 9 February 1990.

swiftly rejected such ideas. Overall, the reformers in South-Eastern Europe preferred a gradual approach to a "shock therapy" – not least because of different starting conditions and a less radical replacement of elites.

Romania was the least indebted country in the former Eastern bloc at the end of the 1980s, when the course was set for transition to a market economy and democracy. This had been achieved through relentless exploitation of the population (i.e. their work effort) and a real decline in the standard of living. All the more surprising is the opinion of Romanians a few years after the beginning of transition and establishment of a capitalist system. When asked about their standard of living in October 1999, 61 percent of Romanians answered that they had lived better in 1989 than at the time of the survey; 11 percent replied that it was the same; and only 24 percent were looking forward to a higher living standard. In 1990, the already very low monthly average wage was about 160 dollars; ten years later it had decreased to almost half that amount – 87 dollars. The number of Romanian pensioners is now much higher than the number of people in employment. Moreover, the number of unemployed grew during transition to the market economy because of the closure of non-profitable enterprises, reaching about 12 percent in 1999. Consequently, there is growing pauperization in Romania: around one-third of the population must live on incomes below the poverty line. Without a shadow economy furnishing additional income, most Romanians would not be able to support themselves (Gabany and Sterbling, 2000).

The transition from socialism to a market economy in Bulgaria has led to deindustrialisation, a return to agriculture, a decline in productivity, job losses, and degradation of social security. Termination of the collective economy and privatisation in the countryside has induced a backslide to the technical level and small family farms of before the Second World War. As a consequence, the post-socialist economy is internationally not competitive. Since the loss of the former socialist market, the pressure of developed industrial countries has grown, because they flood the markets of the post-socialist countries in transition with their products. Reform policy in such countries used to be characterized by the famous "two steps forward, one step back" process, and an excessively slow replacement of elites. Realignment of reform policy at the end of the 1990s was on the other hand closely associated with the process of accession to the EU and with strict requirements imposed by Brussels within the framework of negotiations with the EU.

Things were different in Croatia. As a former constituent Republic of Yugoslavia, it had exceptionally advantageous starting conditions compared with those of the other countries of the so-called Eastern bloc. In support of this contention one may cite a relatively developed and decentralised economy with elements of the market mechanism, with open borders towards the West, a political, economic as well as cultural closeness to Western Europe. The ego of Croats was especially ruffled during the transition process when the northern neighbour, Slovenia, obviously without problems, overcame the obstacles in the accession process. The same happened with Bulgaria and Romania, since both countries were economically far behind Croatia in the 1980s. The reason for this development was, among other things, the specific preconditions that influenced systemic change in Croatia. The simultaneity of transition, state building, and war was not an irrelevant factor in the organisation of capitalism in Croatia, because the long-term focus of policy was on security and recovery of the territorial borders.

6. What lies ahead?

At this point the following questions arise. Will capitalism as it exists in South-Eastern Europe defend its position and maintain its current characteristics in the long run? Is there a sufficient momentum in individual countries to initiate a recovery of the existing system – in the sense of a social market economy. Or are there societal forces that want to "turn the clock back"? Full answers to these questions cannot be provided here because the process is ongoing. Only tentative answers are possible, but not without taking consideration of global developments as well as country-specific ones.

In view of the current situation in the international financial markets and in the real economy of the most important industrial countries, some things seem possible today that seemed impossible a few months or years ago. Let us only consider that calls are made for massive state interventions like nationalisation, state help and guarantees even in such capitalist bastions as the USA and the UK. The protagonists of an alternative way become more enthusiastic as a consequence of such developments. In the meantime, they increasingly look to the public, appear more self–confident, and their speeches do not sound as they did previously. Even more importantly, it seems that they expect to gain growing popularity. In fact, communism is not yet socially acceptable as a proper alternative because of the negative experiences of many decades still fresh in people's minds. Yet a step in that direction has certainly become conceivable for many, even among young people.

This development had already begun somewhat before the financial crisis. It was – so to speak – a creeping process that went together with the decline of the neoliberal doctrine, namely the teachings of Milton Friedman and Chicago economic theory. Wherever the principles propounded by Friedman – privatisation, deregulation and cutting back on state provision – have been pursued with vehemence, the majority of the respective population has not necessarily liked them. As a rule they have been – at least for some time – accompanied by massive prosperity gaps and have hence not been accepted with enthusiasm; sometimes, indeed, they have had to be implemented with force (Klein, 2007). This began in the 1970s in Latin America, made its way in other parts of the world, and found a welcoming "laboratory" in the transition societies of Eastern, Central and South-Eastern Europe. The movement based on the Washington Consensus reached its peak in the 1990s, but for several years the opponents of neoliberal economic policy have certainly been advancing.

It is very difficult today to determine the extent to which the shift to the left noticeable world-wide will find fertile ground in South-Eastern Europe as well. Will it be able to put down roots in that region and exert significant influence on the design and characteristics of capitalism? Experiences from some South American countries show that these developments have durable characteristics, and that they do not have to be ephemeral. On the other hand, the South-East European countries have in the course of accession to the EU – and in the case of Croatia, concrete accession negotiations – been more or less amalgamated with the institutional arrangements of the EU. Hence, solo attempts at radical socio-political change can almost be ruled out. However, a certain shift to the left is conceivable within the entire European family of states as a consequence of the impacts of the global financial and economic crisis. We shall be closer to answering these questions in months to come, and especially after the next elections in some important member countries of the EU.

References

Albert, M. (1993), *Capitalism vs. Capitalism*, New York: Four Walls Eight Windows.

Altmann, F.-L. (2005), "EU und Westlicher Balkan: Eine schwierige Verlobung", *Südosteuropa*, 53(2): 185-212.

Balcerowicz, L. (1994), "Understanding postcommunist transition", *Journal of Democracy*, 5(4): 75–89.

Bandelj, N. (2002), "Embedded economies: social relations as determinants of foreign direct investment in Central and Eastern Europe", *Social Forces,* 81(2): 411-444.

Berger, S. (2000), "Globalization and politics", *Annual Review of Political Science*, 3: 43-62.

Berger, S. and R. Dore (eds) (1996), *National Diversity and Global Capitalism*, Ithaca: Cornell University Press.

Bergson, A. (1987), "Comparative productivity: the USSR, Eastern Europe, and the West", *American Economic Review*, 77(3): 342-357.

Biggart, N. and M. Guillen (1999), "Developing difference: social organization and the rise of the auto industries of South Korea, Taiwan, Spain, and Argentina", *American Sociological Review*, 64(5): 722-747.

Boxberger, G. (1997), *Sozialpolitik und Transformationsprozess: Kosten der polnischen Transformation und ihre Minderung über staatliche Sozialpolitik und Selbsthilfeinitiativen*, Frankfurt am Main: Peter Lang.

Brus, W. and T. Kowalik (1983), "Socialism and development", *Cambridge Journal of Economics*, 7(3-4): 243-255.

Dvornik, S. and C. Solioz (eds) (2007), *Next Steps in Croatia's Transition Process*, Baden-Baden: Nomos.

East West Institute and European Stability Initiative (2000), "Brussels discussion paper: stability, institutions and European integration", available at http://www.esiweb.org/pdf/esi_document_id_12.pdf.

Gabany, A. and A. Sterbling (eds) (2000), *Sozialstruktureller Wandel, soziale Probleme und soziale Sicherung in Südosteuropa*, Südosteuropa-Studien, Band 65, München: Südosteuropa-Gesellschaft.

Heppner, H. (2006), "Ein Mangel an Mitte - Historische Prozesse beeinflussen die aktuelle Situation in Südosteuropa", *Wiener Zeitung*, 18 February.

Klein, N. (2007), *Die Schock-Strategie. Der Aufstieg des Katastrophen-Kapitalismus*, Frankfurt a.M.: Fischer.

König, M. and S. Kušić (2004), "Zemlje istočne Europe na putu u Europsku uniju – od tranzicije do integracije", *Ekonomski Pregled*, 55(1-2): 132-156.

Kornai, J. (1992), *The Socialist System: The Political Economy of Communism*, Princeton: Princeton University Press.

Kušić, S. (2001), *Privatisierung im Transformationsprozess. Das Beispiel der Republik Kroatien*, Wiesbaden: Deutscher Universitäts-Verlag.

Kušić, S. (2002), "Gewinner und Verlierer der Transformation: System- und länderspezifische Ausgangsbedingungen, alternative Transformationspfade und EU-Integration", in M. Neumann and H. Pleines (eds), *Gewinner und Verlierer post-sozialistischer Transformationsprozesse, Beiträge für die 10. Brühler Tagung junger Osteuropa-Experten*, Bremen: Forschungsstelle Osteuropa, pp. 11-15.

Kušić, S. (2003), "Wie wettbewerbsfähig ist Kroatiens Wirtschaft?", *Südosteuropa Mitteilungen*, 43(4-5): 56-69.

Kušić, S. (2006), "Kann Südosteuropa von den erfolgreichen Transformationsländern lernen?", *Südosteuropa - Zeitschrift für Gegenwartsforschung*, 54(1): 107-114.

Kušić, S. (ed) (2005), *Path-Dependent Development in the Western Balkans – The Impact of Privatization*, Frankfurt a.M.: Peter Lang.

Stark, D. (1996), "Recombinant property in East European capitalism", *American Journal of Sociology*, 101(4): 993-1027.

Statistisches Bundesamt der Bundesrepublik Deutschland (2008), available at www.destatis.de.

Sterbling, A. (2001), *Intellektuelle, Eliten, Institutionenwandel: Untersuchungen zu Rumänien und Südosteuropa*, Krämer: Hamburg.

Streit, M. and U. Mummert (1996), "Grundprobleme der Systemtransformation aus institutionenökonomischer Perspektive", *Diskussionsbeitrag Max-Planck-Institut zur Erforschung von Wirtschaftssystemen, Jena* 09-96.

Sozio-ökonomische Perspektiven in Südosteuropa
Socio-Economic Perspectives in South-Eastern Europe

Herausgegeben von Siniša Kušić, Slavko Kulić und Vladimir Cvijanović

Band 1 Siniša Kušić: Zwischen Euphorie und Ernüchterung – Kroatien auf dem Weg in die EU. 2007.

Band 2 Vladimir Cvijanović/Andrea Fumagalli/Carlo Vercellone (eds.): Cognitive Capitalism and its Reflections in South-Eastern Europe.

www.peterlang.de

www.ingramcontent.com/pod-product-compliance
Ingram Content Group UK Ltd.
Pitfield, Milton Keynes, MK11 3LW, UK
UKHW020835290926
15470UKWH00004B/1363

9 783631 604618